Who Is Allah?

Who Is Allah?

THE CONCEPT OF GOD IN ISLAM

Abdur Raheem Kidwai

JAICO PUBLISHING HOUSE

Ahmedabad Bangalore Chennai
Delhi Hyderabad Kolkata Mumbai

Published by Jaico Publishing House
A-2 Jash Chambers, 7-A Sir Phirozshah Mehta Road
Fort, Mumbai - 400 001
jaicopub@jaicobooks.com
www.jaicobooks.com

WHO IS ALLAH?
ISBN 978-81-993555-1-4

First Jaico Impression: 2025

Page design and layout by
Special Effects Graphics Design Company, Mumbai

Printed by
Thomson Press India Limited, New Delhi

For

My teenaged grandson, Shaad Mustafa Hashmi's enquiring, curious mind about religious truths

Contents

In the name of Allah,
most compassionate, most merciful

Preface

Preceding this Preface, as in any Muslim writing, is the customary Islamic invocation, "In the name of Allah, most compassionate, most merciful." Whenever Muslims commence doing anything, right from the devotional prayer to any routine act, they usually recite this Islamic invocation. What this underscores is that Islam is Allah-centric through and through. Muslims live and die for Allah. They venerate the Quran because it is Allah's Word. They hold the Prophet Muhammad (peace be upon him) in great esteem in that he is a chosen servant of Allah. All Islamic devotional acts are dedicated solely to Allah.

While Islam is totally Allah-centred, it is worth-noting that Allah's infalliable book, the Quran is thoroughly human-centric. Far from being a dense metaphysical, or purely theological, or scholastic, or only eschatological (about the hereafter) work threatening humankind all the time with the blazing hell-fire or a polemical diatribe demonising non-Muslims, it consists of Allah's direct, easy to understand address to all humanity, not specifically believers, marked by His compassion, mercy and sincere advice. Allah appears, mainly as humanity's guide and well-wisher, instructing us how to construct a social order standing out for justice, equality, fairness and empathy for the underprivileged. Allah is found talking heart to heart, counselling, exhorting, persuading, commiserating, comforting, counselling, promising His immense reward, and warning against evil, disbelief and Satan, which are self-destructive. He shares with us His profound observations, draws our attention to His marvellous signs, and imparts invaluable lessons applicable to all human activity. In a variety of ways and arguments, He presents truth before us which is in our own interest. Although He has showered His numerous bounties on us and generously sustains us, He does not ask for anything in return. If we serve and worship Him, it fills us with spiritual and emotional peace and tranquility. On reading the Quran, Allah emerges as our best advisor and guide.

Many of us, particularly non-Muslims, know very little about Allah. For some, He being invisible and transcendent, is too abstruse, remote and abstract to find out.

Regrettably in our times, in the wake of some totally un-Islamic, ghastly acts of terrorism in the name of Islam by some perverted, diseased minds, have naturally maligned the image of Islam and Allah. The resultant Islamophobia has turned some of us completely distrustful of Islam and Allah.

Who is Allah: The Concept of God in Islam seeks to familiarise readers with the definition, description, attributes and scheme of things of Allah. The book is based wholly on the Quran, the most authentic source of Islam. As Allah is an Arabic term for God, English-speaking readers will find this book helpful in grasping what Allah means and why He matters all in all in Islam and for Muslims. The book consists of a selection of Quranic verses, which delineate the concept of God in a myriad ways: His self-definition, His guidance, including commands and warnings, and His way to our salvation. This book may answer some such questions which often cross readers' minds:

- Who is called Allah in Islam?
- What type of God is Allah?
- What are His unique features?

- What is His relationship with this universe?
- What is His equation with humankind?
- What are His expectations from us?
- What pleases and displeases Him?
- How can we win His pleasure?
- Whom does He reward or punish?
- Who are Prophets? Where do they stand in relation to Him and his followers?
- Who are angels? Why has He created them?
- What is the way of life prescribed by Him for his followers?
- Is He the God of only believers or Muslims, or the universal God?
- Does He speak only to believers or Muslims?
- What is His view of this and the afterlife?
- Is He the Lord of both this and the next world?
- What are the basic beliefs and duties laid down by Him for us?
- What is He like?
- Does He ask that everyone be compelled into accepting Islam?
- Does He not treat non-believers with justice?
- What are His main arguments for his followers accepting the faith?
- Does He have any partner, son, family or incarnation?
- Does He rejoice in punishing human beings?
- Does He punish the guilty more than that what they deserve?

- Does He reward the pious in a degree equal to their good actions, or more?
- Is He some tribal, ethnic, regional or universal God?
- Does He prescribe a life of monasticism, devoted fully to only worshipping Him?
- Does He approve of our family, social relations, trade, inquiry, critical thinking and worldly activities?
- Is He dependent in any degree on angels, spirits, forces of Nature, prophets or anyone?
- Does He ask for His share in our offerings?
- Does He prefer any particular ethnic group, nationality, colour or linguistic community?
- Is He confined to a particular place?
- Does He have any gender or physical body parts?
- Can we see Him? Does He see us?

Apart from answering these and other questions about Allah, this book also throws some light on the Islamic worldview, its belief system, its socio-moral code and its salvation strategy. Readers are likely to gain some idea about Islam as a way of life practised by around two billion Muslims at present.

Since time immemorial, the concept of God has been part of every community in all times and places. Little wonder then that we note an amazing variety of notions about divinity in history, from strict monotheism to multiplicity of gods, deities, incarnations and what not! Since the objective behind producing this book is to present a very introductory book on the Islamic concept of God for ordinary readers, it does not delve into comparative religion. Nor does it have any polemical design of parading the superiority of the Islamic concept over others. It does, however, aim at informing: what and who is Allah, as depicted in the most authoritative Islamic text, the Quran, with the help of brief, easy to understand explanatory notes. Once again, this explication makes no pretence about being scholarly with some academic paraphernalia. However, the explanation restates more pointedly what features in the Quran and hence it is authentic and accurate. The English translation of the Quranic verses, originally in Arabic, has been taken from my book, *What is in the Quran: Message of the Quran in Simple English* (New Delhi, Viva Books, 2023, Third Edition of the original which had appeared in 2013). Those interested in a further detailed study of Islam or the Quran may draw upon this work. Other helpful introductory works on Islam and the Quran by me are: *The Quran: Essential Teachings* (Mumbai, Jaico Publishing House, 2006) and *The Quran Speaks to You: 60 Great Lessons from Islam* (Mumbai, Jaico Publishing House, 2022). Those interested in a detailed study of God may read the British theologian Karen Armstrong's *A History of God* (Vintage, 1993). Likewise, readers who are keen on studying Islam or the Quran further, may consult the English translations of the Quran by Ahmad Zaki Hammad (2007), Tarif Khalidi (2008) and Mustafa Khattab (2015).

I hope that this book will help readers understand better what Muslims believe about Allah or God. It will cater to the genuine curiosity and interest of readers in a major world religion—Islam. We need better interfaith understanding in today's multi-faith, pluralistic world.

Thanks are due to Mr. Abrar Khan, and Mr. Mohd. Yameen Ansari in Aligarh for their valuable assistance in typing the manuscript.

I am thankful to the team at Jaico Publishing House, Mumbai for their cooperation in the production of this book. My highly pleasant association as an author with Jaico,

Mumbai is now almost two decades old. I am beholden to them for having provided me with this excellent forum for explaining what Islam is, to readers.

Readers are most welcome to favour me with their valuable comments and suggestions.

Professor Abdur Raheem Kidwai
sulaim_05@yahoo.co.in

Aligarh Muslim University, Aligarh
January 2025
Jumadi Al-Thani 1446H

Chapter 1

Allah's Scheme

Allah, the master of the universe has created all of us. It is natural to want to know His likes and dislikes. Does He have any favourites among us? If yes, how can we develop ourselves to become His favourite?

In His Book, the Quran, Allah explains what His favourite, man or woman is like. His scheme of things is as follows:

> **O people, Allah has created you from a male and a female. He has made you into communities and tribes so that you may recognize one another. The most honourable one among you in the sight of God is he/she who fears Him most. Allah is all-knowing, all-aware.**
>
> **(Al-Hujurat 49: 13)**

Unity of humankind is the cornerstone of Islam. Allah has created everyone and provides everything to one and all, irrespective of their religion, caste, colour or ethnicity. He is the Lord of everyone. He has nonetheless, conveyed through His book, the Quran, accessible to everyone, and His messenger, Prophet Muhammad (peace be upon him, 570–633 CE), His guidance, rather roadmap for us. It is up to us to draw on the Quran and the Prophet's teachings, which are available for everyone, for our eternal success in this world and the next.

Allah embodies justice and fairness. He does not take into account our ethnicity, nationality or colour in rewarding us. Nations, races, clans, and other divisions among humankind are mere tags for identification. Piety matters most in the eyes of Allah.

It is a great pity that in the name of these labels (nations, castes, creeds, colours, and regional, ethnic and linguistic communities) there have been horrible wars and ghastly bloodshed in every era of history.

Points to ponder

- This verse points to Allah's plan of creation and our division into various groups—ethnic, linguistic, cultural, regional and religious.
- These divisions among humankind are only labels.
- This is a special Quranic verse which identifies the best and most honourable, according to our Creator.

Chapter 2

Allah's Mercy

Since Allah is our Creator and Master and all of us have to return to Him for His judgement which would decide our eternal life in the next world, it is natural on our part to be curious about His attributes. What features does He embody? An answer to this question would put our mind to rest. Allah introduces Himself thus in the Quran:

> **Ask them: "Whose is all that is in the heavens and on earth?" Say: "All belongs to Allah." He has prescribed for Himself mercy. He will gather you all on the Day of Judgement, about which there is no doubt. However, those who have lost their souls do not have faith.**
>
> **(Al-Anam 6: 12)**

Mercy is Allah's first and foremost attribute. All universe owes its creation, existence and sustenance, thanks to His boundless mercy. Some manifestations of His constant kindness to us are: our amazing body, mental and physical abilities and potential, our parents, spouse and children, friends and wider community, forces of Nature at our disposal such as air, water and sunlight. Generously and prudently He arranges for meeting the needs of a baby even before their birth – provisions in the mother's womb, love and affection for the baby in the heart of not only parents but also in near and dear ones.

For meeting the dictates of perfect justice, which is not possible in this world, Allah has devised the eternal life of the hereafter. We will be rewarded and or punished for our actions in the next world. His judgment will be marked by His vast mercy for humankind.

The Quran opens with this self-introduction: "In the name of Allah Who is most compassionate, most merciful." He constantly asks us to be kind to one another.

Points to ponder

- Since mercy is Allah's predominant feature, we should feel comfortable and assured.
- For drawing upon His boundless mercy, we should devote ourselves to worshipping and serving Him and doing good.

Chapter 3

Allah's Reward

As Allah has created us, watches and records how we lead our life, He would accordingly reward or punish us in the next life.

Let us find out who is rewarded by Him; how can we earn His reward in the next life; and protect ourselves against His punishment?

> **If you believe and are pious, Allah will give you your reward. He does not ask you to give away your wealth.**
>
> **(Muhammad 47: 36)**

In Islam there is no concept of any offering, monetary or otherwise, to be made to Allah. He will adjudge and reward on the basis of only our faith in Him and good actions. Islam, no doubt, prescribes the duty of zakah (2.5% of one's savings beyond a certain limit and animal sacrifice). However, both of these are to be distributed as charity among the poor, which will be rewarded by Allah. Allah does not ask believers to give anything to Him or the messenger. Allah is self-sufficient, independent of everyone and everything. If we do something good in His cause, it is for our own benefit in both the worlds. He is not at all dependent on His worshippers for anything. Even if no one serves and worships Him, He continues to be the Supreme Lord, master of everything and all-powerful.

If we spend what Allah has given us in charity, it becomes a golden opportunity for us to invest in the hereafter. We should consider ourselves as trustees of the wealth granted to us by Allah. This outlook on money helps us protect against greed, craze for amassing wealth and neglecting our obligations to our Lord and Creator, Allah, and to fellow human beings.

Points to ponder

- True faith and good actions on our part entitle us to Allah's reward.
- Allah's criterion for granting His reward to us is not very stringent or taxing. If we lead life with Allah-awareness, He will reward us bountifully.

Chapter 4

Do Not Despair of Allah's Mercy

As human beings we are liable to err. Is there any hope of securing Allah's pardon? Can we earn His pleasure after turning in repentance to Him? Can we attain salvation, notwithstanding our sins and wrong actions?

> **Tell those servants of Allah who have wronged themselves that they should not give up the hope of Allah's mercy. Allah may forgive all sins. He is Most Forgiving, Most Merciful.**
>
> **(Al-Zumar 39: 53)**

Human beings are liable to err because they are, after all, human. Allah's mercy is, however, so boundless that He graciously pardons our sins, provided we repent sincerely. In Islam there is no concept of a revengeful, vindictive God.

The doors of repentance are wide open for everyone. Prophet Muhammad (peace be upon him) on record says that Allah is delighted as we turn to Him seeking His pardon. He forgives even a die-hard sinner. Our ultimate end is thus in our hands. If we do good, He would grant us felicity.

Being unsure about Allah's mercy and forgiveness, polytheists invent His so-called associates/partners/ family members or favourites who may recommend their case to Allah. Islam declares that God–man relationship is one-to-one, direct, without any clergy (the so-called religious authorities) or any intermediary (God's son, angels, incarnations or saints).

Points to ponder

- In Islam there is a direct relationship between Allah and us, without any role of religious or spiritual figures. We should focus only on our belief in Him as the 'one true God' and on doing good to everyone around us.
- Allah's kindness towards us is immeasurable. So during our lifetime we should make most of this golden opportunity of turning to Him, seeking His mercy which would lead to our success and happiness in the next world.

Chapter 5

Allah's Sustenance Scheme

In Islam, the concept of God (Allah) is not some abstraction or notion. As the Creator, He has provided sustenance for all—from microbes to huge whales and billions of human beings who draw upon a vast variety of provisions. More amazingly, the system of abundant provisions has existed since day one of Creation and has still been catering satisfactorily to the needs of all despite the population explosion in our time:

> **Allah increases or gives in a strict measure the provision to whom He wills. The Unbelievers rejoice in the life of this world. However, in comparison to the Next Life, it is brief enjoyment**
>
> **(Al-Raad 13: 26)**

Allah provides sustenance to every living being, including even those who openly reject, oppose or mock Him. He is so forbearing that He does not punish the wrongdoers instantly. With His infinite grace, He grants more or less to all of us as He likes. We cannot fathom the reason behind His bestowal of provisions in a particular degree to someone.

We should not neglect Allah, lost in our worldly joys and material activities. The thought of Allah as our Lord to whom all of us have to return, should always be there in our heart and mind. With this Allah-awareness we are free to carry out any worldly pursuit and this will carry the same reward as we get for our worship. So believers may be top-ranking professionals and highly successful, prosperous persons in this world; Islam does not stand for monasticism.

In Islam, our wealth or poverty in this life is not reflective of Allah's approval or disapproval of our conduct. In contrast, a pious person may starve. It is all part of Allah's test for us in this life.

Points to ponder

- The endless sustenance system for all creatures is a telling proof of the Creator, provider, Allah's existence and His perfect arrangement.
- Allah has ensured such seamless coordination amid the forces of nature, particularly rain, soil and weather that sustenance is found aplenty in all seasons for everyone.
- It is, nonetheless, Allah's discretion to give as much or as little as He wishes to us. We may strive to get more. It again depends on His will if we are successful in our struggle.

Chapter 6

Allah's Role in Our Life

In Islam, Allah is not someone remotely connected with His creation. He listens to our prayers, guides us to good, stops us from evil, watches and records all of our actions.

> **"Allah it is Who has created me, and Who guides me. He gives me food and drink, And He cures me when I fall ill. It is He alone Who will cause my death and then bring me back to life. I look forward to His forgiving of my sins on the Day of Judgement".**
>
> **(Al-Shu'ara 26: 78-82)**

This is part of the Prophet Abraham's dialogue with his unbelieving community as he explains the concept of God to them. As a true believer he is full of praise and thanks for his Lord, the Creator of all that exists in the universe. It is His huge favour to us that He has put in place an elaborate, unmistakable arrangement for our guidance—His Book, the Quran and His final messenger, the Prophet Muhammad's role model reflected in his duly recorded life and sayings. Out of His overflowing love for His servants, Allah cures us. After testing us through disease and suffering as part of His plan, He will recompense us fairly on the Day of Judgement while displaying immense mercy and forgiveness.

This Quranic passage asserts that Allah alone is the Lord, in-charge of everything. So we must turn to only the one true God. He exercises absolute control over our life and death. It is thus foolish to turn to anyone other than Him for all that we need.

Points to ponder

- In Islam, Allah is all in all, to the exclusion of anyone else. All knowledge and power is vested in Him.
- He oversees our conduct in this life, without directly interfering in our actions.
- He will recompense us on the Day of Judgement on the basis of our actions in this life.

Chapter 7

Allah's Command for Worship

For our own spiritual and emotional well-being, Allah asks us to worship Him. Otherwise, being the all-powerful and eternal God, He does not need us worshipping Him. He holds the privilege of being the Supreme Lord, were not one of us to believe in Him.

> **O people, you are in need of Allah while He is Independent, Most Praiseworthy.**
>
> **(Fatir 35: 15)**

It is our duty to worship and serve Allah, as this will ensure our success in the next life. However, Allah is self-sufficient. He does not need at all our glorification of Him. He is per se most praiseworthy. As we glorify Him, it is to our own benefit for its immense spiritual and emotional value. Since Allah is the Lord, Master and Creator of everything, He does not ask us for anything in return. His commands are aimed at our own good and a happy, just social order. It is immaterial for Him, if we worship and serve Him or not. He is eternally Supreme, not dependent in any degree on our service to Him. However, if we obey Him, it will bless us with inner happiness and tranquillity and He will reward us on the Day of Judgement.

Points to ponder

- As creatures it is innate in our nature to turn to our Creator and Lord. The concept of God, though, at times, corrupted beyond recognition has prevailed in every time and place.
- We should focus only on the one true God, our Master

Chapter 8

Allah's Judgment

Perfect, flawless judgement is an essential attribute of Allah. He treats all of us alike, believers or disbelievers, and men and women, as He sustains them all and grants them opportunities, as He deems fit. We differ on a variety of issues. Being all-knowing He would inform us of the truth on the Day of Judgement.

> **Allah will decide all about which you differ. Such is God, my Lord. In Him I trust and to Him I turn.**
>
> **(Al-Shura 42: 10)**

People of all time and place have differed, often bitterly, among themselves on matters of faith. Allah has granted everyone freedom to profess and practise the faith of their choice. Islam recognises the plurality of religions and beliefs and asks us to follow the golden rule of peaceful co-existence. However, bear in mind that at our death all of us have to return to our Lord and Master, Allah and on the Day of Judgement He will call each one of us to account for our faith and actions. Our eternal fate depends on pleasing Allah by following Islam and doing good actions.

Islam does not accept compulsion in matters of faith. When Prophet Muhammad (peace be upon him) migrated to and settled in Madina, a town in Arabia with a considerable Jewish population, he enacted the first written constitution of a state in history, in which Muslims, Jews and others were treated as equal citizens, enjoying religious freedom.

Not only in the next life, Allah has decided all matters of consequence in this life as well for us, as detailed in the Quran and Prophet Muhammad's teachings. He has shown us, through both His Book and His messenger, how to lead life.

Points to ponder

- Allah has granted us free will and an innate ability to discern. We should therefore not engage in polemics, and profess and practise tolerance.
- Since Allah is the Supreme Lord and all-knowing, He would declare the truth of the matters on which we differ, on the Day of Judgement.

Chapter 9

Allah's Lordship

The most outstanding feature of Allah is His being the all-powerful Lord. This verse states the bedrock of the Islamic belief system:

> **Allah is the Lord of the east and the west. There is no god besides He. Take only Him as the guardian.**
>
> **(Al-Muzzammil 73: 9)**

Belief in Allah as the only Lord is the basic Islamic principle. He is omnipresent and omnipotent, without a partner. He is the God of everyone, Muslims and non-Muslims alike. This constitutes the fundamental Islamic doctrine that Allah alone is worthy of all worship. We should repose trust only in Him.

For believers, Allah is the only refuge. They trust Him as their kind, affectionate protector; He is all-powerful and the only Lord. Their belief in Him is the source of immense strength and comfort for them.

Points to ponder

- Islam affirms the supremacy of Allah, ruling out any partner with Him.

- Islam is the Allah-centric faith, which does not admit any plurality of gods. Prophets, though having an exalted rank, are only Allah's servants.

Chapter 10

Allah's Recompense for the Pious

In the following important Quranic verse we learn who is Allah's favourite. His creatures all are alike in His eyes. However, He likes most those whose mind and heart are permeated with Allah-awareness, though they may be engaged in any lawful activity, not necessarily worshipping Him all the time.

> **Allah is with the pious, and those who do good.**
>
> **(Al-Nahl 16: 128)**

We learn from the above that Allah's favourites are His pious servants who do good actions. Piety consists in always bearing in mind the belief that we are Allah's servants, assigned with the duty of believing in Him, and His messenger, the Prophet Muhammad (peace be upon him), following His guidance and doing good which will bring us success in the eternal next life. So winning Allah's pleasure is not something too hard or complicated: only sound faith and good actions are required.

Allah is the Lord of all beings, regardless of their colour, race or any label. He is not the God of only Muslims or Arabs. He has created everyone and sustains them. Likewise, He will call everyone to account.

The Quran delivers the good news of Allah's approval of those who believe and profess and practise good.

Points to ponder

- Allah places a premium on piety, overall Allah-consciousness, not only the ritual acts of worship.
- A pious man is a blessing for his family, his society and his country, for his only interest is in professing and practising good.

Chapter 11

Our Success in the Afterlife

For us entering paradise is the highest felicity imaginable. The following verse indicates the way to paradise.

> **He who gives (in charity) and fears Allah, and testifies to all that is good, Allah will make it easy for him the way to comfort (in the Hereafter).**
>
> **(Al-Layl 92: 5-7)**

We are told the key to our success in the hereafter: constant realisation of Allah's guidance, giving in charity for helping the needy and standing for all that is good. Apart from ensuring our success in the next life, the above conduct will make this world a happy place for everyone, as good and joys will prevail everywhere.

Islam stands for a blend of both faith and good actions, particularly charity for helping the needy. Islam does not approve renouncing life, living like monks. It asks us to fulfil all our obligations to our family, society and country, with Allah-awareness.

Points to ponder

- The way to paradise is easy: helping the needy, leading life with Allah-awareness and doing good.

- In Islam both faith and good actions guarantee success, particularly in the next life which is eternal. Our wealth, social standing or any other worldly consideration would not help us get a place in paradise.

Chapter 12

Allah's Code of Sexual Conduct

Sex is an important aspect of life. We all have natural sexual urges which Allah asks us to fulfil in a regulated way. The verse below outlines the sexual code prescribed by Allah:

> **Those guilty of sex outside marriage, be they male or female, flog each one of them with one hundred whips. Let not mercy move you in their case. For this is about Allah's religion, if you believe in Allah and the Last Day. Let a group of believers witness their punishment.**
>
> **(Al-Nur 24: 2)**

Allah has prohibited sex outside marriage in our own interest. Sexual misconduct breeds a host of social problems and the loss of a woman's dignity. Islam has prescribed a deterrent punishment, public flogging, for those guilty of committing sex outside marriage. Islam has no room for "consensual" sex outside wedlock.

Islam is forthright and candid about the sexual code of conduct. It does not put up with any deviation on this count. In doing so, it seeks to maintain and reinforce the social fabric and upholds broader interests of society, particularly ruling out the sexual exploitation of women. To discourage any sexual misconduct, Islam prescribes that the guilty be punished publicly in the presence of the community which should serve as a lesson to everyone.

Points to ponder

- Allah forbids sex outside marriage. It destroys the social and moral fabric.
- The above Quranic punishment, though it may sound stringent to some, serves as an effective deterrent for curbing the menace of sexual disorder.

Chapter 13

Allah Is One!

The oneness of Allah is the basic, most striking feature of the Islamic belief system. In Islam this belief is totally non-negotiable. Let us study this fundamental article of Islamic faith:

> **Allah says: "Do not take two gods. God is one. So fear Me alone." His is all that is in heavens and on earth. His religion alone is to be followed. Do you fear others besides Allah?**
>
> **(Al-Nahl 16: 51-52)**

Islam is absolutely clear on two points—oneness of Allah and that Islam as the only true religion. No compromise is imaginable on these counts. Allah alone is to be obeyed. He is the only supreme Lord of all.

The idea of one true God is perfectly logical. For the smooth functioning of the universe it is essential that it be governed by a single God. Moreover, monotheism introduces a strong personal note and focus in our direct relationship with Allah. Since Allah alone is the only Lord, we should fear only Him. This belief makes Muslims fearless and courageous, and frees them from all shackles of clergy and rituals.

Points to ponder

- The concept of one God, without any partner is perfectly logical.
- The belief in the one true God ensures a direct, one-to-one relationship between Allah and us, without any third party, which is spiritually and emotionally very fulfilling and reassuring.

Chapter 14

Allah's Justice

In Islam Allah is the God of not only Muslims. He is the Creator, Lord and Sustainer of all human beings, Muslims and non-Muslims alike. Accordingly, perfect justice, fairness and neutrality for all are His attributes, as discussed in the verse below:

> **Allah does not at all wrong people. However, people wrong themselves.**
>
> **(Yunus 10: 44)**

Justice is an outstanding attribute of Allah. He does not force anyone into doing anything good or bad. He has endowed us with free will and faculties to do whatever we choose. He facilitates the course of action we wish to follow.

Since out of our human weakness, we are liable to err, we are warned not to wrong ourselves, as it will have dire consequences in the next life which is everlasting. He has clearly spelled out what is good and what is evil. While abusing our freedom of choice if we do wrong, out of His justice He punishes us for our wrongdoing. So we should be very careful in all that we do.

Points to ponder

- Allah has granted reason to all human beings and shown them the straight and wrong ways of leading life through His messengers and books. He has devised this because He is all-just.
- It is up to us to choose the right way and ensure our entry into paradise.
- While being fair to everyone, Allah has explained clearly what will bring us success or loss in the next life.

Chapter 15

Our Return to Allah

In Islam our life in this world is only a stage, followed by our death which marks our return to our Lord, Allah. Let us note what it signifies:

> **All that is in the heavens and on earth belongs to Allah. Allah's promise is true. However, most of the people do not realize (this truth). Allah grants life and death. All of you will return to Him.**
>
> **(Yunus 10: 55-56)**

Allah is most powerful and most truthful. Lost in this material world we pay little or no attention to this reality. However, when we return to Him at death, we will have to render an account of our faith and actions to Him. We should never lose sight of the fact that it is Allah alone Who grants us life and causes our death, as He wills.

Our eventual return to Allah should make us acutely conscious of our answerability to Him for our life-long actions. Allah has a perfect record of how we spent our mental and physical faculties and money. The belief in Allah's Lordship should impel us to lead a virtuous life.

Points to ponder

- Allah being our Creator will summon us all back to Him for judgement.

- He will reward and punish us in the next life in proportion to our faith and actions.
- The more conscious and well-prepared we are for our next life, the more successful we will be eternally.

Chapter 16

Allah Knows All

Our Lord, Allah is all-knowing. He exercises His boundless power on account of His knowledge of each and every thing. His knowledge of everything does not necessarily indicate His endorsement of all that we do, particularly evil and injustice, as we abuse the free will and mental and physical faculties granted to us by Allah:

> **Allah is a witness to all—in whatever action you may be engaged, or your reciting the Quran or any action you may be doing when you are occupied with it. Nothing, even an atom's weight is hidden from your Lord on earth or in the heavens. Likewise, everything, big or small, is on record in a clear book.**
>
> **(Yunus 10: 61)**

It vividly describes Allah's all-embracing knowledge and power. Since He is all-powerful, He knows everything, open or hidden. His surveillance system is amazingly extensive and error-free. He has devised since the beginning of life on earth DNA and biometric markings, which we have been able to decode to some degree only recently. He has been recording human actions since time immemorial. It will be produced as undeniable evidence on the Day of Judgement for rewarding or punishing us for our faith and actions.

Our accountability to Him should be foremost in our thought. This also underscores the point that Allah's reward and punishment will be totally transparent and just because it will be based on an error-free, empirically accurate record of our actions. Our record itself will speak for or against us.

Points to ponder

- Today we have been able to invent some surveillance gadgets (CCTVs, biometrics, etc.). However, Allah enjoys a perfect recording system of all that happens, good or evil, since eternity.
- Allah would use His error-free record of our actions in deciding our fate in the next life.
- In view of Allah's omniscience we should be all the more Allah-aware in all that we say or do. This evidence would be used by Him in adjudging us.

Chapter 17

Allah's Reward and Punishment

Allah is the fairest, even-handed judge. His mercy and retribution are perfectly balanced. As He has sent us to this world with clear guidelines how to lead life, He expects us to follow His directives and would judge us accordingly:

> **(O Prophet), tell My servants: "I am Most Forgiving, Most Merciful. However, My punishment too, is painful punishment."**
>
> **(Al-Hijr 15: 49-50)**

This underscores Allah's perfect justice and fairness. While He is most compassionate and most forgiving, He is also the Lord of retribution and punishes the guilty severely. We should strive to lead a pious life and thus escape His terrible punishment.

Allah's mercy is vast. We are His creatures and He would naturally not like to harm His own creatures. However, Allah is the just Lord. He would ensure that all of us who wronged fellow human beings, damaged social fabric and brazenly defied Allah's commands are brought to justice. His mercy dictates that perfect justice should be carried out. Avoid anything wrong which may incur His punishment.

Points to ponder

- In the above verse, Allah's use of "My servants" for us is important, underscoring His love, affection and attachment towards us.
- Being the judge on the Day of Judgement, He would recompense us fairly.
- Out of His immeasurable mercy He may forgive us. Yet for meeting the demands of justice, particularly of our wronging fellow human beings, He would punish us for our misconduct.

Chapter 18

Allah's Excellent Attributes

In His book, the Quran, Allah has described some of His attributes by way of self-introduction. These bring into sharper light His perfection and uniqueness. Some of these feature in the following Quranic passage:

> **Allah, there is no god besides He. He knows the unseen and the seen. He is Most Compassionate, Most Merciful. Allah, there is no god besides He. He is the King, the Holy, the source of peace, the source of security, the Guardian, Almighty, the Supreme, and the Greatest. Glory be to Allah! He is far above the partners they take with Him. Allah, He is the Creator, the Maker and the Designer. His are the excellent names. All those in the heavens and on earth glorify Him. He is Almighty, the Wisest.**
>
> **(Al-Hashr 59: 22-24)**

This cluster of Allah's names and attributes helps us to form a mental picture of Allah's grandeur. First and foremost, we are assured about His protection and kindness to us. He is not out there to hurl us into hellfire out of any vindictiveness. We should therefore shun all that displeases Him, particularly ascribing any partner to Him. Being almighty and the wisest, He has drawn up this perfectly balanced scheme of things for us. All creatures testify to His glory, as they praise Him in their own ways and follow the laws prescribed by Him for them.

Points to ponder

- Though Allah is too exalted to be described, all that is the best is reflected in His names and attributes.
- A study of Allah's attributes helps us fathom, to some extent, how glorious and mighty Allah is.

Chapter 19

Allah's Creative Wonders

As we look at ourselves and the world around us, the scenic beauty, the amazing animal and plant worlds, and the mind-boggling sun, moon, stars and galaxies, etc., we cannot deny the existence of their marvellous Creator, the one true God. The following verse draws our attention to the fascinating yet routine phenomenon of the cloud formation and the resultant rain which brings everything to life:

> **Do you not see that Allah makes the clouds move gently and then joins them together, turning them into a thick mass? Then you see rain drops falling from it. He sends down hail from the heavens, thanks to the mountains. He strikes with it whom He likes and removes it from whom He likes. The flash of His lightning almost takes away the sight**
>
> **(Al-Nur 24: 43)**

Clouds, rain, hail and lightning are some of the numerous manifestations of Allah's creative wonders and limitless power. The Quran was initially addressed to the seventh century illiterate Arabs. The Quran therefore states only bare facts about these natural phenomena, which they could observe and verify with their naked eyes. It does not delve into scientific details as to how it rains in that they could not comprehend these. Moreover, the Quran never claims itself to be a book of science. Whatever it states is, nonetheless, scientifically true, pointing as it does to the infallible divine origin of the Quran.

Points to ponder

- Islam does not present any dense metaphysical or philosophical argument for affirming the existence and oneness of our Creator and Master, the one true God.
- Numerous natural phenomena in the human, animal, plant and cosmic spheres point unmistakably to the grand creative genius and ingenuity of their Creator and Originator, Allah.

Chapter 20

Allah Alternates Day and Night

Lost in our mundane activities, we hardly notice the daily yet incredibly strange occurrence: day and night with their opposite features, alternating regularly, without fail. The following verse should awaken us to this great sign of Allah's creativity and power, visible to everyone:

> **Allah keeps changing night and day. In this there is a lesson for those who have sight.**
>
> **(Al-Nur 24: 44)**

The constant alternation of day and night, which we all witness throughout our life, is another illustration of Allah's ingenuity and power. This natural phenomenon is nothing short of a miracle. Allah draws attention to this readily visible sign of His omnipotence. As we take the occurrence of day and night for granted—an ordinary routine matter—we fail to appreciate what a miracle it is, denoting Allah's creative power. The Quran asks us to reflect on these natural phenomena as the signs of Allah's oneness and lordship. The Quran thus adopts a simple, natural way to define and describe Allah and His glory.

The constant passing of day and night alerts one to getting older day by day and one's approaching death, drawing nearer every day. Make most of the time granted to you by Allah for earning His pleasure and thus ensuring a bright, happy future in the next life.

Points to ponder

- Though we take the alternation of day and night for granted, it should open our eyes to the Creator behind this, the one true Allah.

- The Quran asks us to observe and reflect on the numerous natural phenomena around us for grasping the higher truth about God and the purpose of our life which should be to appreciate the grandeur of our Lord, Allah.

Chapter 21

Allah's Grand Scheme of Things

Gifted with the mind and heart and numerous faculties as we are, make it a point to think seriously on these obvious questions: From where have we come and where will we return? What is the purpose of our life? How should we lead life? The Quranic passage below outlines Allah's plan: the objective behind our creation and our ultimate end:

> **All that is in the heavens and on earth glorifies Allah. His is the kingdom and His is all praise. He has power over everything. Allah has created you all. Some of you are unbelievers while some are believers. Allah watches your actions. He has created the heavens and the earth with a purpose. He has given you shapes and made your shapes excellent. To Him is the return. He knows all that is in the heavens and on earth. He knows what you do privately and publicly. Allah knows even the secrets of hearts.**
>
> **(Al-Taghabun 64: 1-4)**

It is a concise statement regarding Allah and His scheme of things. After having brought us into being He has granted us the freedom of choice: to believe or deny Him. Since He has created everything with a purpose, He will take account on the Day of Judgement. We should be constantly mindful of the all-knowing, all-powerful Allah and His recompense.

Allah's big favour to all of us is our excellent body which helps us accomplish numerous mental and physical feats. However, realise that our life is a trust and that we will be held accountable for our beliefs and actions. Since Allah is all-powerful, all-knowing, we cannot escape His grip in any way.

This account of Allah's perfect Lordship makes us all the more obedient to Him.

Points to ponder

- Allah has created us with a purpose: to test us and reward or punish us after our death on our return to Him.
- In view of this clear plan on which rests our eternal success or disaster in the next life, seriously follow it and try utmost to win Allah's pleasure.

Chapter 22

Allah's Knowledge

Allah has not disclosed to anyone, including His prophets, the date when this world would come to an end, followed by our Judgement in the grand assembly. His knowledge embraces even the falling of each and every leaf. Our faith and good actions alone would matter on the Day of Reckoning.

> **The knowledge of the Last Day is with Allah. Without His knowledge no fruit comes from its sheath. Nor does any female get pregnant or give birth to a child without His knowledge. On the Day of Judgement Allah will ask them. "Where are those whom you took as My partners?" They will reply: "We assure you that none of us is a witness (to those partners)."**
>
> **(Fussilat 41:47)**

Allah's knowledge is absolute and total. He keeps track of everything. No one shares His perfect knowledge. He knows all that happens. He has not specified the last day when the present order will come to an end. For us the time granted to us constitutes our test. We should firmly believe in the one true God, to the exclusion of any partner or incarnation. The unbelievers will regret their polytheism or lack of belief on the Day of Judgement and will try to deny their rejection of Allah. They will then see the evident truth of Allah's oneness and lordship. Their remorse at that final stage will not benefit them.

In view of Allah's greatness turn in total humility to Him.

Points to ponder

- Allah's perfect knowledge, being something awe-striking, prompts us to be very fastidious about our faith and actions which do not escape His infinite knowledge.
- On the Day of Judgment, any idol, saint, tie of kinship and worldly consideration (wealth and social status, etc.) would not carry any weight. Idols would disown their devotees. We are totally on our own to face Allah's interrogation and consequent punishment.

Chapter 23

Allah Is Close to Us

Notwithstanding His towering stature as the only unquestioned master and lord of the vast universe, Allah maintains a close, personal rapport with each of His numerous creatures. He listens and responds to our fervent prayers and guides us through flashes of intuition. He is not at all detached, remote from our predicament. On the contrary, He is always near us. We may approach Him without any intermediary. The Quran abounds in His several instructions to certain human beings, not necessarily prophets, for example women such as Maryam, Prophet Jesus's mother, Prophet Musa's mother, Prophet Shuayb's daughters and a woman victimised by her husband's oppressive divorce.

> **Allah has created man and He knows well what dark suggestions his self makes to him. Allah is nearer to man than even his own jugular vein.**
>
> **(Qaf 50: 16)**

Islam does not admit any intermediary or clergy in the direct relationship between Allah and each one of us. He is closer to us than our own jugular vein. He knows even the thoughts crossing our mind. In view of His might, knowledge and proximity with us, we should be all the more careful and attentive. In Islam, Allah is not some abstract, remote or indifferent deity. Be constantly in communion with Him. As man's Creator, He knows well how vulnerable we are to err. Therefore always be on guard.

Allah's constant observation through His absolute knowledge and power infuses Allah-awareness into us.

Points to ponder

- Being our Creator, Allah knows best every psyche. Likewise, since He is all-knowing, even the thoughts crossing our mind come to His notice.
- In view of such constant proximity with us, turn to Him for every help and guidance to strengthen bonds with Him.

Chapter 24

Allah–the Creator

Some reflection on Allah as the Creator of this universe is bound to overwhelm us: His creation of everything out of nothing; His originality in having provided such diversity in every respect (shape, size, colour, working, benefits, etc.); His ingenuity in creating according to habitat and what suits best the survival of His creatures. This amazing spectacle of His creative wonders turns us into His sincere, awe-struck devotees:

> **Your Lord creates and chooses what He wills and they (false gods) have no choice. Glory be to Allah! He is far above the partners they take with Him.**
>
> **(Al-Qasas 28: 68)**

Being Almighty, Allah creates at will. No one else has any role in creation. He is too strong to need any helper or partner. Keep glorifying our Lord, the Master of all. In creation, rather in anything, anyone besides Allah has no hand. False gods have not created anything and hence we should believe in the one true God, which will ensure our deliverance.

Points to ponder

- In comparison to Allah–the Creator, there is no one who may claim to have accomplished anything. We, at best, imitate creation poorly. All of our achievements represent only the mimesis of what has already existed around us, thanks to the great maker and designer, Allah.

- Out of His infinite wisdom and inexhaustible resources Allah creates in no time, anything which pleases Him. We have no role in or control over it. We are too helpless before the forces and elements of Nature, and, above all, death.

Chapter 25

Allah Is in Command of Everything

We have been misled down the ages by the misconception about the multiplicity of gods, and God's incarnations, partners and even children. Emphatically, Islam insists on and vindicates the one all-powerful God, Allah, to be obeyed unquestioningly. Islam does away all notions of priesthood and intermediaries. It establishes a direct, one-to-one contact between Allah and his followers. This logical, alluring concept of God has won over millions of seekers of truth to Islam across the world.

> **He is Allah; there is no god other than Him. For Him is the praise in this world and in the Hereafter. His is the command. To Him all of you will be returned.**
>
> **(Al-Qasas 28: 70)**

All power rests solely with Allah, the one true God. He exercises His power according to will. All of us have to return to Him in order to render the account of our faith and actions.

Monotheism lies at the core of the Islamic faith. Unequivocally the Quran declares this truth at many places. As the Supreme Lord, Allah commands the respect and praise of all beings in both the worlds. His will reigns supreme. In view of this grand stature of Allah, be all the more particular about the eventual return to Him, from which there is no escape for anyone.

This concept of Allah and His accountability infuses piety and humility into us and we should devote ourselves to sound faith and good actions for our eternal success. Also learn to submit to Allah's decisions. This should not be misconstrued as inaction and belief in fatalism.

Points to ponder

- In Islam, Allah is all-in-all, admitting no partner or associate. Even prophets are at His beck and call. He enjoys and exercises all power in every sphere.
- Allah's oneness in pivotal to the Islamic creed. Only He is to be served and worshipped. Only He would sit in judgement on us in the next life. Those lost in the maze of the pantheon of gods, incarnations, spirits and saints, etc. are urged to turn towards this straightforward, readily understandable concept of Allah.

Chapter 26

Allah Is Not Dependent on Our Worship

Since eternity, up to eternity, Allah happens to be the Supreme Lord. Our belief in Him does not confer upon Him the status of being the Supreme Lord. Even if not a single person believes in Him, it does not dent in the least His exalted status. He does not ask any offering in return from His devotees. Prayer and other acts of worship provide spiritual, emotional and moral gratification to believers, having nothing to do with making or enhancing the exalted status of Allah. Numerous objects of Nature willingly obey Him in being bound by its laws ordained by Him for them. The verse below unravels this important theological point:

> **If you refuse to believe, Allah does not stand in need of you. However, He does not like His servants to be Unbelievers. If you thank Him, He is pleased with you. No one will bear another's burden. You have to return to Your Lord. He will then inform you what you did. He knows even what is in your hearts.**
>
> **(Al-Zumar 39: 7)**

Our belief or disbelief in Allah does not make any difference to the exalted status of Allah. However, if we believe and thank Him, He will shower His rewards on us. In Islam everyone is directly accountable to Allah. The all-knowing, all-powerful Allah will recompense us with perfect justice.

Allah's mercy is overarching. He does not want His servants to deny Him which will bring about their eternal perdition. Likewise, though our worship and service does not do any good to Him, out of mercy, He will immensely reward us. As He possesses perfect knowledge of our actions, including our innermost motives, He will deal with us accordingly.

Points to ponder

- Allah is ensconced in His unique position, unperturbed by our belief or disbelief in Him. He is all-independent and does not stand in need of anyone.
- Out of grace, He nonetheless appreciates our service and obedience to Him and would reward us lavishly in the next life, as promised by Him several times in the Quran.

Chapter 27

Allah Would Revive the Dead

As part of His grand plan for human beings, Allah causes our birth, grants us an opportunity to choose a way, including the one prescribed by Him. Then after the appointed term, preordained by Him, He causes our death. On the last day, marking the end of the present world, He would cause all to die, followed by His resurrection of all the dead, from the day of creation up to the last day, summoning them for His requital on the Day of Judgement. This special feature of His unlimited power comes out in the following verse:

> **So consider the tokens of Allah's mercy—how He revives the dead land. Undoubtedly He will give life to the dead. He has power over everything.**
>
> **(Al-Rum 30: 50)**

Out of His immense mercy Allah sends rain which revives the dead land. It is a fairly common natural phenomenon visible to all of us and a telling example of how Allah will bring the dead back to life on the Day of Judgement for the final reckoning. The belief in the hereafter is therefore simple enough to understand.

The rain cycle is life-giving, demonstrating as it does Allah's kindness to all living beings. Without rain, there will be no life. Moreover, this fact convinces us that after our death He will bring us back to life for judgment. Justice demands that the guilty, who went scott-free in this world, and the pious, who suffered for no fault of theirs, should be punished and rewarded respectively. Being all-powerful, Allah will accomplish this on the Day of Judgement.

Points to ponder

- Some of us may naively be skeptical about the phenomenon of Resurrection. However, it is common sight that rain revives the dead, parched land, life-after-death is a reality and all of us will undergo this.
- Life in the next world is a moral, social and legal requirement for meeting out the dictates of justice. Allah alone can dispense justice on such a massive scale—a truth laid bare in the above Quranic verse.

Chapter 28

Allah's Power

Power is an inextricable feature of Allah's being. Without His limitless power, He could not create, design and manage this gigantic universe. His sustaining billions of beings endlessly, once again, is owing to His unimaginable power. The verse below points to another facet of His power: His ability to revive dexterously all the dead from the day of creation up to the last day:

> **Does man imagine that Allah is not able to bring together his bones again? No, Allah has the power to put together in the perfect order even his fingertips.**
>
> **(Al-Qiyamah 75: 3-4)**

The reference is to Allah's ability to re-create us on the Day of Judgement. Since He created us out of nothing in the first place, it is easy for Him to create us again. We will be brought back to life for judgement and this will usher in eternal happiness or pain for us, depending on our faith or the lack of it in the one true Allah, and our good or evil actions in life.

Resurrection is not improbable. Rain reviving dead land is common knowledge. Only those who have a shallow view of life reject the next life. Moreover, divine Judgement is essential and inevitable for dispensing justice. In view of Allah's creative power, of which we see numerous manifestations all around us all the time, our life after death is not hard for Allah Who has created so much out of nothing.

Points to ponder

- Not only has Allah created everything and keeps on doing so every moment even now, on the last day He will bring to life all the dead, by dint of His power, for judgement.
- His power is so consummate that He would replicate the dead up to their fingertips, as they were before their death. Only the Lord, Allah can accomplish such a feat.

Chapter 29

Trust in Allah

In life all of us are confronted with a range of challenges, some of which are seemingly beyond our capacity to cope. The way out is to repose trust in the most merciful, all-powerful Allah Who will graciously grant us the strength to overcome all odds, no matter how onerous these might be. The verse under discussion exhorts us to profess and practise trust in Him:

> **Have trust in Allah Who is Ever Living. He will never die. Glorify His praise. He is fully aware of the sins of His servants.**
>
> **(Al-Furqan 25: 58)**

Allah is unique in every respect imaginable. That He is immortal is one of His awesome features. Therefore, He alone stands out as the only pillar of support and strength for us. In view of His uniqueness we are bound to praise and extol Him. Equally bewildering is His all-embracing knowledge. In recognition of these stupendous attributes, bow down to Him.

Man, being weak, is too vulnerable. He is in constant need of help and support. Allah alone can comfort us. Out of His mercy, He will bless us with eternal happiness in our next life, provided that we profess and practise faith and good actions.

Points to ponder

- Since Allah is everlasting, all around us, the thought of His patronage and refuge for us is so reassuring and soothing.
- He is most merciful to condone our wrongs, provided we turn sincerely to Him in repentance and not indulge again in sins, which He may magnanimously pardon.
- The Prophet Muhammad (peace be upon him) and early Muslims had to undergo terrible persecution for professing and practising the new faith of Islam. However, their unwavering trust in Allah helped them overcome the stiff opposition and emerge victorious in seventh-century Arabia. Within 100 years Islam spread throughout the world.

Chapter 30

Allah's Signs in the Universe

Numerous signs of Allah's power, knowledge and creativity are scattered around us. Take our body as a telling example: what remarkable feats it achieves and what massive potentials, both mental and physical, it has. These signs, according to the following Quranic verse, should help us in our quest for higher truths such as the Creator and creation, and our way and purpose of life as prescribed for us by our master Lord:

> **Blessed is Allah Who has placed big stars in the sky. He has placed in it a great lamp and a shining moon.**
>
> **(Al-Furqan 25: 61)**

Attention is drawn to Allah's celestial signs, underscoring His ingenuity and creative power: the sun, the moon and numerous stars. As one thinks of the gigantic galaxies created by Him, we realise His greatness all the more. It is incumbent upon us to send blessings upon almighty Allah.

These resplendent signs which we witness all the time underscore Allah's creativity and His immaculate functioning of the universe. The Quran urges us to reflect on these signs, appreciate Allah's oneness and greatness and devise ways and means for subjugating forces of Nature for the common good of humanity. Prompted by this directive, Muslims, from seventh to twelfth century, recorded many groundbreaking achievements in various branches of knowledge, as documented in George Sarton's *Introduction to the History of Science.*

Points to ponder

- There are self-evident Allah's signs everywhere, which are as instructive for us today as they were to the illiterate seventh-century Arabs, the immediate addressees of the Quran.
- The sun, the moon and stars are cited in the above example as pointers to Allah's unparallelled power, wisdom and creativity. Even without the highly sophisticated and precise gadgets today, the seventh century, illiterate Arabs too, marvelled at Allah's unmissable signs and recognised His oneness and lordship. With the latest technology unravelling many more fascinating secrets of Nature, Allah's creation, turn all the more to glorifying our magnificent Creator, Allah.

Chapter 31

Allah As Our Sustainer

Allah is our Creator as well as Sustainer. He is so gracious and thoughtful that He arranges for our sustenance even in our pre-natal stage. Inside the mother's womb. Moreover, as part of His larger, benign sustenance scheme, he infuses love and affection for the baby, even before their birth, into the heart and mind of their parents and near and dear ones. His provisions as a blessing for us are at the heart of the following verse:

> **Allah is fully aware of His servants. He gives provision to whom He wills. He is All Strong, Almighty.**
>
> **(Al-Shura 42: 19)**

As the only Provider and Sustainer, Allah feeds all of us. He grants provisions in a certain measure to everyone as He wills. Owing to His limitless resources He has been sustaining all since time memorial and will do so until the last day.

It is a testament to Allah's perfection as Sustainer that notwithstanding the population explosion in recent centuries, the resources provided by Him suffice to meet the varied needs of billions of people. Since He is all-knowing, He provides all that His creatures, need for their existence.

Points to ponder

- Allah's abundant provisions: air, water, food and whatnot are there for everyone, including even die-hard atheists and hostile unbelievers. Being most forbearing and gracious, He ungrudgingly showers His provisions on those who publicly deny and revile Him.
- Being almighty, Allah provides sustenance to everyone and would hold everyone accountable for their conduct on the Day of Judgment.

Chapter 32

Allah's Arrangement for Our Guidance

Throughout history, Allah sent down His messenger and books to various communities in their respective languages. The Bible and the Quran provide their extensive lists. Since He appointed the Prophet Muhammad (peace be upon him) and the Quran as His final messenger and message until the last day, He has made elaborate arrangements for their preservation and dissemination across the world until the end of time. The Quranic verse below informs of the divine arrangement for alerting people to Allah's message:

> **Warners did appear in all the towns destroyed by Allah for advising them. Allah was never unjust to them.**
>
> **(Al-Shu'ara 26: 208-209)**

Through His messengers and books Allah has guided and warned people in all time and place. When they paid no attention to His elaborate warnings and ultimatum, He destroyed the sinful communities. His punishment was a dictate of justice.

Allah does not punish people arbitrarily. Since the dawn of history, He sent down His messengers to all parts of the world. They were human beings and members of their respective communities who conveyed to them in their own language, Allah's message for achieving success in both the worlds.

Prophet Muhammad (570-633 CE) stands out as Allah's last messenger. As the book, the Quran revealed to him and his life and teachings are fully preserved—valid for all time and place — no messenger would appear after Prophet Muhammad (peace be upon him).

Points to ponder

- The main function of Allah's messengers, down the millennia, was to advise their respective communities about Allah's message and the dire consequences of its rejection. The Torah, the Bible and the Quran amply bear out this point.
- Islam's holy book, the Quran, and the last messenger Prophet Muhammad's sayings and teachings (Hadith) originally in Arabic are freely available in all major languages of the world. We may draw upon these to find out the straight way to Allah and eternal success in the next life.

Chapter 33

Allah and Our Conduct

Allah has granted all of us free will and numerous faculties of the heart and mind. He has also arranged for the availability of His guidance to everyone. Likewise, He has eloquently warned us against the horrible consequences of not following His way. Against this backdrop, the following Quranic verse should be studied:

> **He who does good does so to his own good. He who does evil does so to his own loss. Your Lord does not wrong His servants.**
>
> **(Fussilat 41: 46)**

It illustrates Allah's fairness. He has eloquently shown His guidance. The guilty are punished for their own wrongdoing. Allah does not treat anyone unjustly in the slightest. He has given us free will and mental and physical faculties. It is up to us to make or mar our ultimate end. Allah does not instantly seize wrongdoers in this life. This will kill the very purpose of our test and trial in this world. He will recompense us justly for our actions in life-after-death.

Points to ponder

- Allah, the all-just and most forbearing has not imposed His will on us. He has granted us an option and explained its outcome.
- Doing good is emotionally and spiritually very gratifying. Moreover, it makes this world a better place to live in.

Chapter 34

Allah Will Question Us

Our master, Lord, has assigned us a job in this life. It is therefore natural that He will interrogate us, as we return to Him after death. The following verse states emphatically this truth:

> **No one can question Allah about what He does. However, all people will be questioned.**
>
> **(Al-Anbiya 21: 23)**

It posits the Islamic stance on intercession. No messenger, saint or pious person can recommend anyone's case for Allah's pardon. Islam rejects the notion of any redeemer. All of us will have to render our account and will be adjudged accordingly.

Being all-powerful, He will sit in judgement over our record of actions. We should be ever conscious of our conduct as we all have to present our account to Him.

Points to ponder

- The all-powerful would adjudge us in relation to our faith and conduct. Being the master of the Day of Judgement is His important attribute.

- Allah-awareness resides in the constant realisation in our heart and mind that we have to return soon to our Lord and He would question us about our acts of omission and commission. On the basis of our faith and conduct in this life, He would reward or punish us.

Chapter 35

Allah on the Day of Judgement

Our belief in the next life is of paramount importance in Islam. It invests our life with a sense of purpose. Alive to the grim fact of our answerability to our Lord we should lead life driven by the ideals of sound faith and good actions. The following verse sheds some light on the concept of the Day of Judgment:

> **Say: "O Allah, the Originator of the heavens and the earth, Who knows the unseen and the seen, You will judge among people about what they differ." If the wrongdoers had all that is on earth, and as much more, they will offer it on the Day of Judgement in order to save themselves from the painful punishment. Yet there will come to them from Allah what they had not expected. All their evil actions will appear before them. That punishment which they mocked will overwhelm them.**
>
> **(Al-Zumar 39: 46-48)**

Apart from stating Allah's glory, this passage projects a terrifying picture of sinners on the Day of Judgement. Nothing will help or rescue them. We should guard ourselves against this horrible eventuality.

Allah alone, with His perfect attributes of being the Creator, all-knowing, all-powerful will adjudge all of us on the basis of our faith and actions.

The above passage depicts a chilling account of sinners on the Day of Judgment. Let us avoid any loss in the next life.

Points to ponder

- Our fate for eternity would be decided on the Day of Judgment as Allah would take our account. It is high time to prepare for this momentous eventuality.
- No worldly consideration—our power, glory and wealth in this life—would be of any avail on the Day of Judgement. We would be rewarded or punished on the basis of our conduct in this life. Hence, we should pay heed to Allah's warnings.

Chapter 36

Allah and His Messengers

Messengers, Allah's select servants, are an important link between Allah and us. They faithfully conveyed his message to us both verbally and practically. The Prophet Muhammad (peace be upon him) represents the culmination of this series of messengers and hence the role model for all of us to follow. The following verse describes the role of messengers:

> **Allah Almighty, the Wisest sends His message to you (O Prophet), as He did to the Messengers before you. His is all that is in the heavens and all that is on earth. He is Most High, the Greatest.**
>
> **(Al-Shura 42: 3-4)**

Allah's message to all of His Prophets, sent to all parts of the world down the ages, has been identical: believe in Him and doing good actions. Through His messengers and books, He has shown us the straight way, following which we can win His pleasure and get the eternal joys of paradise.

Messengers are the chosen servants of Allah. They are not to be mistaken as His partners or incarnations. They faithfully conveyed His message to their respective communities.

Points to ponder

- Out of His infinite wisdom, for our guidance, in all eras of history and in every nook and corner of the world, Allah sent down His messengers to their respective communities.
- The Prophet Muhammad (peace be upon him) stands out as the final messenger of Allah. His teachings known as *Sunnah,* being the elaboration of the Quran, are there for our guidance in all situations of life.

Chapter 37

The Prophet's Status

Although prophets are the chosen servants of Allah, they do not have any parity with Allah Who alone is the master and Lord. Prophets instruct people in Allah's message, by way of giving them the good news, and warning them for obedience or disobedience respectively to Allah. The verse below describes where prophets stand in relation to Allah:

> **(O Prophet), say: "I am only a warner. There is no god besides Allah, the One, the Supreme. Lord of the heavens and the earth and of all that is between these. He is Almighty, Most Forgiving".**
>
> **(Saad 38: 65-66)**

As directed by Allah, prophets give good news and warn fellow human beings of their era regarding belief and disbelief. All power, nonetheless, rests solely with Allah. He guides us to the straight way and He will recompense us on the Day of Judgement. Messengers or saints do not have any role in our deliverance. Allah will hold each one of us individually accountable for our faith and actions. In the long series of prophets, from Adam, Noah, Abraham, Moses and Jesus to Muhammad (peace be upon them), the last one is Allah's final messenger for all place and time.

Points to ponder

- Some communities have mistaken prophets for god or as His incarnation. Prophets are human beings selected by Allah for performing the assignment of guiding and warning fellow human beings.
- To Allah belongs all power and glory. Apart from being our Creator and Sustainer, He would decide our eternal fate in the next everlasting life.

Chapter 38

Allah Is the Truth

Notwithstanding all its glitter and allure, this world is ephemeral. We are mortal, with a brief life. Allah is the only and ultimate truth. We should never lose sight of this fact and turn wholly to Him. The following Quranic verse presses home this point:

> **Allah alone is the truth. Those whom they call besides Him are false. Allah is Most High, the Greatest.**
>
> **(Al-Hajj 22: 62)**

That Allah is the one true God is the cornerstone of Islam. This rules out any notion of His partner, children or incarnation. Monotheism is the outstanding hallmark of Islam.

All creation is solely Allah's. False gods are man-made, having no power. Allah alone exercises all power.

Points to ponder

- Notwithstanding the self-evident truth about Allah's oneness, many communities have gone astray in having invented false gods. Allah urges us to use reason and reflect in order to realise His lordship and oneness.

- Our adherence to the one true God, His final book, the Quran and His last messenger, Prophet Muhammad (peace be upon him) is the only way out for our deliverance and final success in the next life.

Chapter 39

Allah Is Independent of All

In Islam, the concept of Allah's being is unique. He cannot be likened to anything. Moreover, he has been there since eternity and will last forever. He does not stand in need of any, even worshippers. As the Supreme Being, He enjoys lordship, irrespective of our obedience or disobedience to Him. However, the all-powerful Allah would admit the faithful to paradise and consign the evil to hellfire. The verse below delineates His absolute independence:

> **Allah's is all that is in the heavens and on earth, Allah is Self-Sufficient, Most Praiseworthy.**
>
> (Al-Hajj 22: 64)

Being the master of the universe, Allah owns everything. He is not dependent on anything or anyone in any sense. Praise His magnificence. In recognition of His perfect and unique features, serve and praise Him to the best of your abilities.

Points to ponder

- Allah has brought everything into being out of nothing. This should make us bow down to His greatness, power and glory.

- Since all that is there is at His beck and call, He does not need anyone. He does whatever pleases Him, without anyone's help or assistance. For our bright prospects in the next life, we should serve and obey Him to the extent we can.

Chapter 40

Allah Records Everything

Allah is all-powerful and all-just as well. Owing to His measureless power and knowledge He has devised ways of recording all that happens, particularly our actions and their after-effects. He would not whimsically reward or punish us on the Day of Judgement. Rather, He would produce irrefutable evidence about our conduct and adjudge us accordingly. The truth about His vast knowledge comes out from this verse:

> **Do you not realize that Allah knows all that is in the heavens and on earth? All this is in a record. Judgement is easy for Allah.**
>
> **(Al-Hajj 22: 70)**

All-encompassing knowledge is a remarkable feature of Allah. This equips Him best to adjudge and reward and punish us on the Day of Judgement. It is common knowledge that all that happens, no matter how minor it might be, leaves its imprint. DNA, fingerprints, biometrics, sound waves, etc. are some of the natural manifestations of Allah's recording system. This irrefutable evidence about us will be produced on the Day of Judgement in order to dispense justice in a totally transparent way. We will bear witness to our actions and see its consequences in the form of reward or punishment.

Points to ponder

- We tend to forget that we are not independent, free to do whatever we like. The all-powerful Allah records all of our actions and would use the same incontrovertible evidence for rewarding or punishing us.

- Our belief in the all-knowing, all-seeing Allah is in our own interest. It keeps us alert and serves as a deterrent against doing anything bad in the eyes of Allah. This helps in building a happy, peaceful society.

Chapter 41

Allah Does Not Wrong Anyone

As the Quran was revealed during the Prophet Muhammad's career, it also contains comments on some of the events and characters of the day. Some criticised the Quranic directive for charity. Some disbelievers were guilty of the ghastly crime of having killed Allah's messengers sent to them. Notwithstanding His boundless mercy, Allah sternly punishes culprits, as is evident from the verse below:

> **Allah heard the taunt of those saying: "Allah is poor while we are rich." He has recorded their saying and their unjust killing of their Prophets. He will make them taste the Hellfire. This is because of their own actions. Otherwise Allah does not wrong His servants.**
>
> **(Ali Imran 3: 181-182)**

Some audacious disbelievers mockingly questioned Allah's command for giving charity to the poor and even killed Prophets who called them to follow the straight way. They will be thrown into hellfire. Otherwise, Allah is most affectionate to people. This is very reassuring for those of us who are pious, and have faith and good actions to their credit. Allah will reward them lavishly as He is not unjust to any of His servants.

Points to ponder

- Allah's dispensation of justice is perfect. He does not spare the evil ones who cause mischief. He keeps a vigilant eye on our actions and would recompense us accordingly.

- Allah is not vindictive or given to punishing people for fun. His actions are marked by perfect justice and fairness. We should try our level best to earn His pleasure.

Chapter 42

Belief in Allah

In Islam our belief in Allah as the one true God is the pivot of our faith. The Quran presents a simple, easy way to gain our knowledge of Allah, His working and His lordship. We are urged to study numerous signs of His creativity, ingenuity and might, which are around us. The following Quranic verse suggests the way to know Allah:

> **Allah will show them His signs in this universe and in their own selves. It will thus become clear to them that it is the truth. Is it not enough that your Lord watches everything?**
>
> **(Fussilat 41: 53)**

We are asked to reflect on Allah's creative wonders in our own bodies and in Nature around us. This will convince us of His greatness and lordship. Even with our naked eyes we can see so many marvels of Allah: our body which is able to accomplish so much, animal life, plant life, landscape, rain, mountains and the variety of food and drink. The list is endless. If we reflect on Allah's signs around us, we will turn into His grateful, obedient servants and will attain success in both the worlds.

Points to ponder

- Out of His immense grace Allah has enabled all of us to observe and appreciate His existence and masterly accomplishments.

- The more we study our own selves and things around us, we realise that these represent the handiwork of no one other than the supreme, all-knowing Lord Who has produced numerous things which are essential and beneficial for our existence and are so dexterously interconnected. Take the water or food cycle as an instance. It is amazing how Allah provides these to all living beings and in plenty. Without His perfect arrangement we could not get water or food on our own. We may introduce ways and means for their management and distribution. However, we get these in the first place from Allah alone.

Chapter 43

Allah's Promise Is True

Being the embodiment of truth, Allah's promise is always true. As part of His broader plan, however, He may fulfil some of His promises in the next world. So do not feel disillusioned on noting the apparent ascendancy of evil, injustice and immorality around us and the plight of the pious or innocent victims. Were Allah to settle scores here and now, our test in this life would be pointless. He lets evil prevail so that the culprit may fulfil their base desires. What is nonetheless certain, is that Allah would keep His promise in the next life. According to the above Quranic verse, He would reward the pious:

> **Allah helps whom He wills. He is Almighty, Most Merciful. This is Allah's promise. He does not break His promise. However, most of the people do not understand.**
>
> **(Al-Rum 30: 5-6)**

As Allah is extremely kind to His believing servants, He helps them. Being almighty, He is always true to His promise. The details of His promise appear prominently in the Quran: His mercy; His justice; His sustenance to all living beings; His absolute knowledge and power and His creative wonders.

On reflection, we can verify these promises of Allah. These permeate the world around us.

Points to ponder

- All promises of Almighty Allah are bound to come true, sooner or later. Out of His wisdom He fulfils these at the best, opportune time, though we may be hasty about the same.
- As true believers having full trust in Allah, we should wait for the actualisation of His promises. Most of these are related to the next world when truth would manifest.

Chapter 44

Speech: Allah's Bounty for Us

Allah's favours conferred on us are numerous and equally valuable. In the following verse, one of these, the faculty of speech or communication is cited:

> **Allah created man. He taught him speech**
>
> **(Al-Rahman 55: 3-4)**

Man's creation is a marvel on Allah's part. Equally amazing is that He has granted man the faculty of speech which makes human beings superior to all other creatures. We should be grateful to Allah for this huge blessing.

Without the faculty of speech, life is unthinkable; no communication could be possible among human beings. Knowledge could not be transmitted to future generations. There would have been no literature or culture. We should appreciate it as Allah's great gift to us.

Points to ponder

- We have been able to improve the quality of life and make the forces of Nature subservient to us owing to some special bounties granted to us, especially speech and communication.

- The faculty of speech is indeed precious for us. It is a lifeline for us in every domain of life—business and trade, governance, social relations, entertainment, and what-not! We must thank Allah for blessing us with the faculty of speech which has made our life meaningful.

Chapter 45

Allah's Support for Us

Allah's provision system for us is largely unfathomable. Laws of Nature, our own merit and efforts, no doubt, facilitate in getting us what we have. Nonetheless, it has a big component of luck, chance, being at the right place at the right time, all of which is graciously ordained by Allah for us. This verse asks us to reflect on this truth:

> **Allah gives provision from a place one does not expect. Allah is enough for him who puts trust in Him. Allah does what He decides. Allah has set a measure for everything.**
>
> **(Al-Talaq 65: 3)**

Glory be to Allah for providing us sustenance from even unexpected quarters. Being all-powerful, He executes all that He wills. His scheme of things stands out for its balance and perfection.

We naively think that we earn by dint of our merit and skills. However, it is Allah Who enables us to get all that we have. At times, we do not get something, no matter how hard we might try. We have to accept that everything is ordained by Allah. Accordingly we should be grateful and praise Him.

Points to ponder

- Allah is the provider *par excellence.* Our efforts alone do not help us get everything. Often, we are blessed with Allah's special favour, leaving us speechless and grateful to Him.
- Islam believes in predestination. At the same time, it exhorts us to strive for securing Allah's sustenance. Sometimes Allah, however, confers blessings upon us from nowhere. We should praise and glorify Him for His favours.

Chapter 46

Allah–the Lord of the Worlds

The Islamic concept of Allah as God is wide ranging. He is not the Lord of only Arabs or Muslims. In contrast, He is the universal God, of believers and unbelievers alike and of all that exists. His domain extends to the heavens as well. He is the master of the Day of Judgement, Who will bring back to life all the dead for rewarding and punishing according to the scales of justice. The same trust appears in the following verse:

To Allah belong the Next World and this world.

(Al-Layl 92: 13)

Both this world and the next one lie under Allah's control. It is in our own interest to obey Him for our success and happiness. No one other than Allah has any say in the working of the universe. He does what He wills. Our fate in both this and the next, eternal world depends on His mercy. He has graciously guided us how to worship and serve Him and win His pleasure for achieving eternal joys in the hereafter. Islam represents His guidance for us, for all time and place.

Points to ponder

- 'Allah', the Arabic word for God, should not be taken in a narrow sense, of being the God of only Arabs or, at most, of all Muslims. He is the Lord of the worlds.

- His power reigns supreme in both this and the next world. Apart from being the Creator and Sustainer of all that exists, He is also the master of the Day of Judgement. He would take account of everyone and dispense justice in the most transparent and fair way.

Chapter 47

Allah's Sustenance System

Allah's features are remarkably extraordinary. Take for example, Him feeding His creatures. The scale and distribution system of His provisions befogs our mind. With the latest advanced technology, we cannot dare even plan what He has been accomplishing for eons of time: feeding His creatures, particularly the non-human ones who do not harvest or store food for the next day, and in mountain ranges, deserts, depths of oceans snow-clad regions darkness of night. This is hinted at in the following verse:

> **There are many creatures who do not carry their sustenance. Yet Allah gives them sustenance and He provides sustenance to you also. He is All Hearing, All Knowing.**
>
> **(Al-Ankabut 29: 60)**

Is it not a miracle that millions of creatures (animals, birds, and insects in particular) are fed constantly, thanks to Allah's infallible arrangement? Prima facie, they do not have any food store to draw upon. Since He is all-hearing, all-seeing, the all-wise Lord, He has provided suitably for everyone.

It is Allah Who has provided natural resources for nourishing us. Since the beginning of time up to this day, billions upon billions of creatures have drawn upon His provisions which have not exhausted. He keeps feeding everyone. We have, no doubt, learnt, rather almost mastered, how to utilise the natural resources provided by Allah. Yet, could there be any sustenance for us without the sun, rain, vegetation, cattle, and above all, the human mind, gifted by Allah, for supporting ourselves?

Points to ponder

- Is it not mind-blowing that Allah feeds billions of His creatures who have no means of their own everyday? This divine arrangement has been in place for centuries in every part of the planet earth, including huge oceans.
- Since He is all-powerful, with limitless resources at His disposal, He has been running this incredibly all alone and for so long. He gets things done in no time and without any effort. Such is the supreme Allah! Glory be to Him!

Chapter 48

Allah's Creativity

The world around us abounds in marvels of all sorts—shapes, forms, colours, creatures, patterns, scenes, landscape, seascape, cloudscape, flowers, leaves, trees, fruits, taste, fragrance and what-not! One lifespan is not even sufficient for counting Allah's creative wonders scattered everywhere for us to see and reflect on Allah's inexhaustible mastery over everything of which we can think. The following verse draws attention to only one of His countless wonders—birds, with their flying ability, their habitat, their shapes and sizes and Allah's provision system for them:

> **Do they not think about the birds above them—how they spread and fold their wings? Only the Most Compassionate Allah holds them. He watches everything.**
>
> **(Al-Mulk 67: 19)**

Another miracle from the kingdom of birds! We have been able to attain some advancements in aviation only in the last century. Allah has been accomplishing it in a sustained form for aeons of time. Another proof of Allah's glory and power!

Points to ponder

- We marvel at masterpieces of an artist in one particular sphere. In Allah's domain creative wonders are galore.
- What a pity that we have little time for appreciating Allah's creativity, or even less so for comprehending His glory and power and turning in sheer devotion and admiration to Him for serving and obeying Him.
- The above verse speaks of Allah as the most compassionate one in relation to birds. Indeed, He is the universal Lord, catering to the needs of all creatures.

Chapter 49

Allah Watches Everything

Of Allah's numerous attributes, His being all-seeing, all-aware must merit our attention. This signifies that He records all our actions. This realisation is an effective deterrent against committing any wrong. His omniscience underscores His power and control over everything. The following verse seeks to infuse valuable Allah-awareness into us for our own moral development and fairness in our dealing:

> **Say: "Allah is enough as a witness between me and you. He is All Seeing, All Aware of His servants."**
>
> **(Al-Isra 17: 96)**

In all mutual dealings and interactions with fellow human beings, have this deep belief that Allah watches all our actions. He, being all-seeing and all-aware, records everything and will question us for all we said and did. This consciousness is bound to infuse into us piety, justice and fairness. This, in turn, will make our dealings and social interaction all the more friendly and positive. Islam prescribes self-restraint and a keen sense of our accountability to Allah as the way out for a happy social life, largely free from friction.

Points to ponder

- That Allah watches us all the time should give us a deep sense of security and comfort. We are under His watchful eyes and would be amply compensated for any wrong done to us.
- Allah observes how we act during our lifespan granted by Him to us as a test. He records all that we say and do and would recompense us accordingly on the Day of Judgement. The record produced by Him would be undeniable for us.

Chapter 50

Why Did Allah Send Down the Quran?

Allah is most merciful to us. For our guidance and salvation, He has put in place a permanent, error-free arrangement—His final book of guidance, the Quran which is preserved in its pristine purity since its completion in 633 to this day and His final messenger, Prophet Muhammad's role model life which demonstrates what the Quran teaches in theory. He has provided these two invaluable sources of guidance, which are freely available in all languages of the world, for our success in both the worlds, as is affirmed in the verse below:

> **It is Allah Who has sent the Quran in truth. It is the criterion (to find out good and evil). What will make you know that the Last Day is perhaps near?**
>
> **(Al-Shura 42: 16-17)**

The Quran is Allah's final guidance for mankind of all time and place. It was conveyed piecemeal from 610 CE to 633 CE, conveyed to Allah's last prophet, messenger, Muhammad (peace be upon him) (570–633 CE). The Quran being the Word of Allah stands out as a masterpiece of Arabic, full of literary, rhetorical and presentation skills. It is preserved in its pristine purity. Millions of Muslims have memorised the entire Quran by heart running into around 600 pages, and it is recited every day by billions of Muslims in their devotional prayers. It is addressed to human beings and instructs them in all departments of human activity.

This description of our appearance before Allah and the display of our lifetime record and His absolute power to decide our fate on the Day of Judgement should impel us to lead a pious life in this world, characterised by sound faith and good actions.

Points to ponder

- The Quran stands out as Allah's guidance for us in all walks of human activity. This is the main objective behind the sending down of the Quran.
- As the Quran is the word of Allah, its study keeps us in proximity with Allah, constantly telling us what pleases or displeases Him. It is particularly useful for keeping us on the way to success in both the worlds.

Chapter 51

Fearing Allah

The all-seeing Allah observes and records our personal conduct, particularly our wrongs and sins. This belief should make us all the more cautious about our actions. Nothing escapes His knowledge. Apart from love and awe, believers fear Allah in recognition of His supremacy, His judgement and His absolute power, against which everyone is helpless:

> **Allah knows the cheating of the eyes and the secrets of the heart.**
>
> **(Al-Mumin 40: 19)**

Allah watches all of our actions, and even our innermost motives, desires and objectives. Since nothing is beyond Him, our conduct should be spotless.

Islam aims at our moral self-development. Our belief in the all-seeing, all-knowing Allah Who will take us to task on the Day of Judgment helps us keep following the straight way. In Islam this sense of accountability to Allah imbues us with piety and excellent conduct, without any external agency such as law, police or state. Personal piety lies at the core of the Islamic belief system.

Points to ponder

- Since everything, including even cheating by sight comes to His knowledge in no time, we should be on our guard in our conduct.
- As Allah will take us to task on the Day of Judgment which would decide our eternal success or failure, we should develop a strong fear of Allah and ensure that we do not incur His displeasure.

Chapter 52

Allah–the Best Judge

Justice and fairness are outstanding attributes of Allah. Endowed with complete error-free knowledge of everything and absolute, unquestioning power, He is ideally suited as everyone's judge. For no blemish or partisanship can mar His judgement. The following Quranic verse asserts His role as the best judge:

> **Allah will judge with justice and truth. Those whom the unbelievers call besides Allah cannot judge at all. It is only Allah Who is All Hearing, All Seeing.**
>
> **(Al-Mumin 40: 20)**

Allah's final judgement will be marked by transparency and fairness. No one else will have any role in it. As the Supreme Being, He will be the sole master on the Day of Judgement. That the one true God, Who is all-powerful, will recompense us fairly after our death is morally and emotionally very reassuring. It helps us put up with the problems and excesses in this life. We know that in the next eternal life we will be compensated for all our sufferings in this life. No one, even including Allah's messengers, saints or those whom we erroneously take as partners with Allah, will have any role in Allah's perfect award of reward or punishment to us on the Day of Judgement.

Points to ponder

- Allah alone is entitled to be the judge on the Day of Judgement. For He is all-powerful and all-knowing. It is out of question that false gods, whom some misguided people have made with their own hands or invented, can have any role in the final judgement; they are devoid of power and knowledge.
- Focus on keeping your record straight. Allah would not take into stride any consideration other than your faith and good action in blessing you with paradise or consigning you to hell.

Chapter 53

Allah's Criteria of Justice

Out of His grace and fairness, Allah has explained the basis on which He would recompense us on the Day of Judgement. His ways are not whimsical or arbitrary. His judgment will stem from His thorough, perfect knowledge of our conduct. Owing to His absolute knowledge and power He can easily manage a swift, transparently clear assessment of our record. The same truth is presented in the following verse:

> **Remember, Allah's is all that is in the heavens and on earth. He knows your ways. On the Day when all will return to Him, He will tell you what you did. Allah knows everything.**
>
> **(Al-Nur 24: 64)**

The belief in the next life and Allah's judgement is an integral part of Islamic faith. This serves as a bulwark against committing any sin or excess in this life. A strong moral fibre with its bearings on the next life is special to the Islamic worldview. Allah has put in place an error-free arrangement (finger prints, DNA, biometrics, etc.) for recording our actions, even our innermost thoughts. This record will be the basis of our fate in the next life. Since Allah is all-powerful and all affairs are settled by Him alone, we should better prepare ourselves for the deep, wide ranging consequences of our faith and actions.

Points to ponder

- On the Day of Judgement all of us would appear before Allah, with the faithful record of our beliefs and actions. No recommendation or any other consideration would carry any weight there.
- Apart from trying our best to improve our conduct, we should fervently and frequently invoke Allah's mercy for His forgiveness and mercy for us on the Day of Judgement. His kindness would help us attain salvation.

Chapter 54

Allah–the One True God

Several Quranic passages are by way of self-introduction, spelling out Allah's attributes and His scheme of things. These help in formulating a better concept of Allah and in our approach to Him. The following verse introduces Allah:

> **Allah's is the kingdom of the heavens and the earth. He did not take to Himself a son. Nor does He have any partner in His kingdom. He has created everything in a due measure.**
>
> **(Al-Furqan 25: 2)**

Islam rejects outright the notions of Allah's sonship, incarnations and partners. The one true Allah is all in all. He alone exercises complete control over His unique kingdom. Being all-wise and all-knowing, He has created everything perfectly, suited best for the purpose behind their creation. Little wonder then that we see such diversity, ingenuity and efficiency in the world around us. His oneness, power and knowledge are manifested by His creation. Take the sun as an example: its size, movement, constancy, energy and numerous benefits for us. No human effort can even replicate in the slightest what Allah has created out of nothing.

Points to ponder

- Power and knowledge rest solely with Allah in their absolute sense. No one has any share in these, even remotely. As the one true God, without any partner, Allah is all in all in the Islamic scheme of things.
- The Quran presses home these three truths: Allah's kingship, oneness and creativity. Keep acknowledging His glory and seeking His forgiveness and mercy. Associating anyone with Allah in His lordship is an unpardonable sin which we must shun.

Chapter 55

Allah Appointed Prophet Muhammad His Messenger

The following Quranic passage sheds light on the circumstantial setting of Prophet Muhammad's appointment as Allah's final messenger. For the guidance of his immediate addressees, the seventh-century Arabs and for all people of all time and place Allah sent down His chosen servant Prophet Muhammad (peace be upon him) from among the Arabs of the day in order to show them the way to Allah. He displayed before them through his brilliant example how to lead life in accordance with Allah's will:

> **It is Allah Who sent among the unlettered ones (the Makkans) the Messenger who recites before them His verses. He purifies them and teaches them the Book and wisdom. Before this they were in total error.**
>
> **(Al-Jumuah 62: 2)**

This concisely expounds the role of a prophet—how he carries out the mission assigned to him by Allah. Exactly the same, like earlier prophets across the world down the millennia, was accomplished by the Prophet Muhammad (peace be upon him) in seventh century Makkah, Saudi Arabia. For long there had not appeared any prophet among Arabs. As a result, they were steeped in vices of all sorts, of which polytheism and idol worship was the most serious one. Allah guided His chosen servant Prophet Muhammad (570–633 CE) to instruct initially Arabs in the articles of faith and doing good. He transmitted to them the Quran, Allah's final message conveyed to him by the archangel, Jibrail. Moreover, he taught them morals and manners and showed them by his own example the best way to lead a balanced life.

Out of His kindness Allah arranged for the error-free preservation of His final message, that is, the Quran and Prophet Muhammad's role model teachings for the guidance of humanity until the end of time.

Points to ponder

- A prophet is a bearer of Allah's message. He does not have any share in godhead. He strictly follows Allah's directives in performing his role as His messenger.

- There are three basic functions of a prophet:

    i. To convey Allah's message to people, which he receives through the agency of an angel.

    ii. To instruct people in articles of faith and morals and manners which may help them win Allah's pleasure

    iii. To explain to people the meaning and message of Allah's book verbally and through his own example; in Islam, a prophet is Allah's servant, not His incarnation or associate.

Chapter 56

Allah Is Glorified by All

Allah is the master and lord of all. Little wonder then that He is praised by all. Even the unbelievers who apparently deny Him are bound by His laws of Nature. They are created beings, face hardships in life like all other human beings and would face death. Notwithstanding their rejection of Allah, they have no control over their fate. The following verse relates how Allah is glorified by all, as He is their Creator:

> **The seven heavens, the earth and all those in these declare Allah's glory. There is no one who does not praise and glorify Him. However, you do not understand how they declare His glory. He is Most Forbearing, Most Forgiving.**
>
> **(Al-Isra 17: 44)**

The reference is to the glorification of Allah in the whole universe in recognition of His supremacy. It is clarified that Allah's praise celebrated by non-humans is beyond our comprehension. This verse brings out Allah's greatness, as all creatures in this universe praise and glorify Him, though we, with our limited faculty, do not comprehend their praise for Him.

Points to ponder

- All that is created by Allah, both animate and inanimate, are bound by what Allah has ordained for them. Their submission to His decrees constitutes their glorification of Allah.
- We are unable to comprehend how non-humans express their praise for Allah. Our inability does not rule out the fact that they are engaged in acknowledging the greatness of their Lord.

Chapter 57

Allah Accepts Our Repentance

Mercy is Allah's predominant trait. Notwithstanding His absolute power to punish, He showers His mercy upon everyone, particularly those who turn sincerely to Him, seeking His forgiveness. Prophet Muhammad (peace be upon him) explains: All the manifestations of love and affection, especially parents, kindness towards their children, represents only a tiny proportion of Allah's boundless mercy for His creatures. His numerous favours to us are illustrative of His limitless kindness. The following verse highlights this attribute of Allah:

> **Allah accepts the repentance of His servants and pardons sins. He knows what you do.**
>
> **(Al-Shura 42: 25)**

Pardoning is an amazing feature of the most merciful Allah. He forgives our sins, no matter how many and serious these might be, provided that we repent sincerely. Out of His vast knowledge He discerns our sincerity well.

This is reflective of Allah's boundless mercy, kindness and affection towards His servants. He has prescribed punishments for wrongdoings in order to maintain peace and order in society. Being all-knowing He maintains an accurate record of our faith and actions and will recompense us accordingly.

Points to ponder

- As human beings, we are liable to err. However, immediately implore Allah for His pardon as soon as you realise your mistake.
- Allah's proclamation of His pardoning our sins is very reassuring and soothing. Constantly pray to Him for His mercy.

Chapter 58

Allah Responds to Our Supplications

In Islam, Allah is not some abstract entity, remote and detached from His creatures. His role in our life is consistently dynamic. He watches and records our actions and listens to our petitions submitted to Him. Even if He does not instantly grant us all for which we beseech Him, He would compensate for it later. The following verse is highly motivating:

> **Allah listens to those who believe and do good. He gives them more out of His grace. There is terrible punishment for the Unbelievers.**
>
> **(Al-Shura 42: 26)**

Allah is most affectionate to believers who have good actions to their credit. He generously and graciously rewards them. By the same token He punishes those who go astray. It is worth clarifying that He will give us this reward and punishment in the next world. In this life the results of our conduct do not appear immediately. Otherwise the whole point of testing us would be lost. On observing the instant punishment for our sin in this world, none of us will dare commit any sin. The same holds true for doing good.

Allah is most gracious to appreciate us if we profess and practise faith and good actions. Being just, He will take to task those who had disobeyed Him. Out of His mercy He has shown this clear path.

Points to ponder

- Being all-knowing and all-powerful, Allah listens and responds to our supplications in the way He deems fit. Nothing escapes His attention which is all-embracing. He pays particular heed to the cries of the wronged, oppressed persons.
- It is a very reassuring belief that Allah, the Supreme Lord, responds to our petitions. We may not always get the desired outcome. However, He would graciously reward us in another way.

Chapter 59

Allah Alone Knows the Unseen

In Allah's scheme of things many items belong to the realm of the unseen, known exclusively to Allah—when will be the last day, our lifespan, the quantum of our reward and punishment in the next life, Allah's pardon for our sins, and the duration of our stay in hell, etc. Even Allah's messengers and angels who enjoy proximity with Allah have no clue about these highly important matters. We should pray to Allah alone for being kind to us about these. The verse below states this truth about the unseen, something which lies beyond the ken of our sense perception and which is not even known to Allah's messengers and angels:

> **Allah alone knows the Unseen. He does not inform anyone of the Unseen matters, except His Messenger whom He wills. He then appoints guards (angels) who go before and behind him.**
>
> **(Al-Jinn 72: 26-27)**

The knowledge of the unseen rests solely with Allah. He may impart some of it to His chosen prophets who are under the care of angels, who guard any corruption in this special knowledge. Allah has provided this knowledge to them for our guidance.

Allah's knowledge is limitless. Through His books and messengers, He has imparted some knowledge to humanity. However, much belongs to the realm of the unseen, unknown to us. Faith demands that we believe in all that rests with Allah. We will be rewarded for this faith.

Messengers only have a limited role in Allah's scheme of things.

Points to ponder

- The knowledge of the unseen is only Allah's prerogative. He has not disclosed a range of vital matters to anyone, including His messengers.
- At times He shares some of this information with His select messengers. However, these matters do not come up in the public domain. We should pray to Allah for our best in the next life.

Chapter 60

Allah Is Without Any Partner

That Allah does not have any partner or associate is the cornerstone of the Islamic belief system. Islam stands distinct for its insistence on the oneness of Islam. In their creedal statement, devotional worship and rites and rituals, Muslims strictly profess and practise monotheism. Allah's perfection is pressed home in the following verse:

> **All praise belongs to Allah. He has not taken to Himself a son. Nor is there any partner with Him in His kingdom. He does not need anyone to protect Him from any weakness. So praise Him for His greatness and glory.**
>
> **(Al-Isra 17: 111)**

Allah, the most glorious, is far above having a son or any partner or protector. Rather, He protects everyone. He is all-powerful and hence He does not need anyone. While reflecting on creation and Allah's numerous signs around us (our body and family, plant and animal life, natural phenomena and above all, death), we recognise what a supreme lord He is! It is therefore our duty to praise and glorify our Creator and Master. Allah's greatness is unique, not to be compared with that of anyone who is mortal.

Points to ponder

- Islam rules out all notions of God's sonship, partners and pantheons of gods. The one true God, Allah, is all in all. He embodies all the excellent attributes and traits and hence His dependence on anyone is out of question.
- Since He is all-powerful and protector of all that exists, He does not ask His devotees for any offering. All charity in His cause, including animal sacrifice, is to be distributed among the poor and the needy. He is independent whereas we all are in need of Him for everything.

Chapter 61

Allah's Punishment

Notwithstanding His vast mercy and affection for us, Allah is also our all-just ruler and master. He has created us for a purpose and provided us with numerous bounties. As the king and supreme lord, He has prescribed a test for all of us: to believe in Him and do good. He has explained the rules of the test very clearly to us through His book and messenger and granted us the faculties of the heart and mind to follow the straight way. To ensure justice, He rewards those passing this test and punishes those who rebel against Him and commit wrongdoings, as is stated in the following Quranic verse:

> **Among people some dispute about Allah, without any knowledge or guidance or the Book to direct them. He arrogantly misguides others from Allah's way. There is humiliation for him in this life. Allah will make him taste the punishment of the Hellfire on the Day of Judgement. (It will be said to him): "This is because of the actions of your own hands. Allah never wrongs His servants."**
>
> **(Al-Hajj 22: 8-10)**

Contained in this passage is the rationale behind Allah's punishment of disbelievers. He does so because justice demands it. He is not at all unkind to His servants. Throughout history and even today, many people have rejected Allah out of their ignorance, arrogance, or their blind servitude to their ancestors and customs. Some of them are so audacious that they drive people away from Allah's path. Such wrongdoers will face humiliating punishment after their death in the next life.

Points to ponder

- We are Allah's creatures and exist owing only to His kindness. He does not rejoice in punishing His own creatures. However, He would take to task those of us who deliberately disobey Him and destroy the social order by their wrongdoings.
- Allah punishes only those who opt for the path of self-destruction. They refuse to obey Allah and spread evil and corruption which makes life miserable for everyone.

Chapter 62

Allah's Glory

Allah is the most glorious in the entire universe. He created all that we see, out of nothing. Moreover, He provides endless provisions to all of us for our existence. He would bring all of us back to life after our death for judgment. We must therefore believe in this supreme Lord, unmatched by anyone in power, knowledge and glory. The following verse justifies why we should glorify Allah:

> **Allah created you and gives you sustenance. He will then cause your death and will create you again. Is there any among your associate gods who can do any of the above tasks? Glory be to Allah! He is far above the partners they take with Him.**
>
> **(Al-Rum 30: 40)**

A clear manifestation of Allah's power is causing our life and death and feeding us throughout our lives. It is adduced also as proof of Allah's oneness. Had there been any associate with Allah, the present flawless order could not be in place.

It underscores Allah's oneness and supreme power. No one other than Allah has any role in managing this universe. We should therefore believe only in Him.

Points to ponder

- There is no one even remotely comparable to Allah in His might and glory. Even the so-called high and powerful among us are mortal and vulnerable to numerous failings—disease, old age and flaws in character and conduct.
- It is the highest privilege imaginable for us to celebrate and glorify our most generous benefactor Who has granted so much—life, health, wealth and social relations. We cannot even count the bounties showered on us by the most merciful Allah. Our praise and glorification of Him represents, in a very small way, our acknowledgement of His unique glory and majesty.

Chapter 63

Allah's Judgement

Allah's control over our life is all-embracing: He alone causes our life and death and would decide our ultimate end on the basis of our faith and conduct, with perfect justice and fairness. This constant awareness about the next life and our answerability to Allah instils into us faith, discipline and good character. This, in turn, makes our individual and collective life happy and peaceful. The following verse points out how Allah will execute His judgement:

> **Allah manages all affairs of the heavens and the earth. Every matter will be referred to Him on the Day of Judgement, which is equal to one thousand years of your calculation. He knows all that is hidden and open. He is Almighty, Most Merciful.**
>
> **(Al-Sajdah 32: 5-6)**

Allah has not detached Himself from this universe after having created it. Rather, He runs the affairs of the universe. He will finally settle all matters on the Day of Judgement. His absolute power and wisdom are behind all that happens in the universe. Since He is most glorious, His one day equals 1,000 years of our reckoning. More important is His knowledge of all that we believe and do. Out of His power and mercy, He has given all of us life and numerous favours. It is up to us to obey or reject Him. If we deny Him, we will be utter losers on the Day of Judgement.

Points to ponder

- Allah's judgement in the next world is a moral necessity. The good and the evil are not recompensed in this life. The powerful culprits often escape any punishment owing to our defective political and legal system. It is Allah's mercy that He has established the Day of Judgement for us.
- Allah constantly watches all that we say and do. He would make us pay for our actions. It is imperative for us to lead an Allah-aware life which alone can help us follow the straight way and secure our eternal success in the next world.

Chapter 64

Our Creation by Allah

The Quran is the book of guidance, instructing us in articles of faith and morals and manners. It is not a book of science, as it was addressed initially to the seventh century illiterate Arabs. Rather, no one could then appreciate any scientific account of our creation. The Quranic description is generic, yet accurate according to the scientific stance of our time. We are able to achieve so much in various domains, thanks to the amazing body granted to us by Allah. The following verse lays emphasis on our creation:

> **Allah has created everything in the best manner. He originated the creation of man from clay, and made man's children from the extract of a mean fluid (semen). He proportioned man and breathed into him of His spirit. He has granted you the ears, eyes and hearts. Yet you hardly thank Him.**
>
> **(Al-Sajdah 32: 7-9)**

It gives us some idea of our creation by Allah. We know that each body part is precious and irreplaceable. Yet we hardly thank Him for having blessed us so much. A major part of this account of our creation is readily understandable to us as it was to the seventh-century Arabs, the immediate audience of the Quran. Some of its portions (His spirit breathed into us) belong to the realm of the unseen (beyond the ken of our sense perception). The takeaway is that we should thank and worship Allah Who has provided us with the priceless faculties of hearing, seeing and feeling. Notwithstanding the self-evident truth of Allah's countless bounties to us, we hardly obey and glorify Him.

Points to ponder

- It is so wonderful to enjoy the faculties of sight, hearing, thinking and feeling, which make our life meaningful. This calls for thanksgiving to Allah, our Creator Lord Who has blessed us thus.
- Perfection characterises Allah's creation. Take our body as an illustration. It performs numerous, complex jobs and helps us achieve so much. We should be on our guard against any abuse of these precious gifts bestowed upon us by Allah.

Chapter 65

Day and Night As Allah's Wondrous Signs

Of Allah's numerous creative wonders, the most common which we witness every day is the alternation of day night, the two opposites replacing each other so seamlessly. It is a great pity that we pass by this marvel, without acknowledging Allah's mastery. The cycle of day and night is essential to our life and well-being. The following verse underscores this big favour done to us by Allah:

> **It is Allah Who has made night for you so that you may have rest in it. He made the day bright. He is full of favours to people. Yet most of the people do not thank Him.**
>
> **(Al-Mumin 40: 61)**

Another marvel of Allah's creative power: night and day for sleep and work. We take these natural phenomena for granted and do not appreciate Allah's favours to us. The biological cycle of sleep and rest, which equips us for work the next day, is another marvel. We realise its immense value if we suffer from sleeplessness. Although Allah has devised so much for our comfort, it is the height of our ingratitude that we do not acknowledge His favours.

Let us make most of the opportunities granted to us by Allah and serve and worship Him.

Points to ponder

- Allah's power and glory are at work in numerous objects around us. We should make it a point to reflect on these. This would spiritually and emotionally strengthen us.
- Allah's creative wonders are of tremendous benefit to us. Take daylight to illustrate this. How fortunate we are in getting this huge supply of energy for free. Allah's favours to us should humble us. We should turn sincerely to our most magnificent and beneficent Creator and Lord.

Chapter 66

Allah's Favours to Us

Throughout the Quran, Allah's message to humanity for all time and place, keeps drawing attention to the immeasurable quantity and quality of Allah's bounties which He has placed at our disposal. We draw upon these freely, without making any effort. The Quranic passage below cites water as an invaluable favour of Allah to us:

> **(Are these false gods better) or Allah Who created the heavens and the earth and sends down for you water from the sky? He causes beautiful orchards to grow with water. You could not grow those trees. Is there a god associated with Allah? No, they are given to straying from the straight way.**
>
> **(Al-Naml 27: 60)**

Rainfall and the subsequent blossoming of plant life, particularly grain, is essential for life. It stands out as the proof of Allah's mercy. No associate god has any role in this phenomenon.

The signs of Allah's absolute power and greatness are all around us: creation, rain, and the plant kingdom. Rain is our lifeline. Out of His mercy, Allah has set this marvellous phenomenon in place for our benefit. No one has any role in bringing rain to us. Given this, we must shun polytheism and not take anyone as His partner. Rather, we should acknowledge His big favours to us.

Points to ponder

- The value of water for us does not call for any elaboration. Life without water supply is unthinkable. Out of His immense kindness for His creatures, including the human, animal and plant domains, He has provided water supply for us.
- While reflecting on the marvels of creation, we should seriously think about the Creator. Helpless false gods made with our own hands have nothing to their credit. We should profusely thank and glorify the one true God Who has granted us so much.

Chapter 67

Allah Is Sovereign

In Islam Allah is all-powerful, the sovereign, to the exclusion of any associate or partner. Everything is at the beck and call of this one true God. The oneness of Allah is the most striking feature of the Islamic faith. He exercises all power as it pleases Him, without answerability to anyone.

> **Allah has no fear of the results of His actions.**
>
> **(Al-Shams 91: 15)**

While we are answerable to Allah for all that we say and do, Allah being independent of all and almighty, is not accountable to anyone. He does whatever pleases Him.

It is on record that many mighty unbelieving communities, raking in their splendor, were destroyed by Allah as punishment for their misdeeds. Ruins across the world are reflective of their downfall. They could not at all resist divine penalty which devastated them.

We should be careful about the consequences of disobedience to Allah and keep following the straight way.

Points to ponder

- Islam is an Allah-centric faith, with all power lying with Allah alone.

- No one, including angels, prophets and saints, has any role in the working of the universe.
- Allah decides whatever He wills in His infinite wisdom.
- No one can prevail over Allah in any respect.

Chapter 68

Allah's Dominion

Allah is the incontestable king and master of all that exists. It is a cardinal sin in Islam to take anyone as Allah's associate or partner. His control over all that exists in absolute.

> **To Allah belongs all that is in the heavens, on earth, between these, and also underneath the earth.**
>
> **(Ta Ha 20: 6)**

This is a comprehensive statement about Allah's absolute power across the universe, leaving no room for any deity other than Him. This underscores how almighty He is. We too, are totally under His control. Birth and death are the most important aspects of our life. Yet we have no choice or control over these. Notwithstanding our free will and our varied faculties we are absolutely helpless regarding our fate. Moreover, we should not forget that all that we possess (health, family, money and social status, etc.) are granted to us by the superior power, Allah.

We should therefore be thankful to Him and lead life as prescribed by Him, of which the details appear in His unaltered book, the Quran, and His final messenger, Prophet Muhammad's teachings.

Points to ponder

- Allah is an all-encompassing entity.
- His power prevails over everything, irrespective of time and place.
- He has not assigned any authority to anyone in the entire universe.
- His universal being overwhelms all.

Chapter 69

Winning Allah's Pleasure

Out of His immense mercy and kindness Allah has instructed us in the ways and means for winning His pleasure. Our satisfaction and happiness in this life and our success and joys in the next depend on following Allah's ways, which is spelled out in the following verse:

> **Allah is Most Forgiving to him who repents, believes, does good and follows guidance.**
>
> **(Ta Ha 20: 82)**

Allah's statement is very assuring and comforting as we human beings are liable to err. Allah, however, promises us His gracious pardon.

In Islam our roadmap is very simple, clear and practical, free of rituals and mythology. We are asked only to believe in Allah and do good. We are free to pursue any activity of our choice with Allah-awareness, and that will be reckoned as good as an act of devotional worship. Allah will lavishly reward us if we make others' lives better.

Allah is gracious and forbearing enough to forgive us for our lapses, provided that we repent sincerely and refrain from doing any further wrong. We should lead life, following the straight way shown by Allah and His messenger, Prophet Muhammad (peace be upon him).

Points to ponder

- The Quran and Prophet Muhammad's role model prescribe for us the way to win Allah's pleasure.
- The way to Allah is simple and easy to follow, not involving any onerous exertion.
- Our efforts to win Allah's pleasure are in our own interest. These bring inner happiness and tranquillity to us and make this world a better place to live in.

Chapter 70

Allah Alone Is the Master

Monotheism, that is, the belief in the one true God as our only master and lord of the universe is the cornerstone of Islam. The Islamic faith and practices, specifically all acts of worship, revolve around the same axis. The following verse introduces Allah as our master who causes our life and death. For our life and death we are totally dependent upon Him, as is evident from the following Quranic assertion:

> **It is Allah Who gives life and death. To Him is the return.**
>
> (Qaf 50: 43)

This important truth about Allah lies at the core of the Islamic belief system: We are from Allah and to Him is our ultimate return. It is Allah alone Who causes our birth and death. It is equally important to bear in mind that He will bring us back to life after our death, and will call us to account on the Day of Judgment. He will reward or punish us in proportion to our faith and actions. The belief in our ultimate return to our Creator and master, Allah, should always be at the back of our minds. It helps us to keep following the straight way.

This verse is an excellent reminder of Allah's power, our dependence on Him and our ultimate end, the eternal life in the hereafter.

Points to ponder

- Notwithstanding all of our accomplishments, we are absolutely helpless about these two most important matters about us: our life and death. Is it not something worth reflecting on?
- The constant thought of death and our accountability to Allah for all of our actions helps us to keep following the straight way.

Chapter 71

Allah As the Ruler

In Islam Allah is not some abstract, remote deity. He is not the Creator who has nothing to do with us. On the contrary, He has been constantly and consistently managing every affair, including the functioning of this universe and deciding everything for us. According to the Quran, He manifests His glory every moment:

> **When Allah decides something, He only says:**
> **"Be" and it is.**
>
> **(Al-Mumin 40: 68)**

Such is Allah's power and mastery that He instantly gets done whatever He wills. He executes whatever He wants in no time, and without any help from any partner. Angels are at His beck and call and He assigns them duties which they perform unquestioningly. In Islam, angels are a special species, without free will. Like robots they implement Allah's commands. His word is final and instantly comes into force. All this is part of His grand, pre-ordained plan to ensure that things are done at their appointed time. No one can advance or defer His commands. Since He is all-powerful, He decides everyone's life, death and all matters.

Points to ponder

- Allah is always near us, closer to us than our own jugular vein.
- He is all-glorious and gets everything done in no time whatever pleases Him.
- In view of His might and nearness with us, we should turn all the more to Him.

Chapter 72

Allah's Forgiveness

Allah is all-merciful. He has declared in His book that He has decreed mercy and kindness for Himself. We get our sustenance and survive only because of His vast mercy. Being the most kind, He overlooks our numerous failings. His doors of mercy and forgiveness are always wide open for everyone, as is clear from the following Quranic verse:

> **Your Lord is Most Forgiving, Most Merciful to him who does some evil out of ignorance and then repents and reforms himself.**
>
> **(Al-Nahl 16: 119)**

Allah is most forgiving and most forbearing. He pardons even our atrocious sins, if we repent sincerely and lead a pious life afterwards. Allah's mercy is His most outstanding attribute. He declares in His book: "He has prescribed mercy for Himself" (Al-An'am 6:12 and 54).

At times we do some wrong unknowingly or even intentionally. Allah is kind enough to show us the way out: we should repent and mend our ways. Since Allah is most compassionate, most merciful, He may forgive us and admit us to paradise, which is the highest felicity imaginable for us.

Let us draw upon His boundless mercy by invoking His kindness and graciousness in order to cleanse ourselves before our return to Him.

Points to ponder

- In Islam, Allah is not some stern, vindictive deity, ever ready to unleash His punishment.
- Graciously, He keeps pardoning us for our acts of omission and commission, provided that we repent sincerely to Him and refrain from committing the same sin again.

Chapter 73

Prophets As Allah's Servants

Many communities have been guilty of mistaking prophets, saints and sages for God or Allah, or as His partner. Emphatically, Islam denies any role of prophets in godhead. They are Allah's chosen servants who faithfully practise and preach His message to people. The Quran states their mission thus:

> **(O Prophet), do you ask them for any reward? The reward of your Lord is the best. He is the best to give provision.**
>
> **(Al-Muminun 23: 72)**

Allah's prophets carry out their mission without any financial motive. Allah will reward them suitably. He provides plenty and variety of provisions to everyone. He chooses His best servants as His messengers who have appeared in almost every part of the world at some point of time. Allah's archangel, Jibrail, conveys to the prophets Allah's message which they preach and also demonstrate through their own example. That is why in Islam the Prophet Muhammad (peace be upon him) is the role model. He, like every other messenger of Allah, was a paragon of virtues and selflessly spent his whole life conveying Allah's message to one and all. In so doing, he faced ghastly persecution, had to migrate from his hometown Makkah, to Madina, another town some 430 kms away, and was wounded in a battle as the Makkan unbelievers invaded Madina. He never sought money or any position for his lifelong devotion to his mission and hard work. We should trust Allah in that He is the best to grant us provisions. His reward is the highest felicity imaginable for us.

Points to ponder

- Prophets are Allah's selfless servants. They do not have any monetary or political motive behind their mission.
- In Islam, there is no concept of any offering or religious tax payable to the prophet, clergy or place of worship.
- It is on record that Prophet Muhammad (peace be upon him) did not behave as a king or ruler, though he enjoyed power, owing to the phenomenal success of his mission.

Chapter 74

Allah's Perfect Management of the Universe

Allah's creativity and ingenuity are in created objects and natural phenomena. Not only are these awe-inspiring in their appearance, their inter-coordination resulting in the perfect functioning of the universe is equally amazing. The Quran repeatedly cites these signs as the proof of Allah's existence and lordship. The following verse urges us to reflect on the smooth functioning of the universe:

> **Were the truth to follow people's desires, the heavens and the earth and all those in these would have faced confusion and corruption. Allah sent them what is good for them. Yet they turn away from what is good for them.**
>
> **(Al-Muminun 23: 71)**

Allah's guidance, which He has sent us through prophets and scriptures, is the most precious gift to us. Otherwise, we could not see or follow the straight way on our own. Regrettably, many of us refuse to accept divine guidance for which we will face dire consequences in the next life.

Allah's dispensation is perfect. Out of His wisdom, He decrees matters for us which are not decided according to our desires. Otherwise, there could be utter chaos. With our limited knowledge and selfish outlook, we cannot appreciate what is good for us.

Far from following our desires we should abide by Allah's guidance which is in our best interests. Almighty

Allah has set everything perfectly in place. Owing to our limitations we do not and cannot grasp His grand plan.

Points to ponder

- Allah's creation is marked by perfect balance and efficacy.
- Out of His infinite wisdom Allah has bound everything to laws of nature which ensure equilibrium.
- Nature points unmistakably to Allah's power and wisdom.

Chapter 75

Allah Forbids Unbelief

Allah has, no doubt granted his free will and we have the option for affirming our belief in Allah as the one true God or rejecting Him. However, He has expressly warned us not to take unbelief as an option. It betrays ingratitude to His countless bounties which we enjoy day and night. Moreover, as He disapproves unbelief, it would incur His wrath and ruin our prospects in the eternal next life. This note of warning is to the fore in the following verse:

> **This is Allah, your Lord. He is the Creator of everything. There is no god besides Him. How are you then misled?**
>
> **(Al-Mumin 40: 62)**

It is indeed strange how in the face of numerous self-evident signs of Allah all around us, many people have the audacity to reject Him. All creation is by His command. Moreover, He has been constantly feeding us and catering to all our needs. In view of this self-evident truth, it is unthinkable not to believe in Him or turn to others who have no role in our creation, sustenance and deciding our fate.

We should affirm His lordship, shun polytheism in any form, and refrain from evil and sin.

Points to ponder

- Since Allah alone is our Creator, master and benefactor, it is the height of injustice and foolishness to deny this reality.
- Unbelief as an option is something shocking. It amounts to choosing self-destruction.

Chapter 76

Allah's Countless Bounties for Us

As the most beneficent and generous lord, Allah has blessed us with numerous favours. These enable us to accomplish what we seek in every domain of our choice. Without His generosity we could not achieve anything. The verse below draws attention to this self-evident reality:

> **It is Allah Who made for you the earth a place to live and the sky a structure above you. He gave you shapes and made your shapes beautiful. He has given you pure and good things to eat. This is Allah, your Lord. Blessings be on Allah, the Lord of the universe!**
>
> **(Al-Mumin 40: 64)**

We should be thankful to Allah for having showered His innumerable blessings on us, some of which are listed above. We should be grateful to Him, in particular, for our amazing body and the variety of things to eat and drink. This impressive, though very brief, catalogue of Allah's big favours to all of us, believers and unbelievers alike, should make us reflect on His glory and kindness. How can we turn away from such a compassionate, loving lord, Who has provided us with so much? He is the only source of blessings for all beings. Given this, we should glorify Him as He is all-powerful. It is in our own interest to turn to Him wholly.

Points to ponder

- To begin with, we should be grateful to Allah for having provided us with such an amazing and suitable habitat as the earth.
- We owe profuse thanks to our maker, Allah, for having blessed us with such a marvellous body that enables us to achieve so much.

Chapter 77

Allah Is Eternal

Islam asserts that Allah is eternal, without a beginning or end. It might sound strange to some. However, this extraordinary statement befits the stature of the almighty. By definition, He transcends gender, form, birth, death, flaw or any human attribute. His being is beyond comprehension. Instead of speculating about His appearance, which lies beyond the ken of our sense perception, we should focus on following His way in which lies our success:

> **He is the Ever Living. There is no god besides Him. So call Him, with true devotion. Praise be to Allah, the Lord of the universe.**
>
> **(Al-Mumin 40: 65)**

In recognition of Allah's wondrous attributes, turn sincerely to Him. Allah, the lord of the universe is without any partner. The eternal Allah has brought the entire creation into being. Nothing preceded Him. Nor will anyone outlast Him. He has been there since the beginning and will always be there, as decline, or death, or any weakness is out of the question with regard to Him. Since He is the only Creator and Lord, He alone should be invoked for every help. Our belief in Him should be, nonetheless sincere, not merely ritualistic, without true faith and good actions to our credit. Being the Lord, He deserves our praise as much as we can manage.

Points to ponder

- Allah is unique in every respect. His being eternal is inextricably linked with His majesty.
- In view of His awesome attributes, of which His eternity is the most staggering and unmatchable, we should turn in all humility to Him.

Chapter 78

Allah's Creation in Pairs

While stating Allah's creative power, the Quran points to one of its fascinating aspects: Allah has created living beings in pairs that are so similar, yet so dissimilar. This ingenuity on Allah's part has ensured constant procreation, perpetuity of species and mind-boggling variety. This arrangement underscores His might and glory:

> **Allah is the Originator of the heavens and the earth. He made for you pairs of your own kind (male and female). Likewise, He made pairs for cattle. He lets you grow. There is nothing like Him. He is All Hearing, All Seeing.**
>
> **(Al-Shura 42: 11)**

We are asked to ponder over the bewildering phenomenon, which we see all the time: creation of living beings in pairs of male and female, which ensures perpetuity of generations. Equally stupendous is the process of the growth of every living being. Only the peerless Allah could accomplish all this. These and numerous other creative wonders of Allah are the signs through which we can gain faith and turn into pious servants of Allah. Throughout the Quran, Allah asks us to reflect on these signs. Islam is thus a rational religion, urging us to believe after studying these wondrous signs of Allah. Apart from being the Creator of everything out of nothing, He is also all-seeing, all-hearing and all-powerful. Hence He does all that He wills. No deity or idol matches Him in the slightest.

We should appreciate His creative power through our acts of worship and good behavior towards fellow human beings.

Points to ponder

- Allah's arrangement for the multiplication of living beings is yet another facet of His creative wonders.
- Being all-knowing and all-wise He has put in place such an amazing system, working since day one to this day, and will last till the end of time.

Chapter 79

Allah's Plan to Provide for Us

Is it not something seemingly incredible that Allah has been feeding billions and billions of living beings since the beginning of time until now. He has granted us physical and mental faculties and skills to earn bread from numerous natural resources which He has magnanimously placed at our disposal. Owing to our own greed and mismanagement some people, no doubt, suffer from hunger, even starvation. However, the beneficent Lord has provided for us in plenty. As part of His trial, He grants more to some and less to others, as indicated in the following verse:

> **To Allah belong the keys of the heavens and the earth. He increases and restricts the provision of whom He wills. He knows everything.**
>
> **(Al-Shura 42: 12)**

Allah is the master of all that exists. Out of His fathomless wisdom He decides what and how much to give to each of His creatures. He alone knows the rationale behind His scheme of things, on which we can only contemplate; we cannot alter it. His bestowal of more provisions on some of us and less on others does not at all indicate that He is happy with the rich and unhappy with the poor. Some sinners may have all the comforts and plenty of wealth in this life while some devout persons may be found starving. This arrangement is not haphazard. Allah has devised it in order to test if we remember Him in prosperity and adversity. We should accept His dispensation as His obedient servants. We should nonetheless strive for earning and raising our lawful income for which Allah has provided equal opportunities to everyone.

We should realise Allah's immense power, wisdom and knowledge, as manifested all around us.

Points to ponder

- Our prosperity or adversity do not signify Allah's approval or disapproval of our conduct
- His provisions to us should fill our heart and mind with thanksgiving and humility.

Chapter 80

Allah's Reward and Punishment

As the king and master of the Day of Judgement, Allah will reward and punish us. His recompense would be characterised by perfect justice and transparency, as it would be wholly based on the incontrovertible, demonstrable record of our faith and actions. He may punish and reward us in this life. However, His final judgement, which would affect us eternally, would be pronounced after we appear before Him along with an accurate and complete record of our actions in this life:

> **This Book is from Allah, Almighty, All Knowing. He forgives sins and accepts repentance. He is strict in punishment and full of power. There is no god besides Him. To Him is everyone's return.**
>
> **(Al-Mumin 40: 2-3)**

The Quran, revealed to the Prophet Muhammad (peace be upon him) through the agency of the archangel, Gabriel, is the word of Allah which is preserved in its pristine purity. We should fear almighty Allah and, at the same time, try to win His pleasure by following the straight way, of which the main planks are: faith and good actions. Being all-powerful and all-knowing, He has given us perfect guidance, found in His book, the Quran, and His messenger, Prophet Muhammad's brilliant example, which is recorded faithfully and easily accessible for emulation. Justice and mercy are outstanding features of Allah: He generously forgives us if we repent sincerely. However,

He will inflict terrible punishment on unbelievers and those who wronged fellow human beings in any way.

This verse represents a comprehensive description of Allah's main attributes.

Points to ponder

- Since Allah is almighty and all-knowing, He alone can pronounce judgement on us.
- His justice would be tempered with mercy and transparency.

Chapter 81

Proceedings on the Day of Judgment

In several passages the Quran graphically recounts the horrible spectacle on the Day of Judgement: All of us brought back to life and summoned to Allah's court for our interrogation and our dispatch to hell or paradise. Allah alone would exercise all power on the day. Unbelievers reject the belief in the hereafter, as something improbable. Allah Who has created us in the first place can easily resurrect us and take our account, as detailed below:

> **All those who are in the heavens and on earth will appear as servants before the Most Compassionate One. He takes account of and counts them all. On the Day of Judgement each one of them will appear before Him, one by one, Allah will pour love on those who believe and do good.**
>
> **(Maryam 19: 93-96)**

Here we have a vivid picture of the Day of Judgment. It is so delightful to note that Allah will heap His love and mercy on those who have faith in Him and are engaged in doing good. Since Allah is all-powerful and each one of us has to face death, we should prepare ourselves for the unavoidable Day of Judgement. Allah will reward or punish us on the basis of our belief in Him or otherwise, and our actions, good or bad. Allah alone will pass judgement on us with perfect justice and fairness. No one can save us from Allah's reckoning. It is therefore time for us to accept truth and ensure our ever-lasting success in the hereafter. It is also worth remembering that Allah will take each one of us to account individually, without consideration for anything else.

Points to ponder

- The next world is essential for rewarding the pious and punishing the wicked, as perfect justice is not possible in this world.
- Allah's judgement would be marked by fairness and transparency. We would be rewarded our punished exactly in line with our faith and record of actions.

Chapter 82

Allah's Boundless Knowledge

All-embracing knowledge is an outstanding feature of Allah. He knows even the thoughts crossing our minds. He directly watches everything simultaneously and is not dependent on anyone for reporting matters to Him. In our age, bristling with comprehensive, sophisticated surveillance gadgets, it is easy for us to perceive Allah as the all-knowing Lord.

> **Allah knows all that is in the heavens and on earth. He knows what you do privately and publicly. Allah knows even the secrets of hearts.**
>
> **(Al-Taghabun 64: 4)**

Since Allah is all-knowing, we should be very careful about our actions. Even the thoughts crossing our mind are known to Him. As He knows our actions, and He will judge us in the light of His perfect, all-embracing knowledge, we should be very careful. In this life we may get away by using any means after doing something wrong. However, we cannot escape Allah's absolute, accurate knowledge. We cannot even hide from Him the thoughts crossing our mind. This calls for our self-control and good conduct. We should think carefully about what we say and do in the light of the fact that Allah is all-knowing.

Points to ponder

- Perfect knowledge befits the almighty. Godhead is inconceivable without all-inclusive knowledge.
- Allah's perfect knowledge lies at the heart of the smooth functioning of the universe, of meeting all our needs and of fair recompense for us on the Day of Judgement.

Chapter 83

Criteria for Getting Allah's Reward

Out of His immense kindness, Allah has clearly explained in a variety of ways what pleases or displeases Him. As He has spelled out graphically His way; we can discern its merits and realise our loss if we refuse to follow it. It is not beyond our capacity to earn His reward. We do not have to renounce life or undergo strenuous, enervating devotional worship for getting His reward, as elucidated in the following verse:

> **Allah promises forgiveness and a great reward to the men and women who surrender to Allah, the men and women who have faith, the men and women who are obedient, the men and women who are truthful, the men and women who are patient, the men and women who humble themselves (before Him), the men and women who give in charity, the men and women who fast, the men and women who guard their chastity and the men and women who remember Allah much.**
>
> **(Al-Ahzab 33: 35)**

This is an extensive description of the men and women whom Allah gives the good news of His pardon and reward in the next life. In Islam there is no discrimination against women in matters of faith. The note of total gender parity in this passage is striking, as both men and women are addressed in an equal degree, instead of using the generic 'man', generally employed to address humanity comprising both men and women.

More importantly, it lists the traits desirable in the sight of Allah: submission to Him, faith, obedience, truthfulness, patience, humility, giving in charity, chastity and remembrance of Allah.

Our objective should be to develop these traits as much as we can. For this will win Allah's pardon and huge reward.

Points to ponder

- Allah's reward is open to all, men and women of any ethnicity, colour, linguistic community.
- The criteria for securing Allah's reward are anchored in faith, and more importantly, in our excellent social relations and charity.

Chapter 84

Response to the Hereafter

Although the concept of the hereafter is logical enough, some people consider it to be improbable. The life-death-rebirth cycle is commonplace. Rain revives dead land and plants blossom in little time. Allah–the Almighty Lord can easily resurrect us, and adjudge us, resulting in our landing in paradise or hell. Justice demands this recompense, as in this world the dictates of justice are hardly met. The Quran comments thus on the response to the hereafter:

> **(O Prophet), say: "No one in the heavens and the earth knows the Unseen, except Allah. They do not know when they will be raised (for the Judgement). Their knowledge cannot comprehend the Hereafter. That is why they are in doubt about it. Rather, they are blind to it."**
>
> **(Al-Naml 27: 65-66)**

Allah's oneness and His absolute power are manifest all over the universe. The disbelievers, however, either do not want to understand this truth or doubt it or knowingly reject it, especially about their life-after-death and the judgement. The knowledge of the unseen, including the date when the present world would end completely, is known only to Allah. The unseen is beyond the range of our comprehension. We should not therefore waste our time on it. If the last day could be specified by date, the whole point of our test and trial, as devised by Allah, would be lost. Once the truth becomes manifest, even a die-hard unbeliever would have to accept it.

What is more important for us is to prepare ourselves for the happy next life by embracing true faith in Allah and Islam and doing good to everyone around us.

Let us recognise this logical truth that there is life-after-death in which Allah, our lord and master, will recompense us according to our faith and actions.

Points to ponder

- Foolish people ask pointless questions about the hereafter, for example, the exact date of the Day of Judgement.
- We should focus on our faith and actions for our happy end after death.
- Owing to their denial mode and stubborn attitude, unbelievers refuse to realise self-evident truths about the eternal life-after-death.

Chapter 85

Allah's Treatment of Unbelievers

Although Allah has provided extensive guidance to us for accepting the faith, some of us refuse to believe in Him. In so doing, they abuse the free will granted to them and act ungratefully towards their Creator. As they choose a self-destructive path, they will face its dire consequences, as explained in the following verse:

> **It is Allah Who has settled you on earth. One who refuses to believe will bear the burden of his unbelief. Their unbelief will invite God's wrath against them. Their unbelief will add to their own loss.**
>
> **(Fatir 35: 39)**

Out of His boundless mercy, Allah has made human beings the supreme creature on earth by way of having endowed them with knowledge. It is regrettable that disbelievers refuse to acknowledge this truth. Allah will inflict His horrendous punishment on disbelievers.

Allah does not punish us wantonly. He has shown us the straight way. Those of us who reject truth will have to face the consequences of their disbelief in the next life. On the Day of Judgement they will realise that they are utter losers. However, it will be too late then to mend their ways.

It is time now to accept the truth and gain everlasting success in the next life. Allah has sent us to this world to undergo a test whether we believe in Him the unseen or not. If we do, we would enjoy the eternal bliss of paradise. However, if we do not, hellfire awaits us.

Points to ponder

- Allah, the most merciful, does not seek to punish us. He has bestowed numerous favours on us and asks us to follow His way, which is to our own benefit.
- As unbelievers deliberately defy their Creator and master, they would end up as losers.

Chapter 86

Allah's Dispensation

In His wisdom, our Lord has devised a system for bestowing His blessings upon us. Some of us get more, whereas others get less. Rather than begrudging this, we reconcile to fate and keep trying our best to get what we want. We would be amply compensated for our patience and resignation to our Lord's will. The following Quranic verse advises us cogently:

> **Do not be jealous over what Allah has given more to some than others. Men will get a share for what they do and women a share for what they do. Seek from Allah His bounty. Allah knows everything.**
>
> **(Al-Nisa 4: 32)**

Men and women differ in their constitution, as devised by Allah. The anatomical differences, however, have no bearing on their status in the eyes of Allah. Allah will fairly recompense both in accordance with their faith and actions. Allah has ordained provisions for everyone out of His wisdom: some have more while others have little. Far from resenting this we should turn to Allah, embrace faith and pray for His bounties. Even if we do not get anything in this life, by dint of our true faith and good actions, we are bound to have amazing success in the next life.

We should rest content with what we have, along with constantly striving to earn lawfully more and more. Moreover, we should be concerned about our ultimate end in the hereafter, which depends on our true faith and good actions. We should invoke Allah for improving our prospects in both this and the next life.

Points to ponder

- In Allah's eyes, men and women are alike. The verse mentions both in equal terms. Women may be more gifted than men.
- Far from growing jealous, we should strive to achieve as much as we can. The Quran encourages positive thinking.

Chapter 87

Allah Would Bring the Dead Back to Life

One of the three basic articles of faith is that after death we would be brought back to life on the Day of Judgement, of which the date is known to Allah alone. All of us would appear before Him in the grand assembly. He would call each one of us to account and would reward or punish us, depending on our faith and actions in this life. This would be an eternal decree and for ever we would live in paradise or Hell. Unbelievers disregard this truth and are destined to suffer eternally:

> **And man makes comparisons for Allah while forgetting his own creation. He asks: "Who will revive the bones after they have decayed?" (O Prophet), say: "Allah will revive them as He created them in the first place. He knows best about every kind of creation."**
>
> **(Ya Sin 36: 78-79)**

The disbelievers' doubt is allayed by this assertion that Allah created human beings in the first place out of nothing, so it is quite easy for Him to resurrect and recreate them for judgement at the end of time. Resurrection, that is, Allah bringing the dead back to life on the Day of Judgement for rewarding or punishing them had been an incomprehensible idea for the immediate audience of the Quran, the seventh-century Arabs and all disbelievers throughout history. Take the common spectacle of rain as instructive: how it revives the dead, parched land. Moreover, since Allah is the all-powerful Creator, it is not at all difficult for Him to cause the rebirth of the dead. The undeniable signs of His absolute power are all around us.

Let us reflect on the constant phenomenon of resurrection in Nature, which we can see even with our naked eye, and believe in the doctrine of life-after-death. It is perfectly logical that this life in the world which constitutes our test should conclude with our reward or punishment, depending on our conduct.

Points to ponder

- Since Allah is the all-powerful Creator *par excellence* who brought into being everything out of nothing, He would resurrect all of us on the Day of Judgement.
- We should prepare ourselves for this eventuality. True faith and good actions in this life would result in our success on the Day of Judgement.

Chapter 88

Prophets As Allah's Messengers

Islam draws a very clear line of demarcation between Allah and His prophets. All power and knowledge rests solely with Allah. For the guidance of people Allah selected some pious human beings, His servants, as His messengers for instructing people in the straight way. These messengers belonged to their respective communities in various eras. Prophet Adam (peace be upon him) is the first in this series and Prophet Muhammad (peace be upon him) the last. Allah grants His messengers miracles and knowledge. They accomplish everything by Allah's permission. They take pride in being Allah's servants and do not lay any claim to godhead. The following Quranic passage presses home these truths:

> **Your Lord is Allah. There is no god besides Him. His knowledge covers everything." (O Prophet), this is how God relates to you the account of the past. He has given you advice from Himself."**
>
> **(Ta Ha 20: 98-99)**

People are informed of Allah's grandeur and oneness. Moreover, He is all-knowing, all-powerful. The above account gives us some idea how Allah has communicated with us, through the agency of His books and His chosen servants, messengers. The final, latest message from Allah is faithfully recorded in the Quran and Prophet Muhammad's teachings. On studying these we learn how Allah created this universe, what message He conveyed to earlier communities and how He punished those who rejected Him. These also instruct us in the straight way and how we can achieve eternal success and all the joys in the next life with our true faith and good actions.

Out of His boundless wisdom and mercy, Allah has provided His extensive guidance to us. It is up to us to make or mar our prospects in the next life. We should devote ourselves to earning Allah's pleasure.

Points to ponder

- Messengers have been misconstrued by some as God or His son or incarnation. Essentially they are only His obedient servants.
- They are the best human beings, with excellent character and conduct. However, their knowledge is limited to what Allah grants them.

Chapter 89

Recipients of Allah's Mercy

Allah's mercy and kindness extend to everyone. He showers His blessings even on die-hard unbelievers. Were He to starve them in this world, it would render His test of us as pointless as everyone would be forced into believing in Him. The following Quranic passage informs who will receive Allah's mercy and reward in the next life:

> **[They implored:] "Grant us good in this world and in the Hereafter. We have turned to You." Allah replied: "I punish whom I will. However, My Mercy extends to everything. I will have mercy on those who fear Me, pay Zakah and believe in My signs. And those who follow the unlettered Prophet (Muhammad). They find him mentioned in their Books—the Torah and the Gospel. The Prophet instructs them in good and forbids them evil. He allows them as lawful what is good and pure. He disallows them as unlawful what is bad and impure. He removes from them their burdens and the restrictions which were upon them. As to those who believe in this Prophet, help and support him and follow the light of guidance with which he is sent, they will achieve true success."**
>
> **(Al-Araf 7: 156-157)**

This passage, apart from giving us the good news of Allah's measureless mercy, defines the recipients of His mercy and predictions about the advent of the Prophet Muhammad (peace be upon him) in earlier scriptures. Also, it expounds the functions of a prophet of Allah. Believers are promised Allah's help and support.

This passage represents a clear road map: what we should do to attain our deliverance in the hereafter. Allah graciously sent down His book, the Quran, and His messenger, Prophet Muhammad (peace be upon him). As the benefactor of humanity, the Prophet (peace be upon him), through his own bright example and life-giving teachings showed us the straight way. Allah promises success and happiness to us if we follow the straight way in our life.

Points to ponder

- Allah's mercy in the next life is exclusively for believers who adhere to the Quran and the Prophet's practice.
- Those who strive sincerely in Allah's way would receive His choicest reward.

Chapter 90

Reasons for Allah's Punishment

The Quran informs that Allah has ordained mercy for Himself. We see the entire creation flourishing owing to His kindness and beneficence. Given this, the question arises as to why Allah would punish some people. He is the master and ruler of this universe and has to dispense justice. As He has eloquently warned against the disastrous consequences of defying Him, He is perfectly justified in bringing to book those who chose not to obey Him and hence punishment for them:

> **This punishment is because of your own actions. Allah does not wrong His servants.**
>
> **(Al-Anfal 8: 51)**

Justice permeates Allah's treatment of His servants. Only wrongdoers incur His punishment. Notwithstanding His vast mercy and kindness, Allah has prescribed punishment for us as a deterrent. It helps us keep on the straight way which makes our life peaceful and pleasant. Islam does not admit any concept of a jealous, vindictive god who rejoices in tormenting His own creations. Nor is He partisan, preferring a particular race, nation, colour, or linguistic group to others.

His reward and punishment criterion is simple and logical: those of us who embrace true faith and do good will have an excellent end; those who do not would be hurled into hellfire on account of their own evil actions. Allah's recompense is marked by perfect justice and transparency.

May Allah save all of us against His punishment. We can escape it with our faith and good actions.

Points to ponder

- Our own disbelief and misconduct accounts for Allah's punishment against us.
- On the Day of Judgement, we would be a witness to our sins and misdeeds, recorded meticulously by Allah. He will punish us accordingly.

Chapter 91

Purpose behind Allah's Creation

Throughout the Quran makes it perfectly clear that Allah has created this universe with a clear objective: To test us if we obey or disobey Allah's commands. This life does not end with our death. We are then transported to the next world and would be rewarded and punished for all what we believed and did. If we bear in mind the purpose of our life—to lead life according to Allah's way—we would be blessed with satisfaction and happiness and earn eternal joys in the next life. The following Quranic verse alerts us to the meaning of our life:

> **Allah created the heavens and the earth with a purpose. He makes the night cover the day and the day cover the night. He has subjected the sun and the moon (to His law), each running its course until the appointed day. Allah is Almighty, Most Forgiving.**
>
> **(Al-Zumar 39: 5)**

Cosmology—the sun and the moon abiding by Allah's law since time immemorial is cited as another proof of Allah's glory and might. The seventh-century Arabs and many people, in our time as well, have failed in thinking over the purpose behind life and creation around them. Lost in worldliness, materialism, lust for more and more money or joys of flesh they have no time or inclination for reflecting on the self-evident questions: Who are we? Why are we here? How should we lead our lives? What will happen to us after death?

Allah has not brought this gigantic universe into being as a plaything. We are granted life in order to find out our acceptance or rejection of Allah and His message.

We should give a serious thought to life, this universe and more importantly, the purpose of our life.

Points to ponder

- All objects of Nature have been performing the duty assigned to them. Likewise, we should also serve and worship our Creator, Allah.
- We have a limited lifespan. Let us utilise it for improving our prospects in the next life.

Chapter 92

Allah Has Devised Death

We all have to die. Death is imminent. Far from dreading this inescapable reality, we should realise that it is only a stage, taking us to the next world. We would face our answerability to Allah and His judgement which would be based on what we believe, do or say in this life. So if we adhere to Allah's way, as illustrated in the Quran and Prophet Muhammad's illustrious life, we would not have any fear of death. Allah's objective behind devising death is clarified in the following verse:

> **Blessed is Allah in Whose hand is the kingdom. He has power over everything. He has created death and life so that He may test as to who is best in action. He is Almighty, Most Forgiving.**
>
> **(Al-Mulk 67: 1-2)**

Allah has brought us into being in order to test as to how we lead our life: in accordance with, or in defiance of His will. Accordingly He will punish or reward us. For us, death is a baffling matter. We find it very hard to come to terms with it. However, death is an undeniable grim reality which we witness every day around us. More importantly, each one of us has to die one day. Allah explains the rationale behind death which He causes. It transports us to the next world which is eternal. We will be judged there according to our faith and actions.

In Islam death is not the end; it is a stage, leading us to the hereafter. This life is a period of our test which will end with our death. So we should bear the fact of our imminent death all the time in our mind and keep following the straight way. Otherwise we will undergo humiliating, agonizing punishment after our death. As Allah is most forgiving, most merciful, He will graciously pardon our sins in view of our sincere repentance.

Death is a clear, open reminder of Allah's absolute power, as we are totally helpless against death, notwithstanding all the mind-boggling advances in medical technology.

Points to ponder

- The all-wise Allah has drawn a comprehensive scheme for us, of which death is an integral part.
- Death will mark the end of the term granted to us, followed by Allah's judgement. We should be ever prepared for the next life.

Chapter 93

Allah's Perfect Creation

The Quran throws a challenge: No one can identify any flaw in Allah's creation. Each and every object is best suited for the purpose it has been created. Moreover, all natural phenomena, apart from being hugely beneficial for us, are interconnected. Their coordination contributes to making the planet earth a highly suitable habitat. We should appreciate Allah's creative wonders and glorify Him:

> **Allah created the seven heavens, one upon another. You will not find any defect in the creation by the Most Compassionate One. See again, do you find any defect? Again see, another time and then again. (In the end) your vision will come back to you, tired and frustrated.**
>
> **(Al-Mulk 67: 3-4)**

The perfection in the universe testifies to Allah's creative power and infinite knowledge and wisdom. The Quran throws open a challenge about identifying any disorder in the working of the universe. As we study Nature scientifically with the latest technology, we learn more marvels of Allah's creation. Throughout the Quran, Allah urges us to reflect on and harness natural phenomena for improving the quality of our life and for appreciating Allah's creative wonders. The seamless functioning of the universe testifies to the presence of the perfect, all-powerful lord.

Every object in the universe has some purpose. We should reflect on the purpose of our life and ensure that we keep serving and worshipping Allah and doing good.

Points to ponder

- In recognition of Allah's greatness, as reflected in the splendid natural phenomena, we should turn all the more humbly to our all-powerful Lord.
- Natural phenomena and our own selves stand out as signs for reflecting on Allah's glory and for gaining an understanding of truth.

Chapter 94

Allah's Communication with Us

As Allah transcends our vision and sense perception, He has ingeniously devised ways of authentic communication with us. He has gifted all of us with intellect and sparks of intuition which helps us grasp even tough issues. Moreover, He has put in place an elaborate system of the transmission of His guidance via the agency of angels in all time and place through His book, prophets sages and the pious. They faithfully convey His message to us in our own readily comprehensible language. The following verse points to modes of His communication:

> **It is not possible for any human being that Allah may speak to him. Allah communicates to man by revelation, or from behind a veil, or by the sending of an angel to him who reveals to him by Allah's permission what He wills. He is Most High, the Wisest.**
>
> **(Al-Shura 42: 51)**

It explains the fascinating phenomenon of Allah's message to us. He has devised an elaborate arrangement for our guidance. It also underscores Allah's love and mercy for us. He has sent down a long series of His messengers in every part of the world and His books which clearly state what Allah expects us to do: act in true faith and good action. His final, up to date guidance is contained in the Quran and the Prophet Muhammad's role model.

We should act on Allah's message as communicated to us with utmost attention. On it depends our success in both this and the next world.

Points to ponder

- Out of His inexhaustible wisdom, Allah has devised a perfect system of communication which enables us to find out His will.
- Angels and Prophets communicate to us only as much as Allah has assigned to them. They cannot do anything on their own.

Chapter 95

The Earth As Allah's Sign

We know the earth as our habitat since our birth. We hardly pay any attention to this great blessing which Allah has generously provided to all of us, irrespective of our caste, colour or creed. The earth's ecosystems provide net worth $33 trillion per year! For our basic food, water, mineral and energy supplies we are totally dependent on the earth's ecosystem. Life is unimaginable without all that we get from the earth. In the following verse the earth is likened to a carpet metaphorically, signifying our smooth life on it:

> **It is Allah Who has spread the earth as a carpet for you. He has made roads for you in it so that you may find the way.**
>
> **(Al-Zukhruf 43: 10)**

One of Allah's big favours is that He has made the earth habitable for us. We draw numerous benefits from the earth. The natural signposts on earth are of tremendous value to us. The earth with its numerous resources (water bodies, mountains, forests, valleys, plains, minerals, natural gas, plants, animal and human habitats, soil, life forms, gardens, coasts, agricultural fields, etc). It is Allah's huge favour that He has made the earth not only habitable for us, but also as a vital source for our sustenance (agriculture, cattle, mining etc.). Moreover, it is another marvel of Allah's creative power that despite its diversity, we can easily find our way, as it is dotted with so many signposts (rivers, mountains, forests, etc.).

We should express our thanks to Allah for these bounties and follow the straight way as spelled out by the Quran and Prophet Muhammad's practice.

Points to ponder

- Of Allah's numerous bounties available to us, the earth is the self-evident one.
- We draw upon the earth in countless ways. It has been the source of our subsistence since time immemorial.

Chapter 96

Rain As Allah's Sign for Our Resurrection

That Allah would revive all the dead beings on the Day of Judgement for His recompense is a basic belief of Islamic faith. Since the immediate addressees of the Quran, the seventh-century illiterate Arabs, among whom no prophet had appeared for ages, found it hard to appreciate the doctrine of Resurrection. For instructing them in this self-evident truth, the Quran has often cited the phenomenon of rain, which brings to life dead land. The barren, parched land teems with life in no time. By the same token, the following Quranic verse asserts, we would be resurrected after death.

> **Allah sends rain from the heavens in due measure. He brings with it the dead land back to life. This is how you will be raised (from your graves on the Day of Judgement).**
>
> **(Al-Zukhruf 43: 11)**

Rainfall represents another precious gift from Allah, which is essential for life system on earth. The blossoming of the dead land after rain stands out as a readily understandable proof of how Allah will bring back the dead to life on the Day of Judgement. Resurrection should not therefore be considered as something improbable or incomprehensible. Equally important is that Allah blesses us with rain in a certain measure. Were it to rain incessantly, life would come to a standstill. Being all-wise and almighty, He accomplishes everything, marked by a sense of proportion and balance.

The analogy between rain reviving the dead land and our coming back to life after our death helps us understand easily the reality of resurrection. Those with shallow thinking miss this obvious point altogether.

The natural phenomena, including rain, prompt us to reflect on Allah's greatness and ingenuity.

Points to ponder

- As Allah has brought all creation into being out of nothing, it is naturally simple enough for Him to recreate us.
- Allah's plan of Creation has Resurrection as an essential part of His scheme.

Chapter 97

Cattle As Allah's Favour to Us

Cattle is yet another bounty of Allah, which is of immense benefit to us. We have been drawing upon them for aeons of time. Our economy—farming, transport, and food and drink supply, have been largely owing to the highly beneficent cattle. Islam recognises their right in stating that Allah arranges for rainwater and grain both for us and the animals.

> **Allah created all living beings in pairs and gave you ships and cattle on which you ride. You sit firm on their backs. When you ride them, remember the favour of your Lord and say: "Glory be to Him Who subjected this to us. Otherwise we could never have it. To our Lord is our return."**
>
> **(Al-Zukhruf 43: 12-14)**

Our creation in pairs of male and female and our ability to draw upon cattle and ships for transport are some of Allah's favours to us for which we should thank Him. Let this be realised that in the seventh-century Arabia when the Quran was revealed and up to a much later period, before automobile revolution, animals were commonly used as a mode of transport. Cattle's milk, meat, bones, skin, etc. have been of immense benefit and value to us since time immemorial. This is one of the numerous favours of Allah to us for which we should worship and praise Him.

Likewise when we use cattle or any vehicle today for transport, we should make the above-mentioned supplication. Without Allah's kindness, we could not have so much ease and comfort. Moreover, any travel should bring to our mind our final journey to the next world, that is, our death. It would help us keep steady on the straight way. We must return to our Creator as His obedient, pious servant.

Points to ponder

- Domesticated animals, which are our best friends, represent another amazing sign of Allah.
- It is a pity that animals, who are subservient to us, have been idolised by some communities. On the contrary, we should praise and glorify the all-powerful Creator of cattle.

Chapter 98

Allah and Angels

As part of His grand design of creation, Allah has created a special species – angels who obey Him unquestioningly. As they are not invested with free will, they discharge their duty like robots or AI gadgets. They are invisible to us and have no role in our life. They are another testament to Allah's power and glory, as it comes out in the following verse:

> **To Allah belong all those who are in the heavens and on earth. Those who are with Him (the angels) are not averse to serve Him. Nor do they ever tire of (serving Him). They glorify Him day and night. They never stop.**
>
> **(Al-Anbiya 21: 19-20)**

This Quranic passage corrects the misperception of some people regarding "the fallen" or "rebellious" angels who had revolted against Allah under Satan's leadership. Angels, like everyone else in the universe, are completely submissive to Allah. In Islam, angels are Allah's special species, invisible to human beings. As they do not have free will, they unquestioningly execute Allah's commands in no time. Angels do not have any role at all in divinity. They are always at Allah's beck and call and serve Him humbly. Their special constitution does not let them feel any fatigue. They keep glorifying Allah all the time.

We should try to emulate angels in obeying and praising Allah and not deviating in the slightest from His way.

Points to ponder

- In Islam the concept of angels is not problematic. Islam does not admit any notion of the "fallen, good or bad" angels. Nor does it assign them any part in godhead.
- It is part of Islamic faith to believe in angels as Allah's absolutely faithful servants.

Chapter 99

Allah's Partner(s)

Islam is very clear and insistent on the doctrine that the one true God is the only Lord, enjoying all power, knowledge and excellent attributes. There is no one like Him – be they angels, Prophets, saints or anyone. He reigns supreme, to the exclusion of any partner or associate. Associating anyone with Him in divinity is an unpardonable sin in Islam:

> **Say: "Allah knows best how long they [people] stayed. With Him alone is the knowledge of the Unseen of the heavens and the earth. How well He sees and hears! There is no protector besides Allah. He does not share His power with anyone."**
>
> **(Al-Kahf 18: 26)**

Allah is all-knowing, all-seeing. Only He provides protection and support to everyone. He does not have any partner. He alone reigns supreme. He keeps an exact record of our lifespan and has exclusive access to and control over the Unseen. So He is peerless, not having anyone like Him. By dint of His absolute power and knowledge He does not stand in need of anyone. He is unique in every respect. It is in our own interest to turn to this almighty Lord. Our obedience to Him might improve our prospects in the hereafter. For He is the only protector!

Points to ponder

- As Allah is all-knowing, all-powerful and the Creator and master, He alone is to be worshipped and served.
- While Islam endorses the plurality of religions and rules out compulsion in matters of faith, it does not budge even an inch about the belief in only the one true God, Allah.

Chapter 100

Allah's Assignment for Messengers

As Islam is the natural way, it has devised a simple yet error-free and elaborate system for our guidance. First, the comprehensive book of guidance running into hundreds of pages, the Quran, which has been preserved in its pristine purity since its revelation and is readily available in all languages of the world. Moreover, we have the minutely recorded life, sayings and actions of Prophet Muhammad (peace be upon him) which demonstrate what the Quran teaches. The mandate of messengers is described in the following verse:

> **Allah sends Messengers as bearers of good news and warners. However, Unbelievers dispute falsely in order to reject the truth. They mock Allah's signs and warnings.**
>
> **(Al-Kahf 18: 56)**

This spells out the role and position of Prophets. While those possessing knowledge greet truth, disbelievers stubbornly reject Allah's signs and warnings presented by prophets. Allah's messengers clearly convey the divine message by their word and deed. They perform the twin roles: 1) of stating the truth and promising those who follow them Allah's reward, that is, entry into paradise 2) They warn disbelievers that their rejection of truth will land them in eternal hellfire. They do not force anyone into believing. Their excellent character and conduct attracts people to accept the truth preached by them. This is best illustrated by the Prophet Muhammad's example. In 23 years of his prophetic career, he was successful in winning over the hearts and minds of hundreds of thousands of people who were ever-ready to lay down their lives at his command. Up to this day, he is the role model for around two billion Muslims the world over.

Points to ponder

- As messengers are from among their own community, it facilitates the communication and comprehension of their message.
- Messengers are not supra human beings. It is therefore easy to emulate them.

Chapter 101

Allah Is Immortal

The only immortal being is Allah: All others, great or small, are mortal, which is a common sight. Being the Lord and Creator Who is unique is every respect, Allah is eternal, without any beginning or end. There cannot be godhead without the essential feature of immortality. He has to settle everything. Moreover, death would betray His imperfection whereas He is the Creator and Master of death itself.

> **God alone will inherit the earth and all that is on it. Everyone will return to Him.**
>
> **(Maryam 19: 40)**

At the end of time everything will return to Allah, the real Master and Owner. We are only a trustee of all that we have, and only during our lifetime. Being a trustee we should be very careful, as we will be held answerable.

As the Lord, Master and Creator, Allah alone is immortal. He has always been there and will remain so. All else, including Allah's messengers are mortal as they faced death. Of His numerous unique attributes, Allah's eternality is very striking. He has brought everything into being, including this universe, as part of His grand design. He has created us, sent us to this world up to an appointed term. However, on the last day He will end the present order, resurrect us and adjudge us, on the basis of our faith and actions and will accordingly award us eternal paradise or consign us to eternal hellfire.

We should keep in mind this divine scheme of things which helps us adhere to the straight way. In Islam, the purpose of our life and our fate in the next world are stated very clearly, free from any metaphysical, philosophical or mythological jargon or superstructure. We should remember all along the bare fact of Allah's Lordship and our return and answerability to Him.

Points to ponder

- Death represents our transition from this world to the next one. It is not synonymous with end.
- Allah will adjudge as all of us would return to Him on the Day of Judgement.

Chapter 102

Allah's Treatment of Earlier Communities

As part of advice to us the Quran recounts the history, though briefly, of some of the communities that lived down the ages. Allah sent down to them His book and messengers to guide them to the straight way. Notwithstanding their witnessing a range of miracles and severe warnings to them by messengers, they persisted in unbelief and idolatry. They even slew some messengers of Allah. It was then that Allah destroyed them in no time. Their ruins, found even today, bear out the devastating divine penalty which overwhelmed them. Though they were affluent, nothing helped them against the calamity which they had incurred for themselves. The following Quranic verse urges us to reflect on their catastrophic end:

> **Do they not travel through the earth? They should see the end of those before them, though they were even stronger. There is nothing in the heavens or on earth that may defeat Allah. He is All Knowing, All Powerful.**
>
> **(Fatir 35: 44)**

We are asked to reflect on the ruins of vast ancient empires and their mighty rulers. All of them have been reduced to dust. As we go for sightseeing to historical places, we should realise all the more that we too, are mortals and will disappear soon like them as no one can outpace Allah.

Throughout the Quran we are asked to learn lessons from the past communities. Each of them, in their day, had everything granted to them by Allah: wealth, glory, political power, material resources and sway over others.

It should serve as an eye opener. Allah is supreme and His will alone matters. Let us seek His forgiveness and try our level best to win His pleasure for our eternal success and happiness in the next world.

Points to ponder

- After the advent of the final messenger of Allah, Prophet Muhammad (peace be upon him), large scale divine penalties have ceased. The well-preserved divine guidance is there for everyone who will now be recompensed on the Day of Judgement.
- We are asked to visit historical places, particularly ruins, in order to strengthen our belief in Allah's might, our mortality and our ultimate return to Allah.

Chapter 103

Allah's Foreknowledge

As the Supreme Lord Allah knows everything well in advance. Rather, He has pre-ordained everything. Calamities on a wider scale and suffering and grief at the individual level have also been sanctioned by Him as part of our test and trial. Since we live in the age of Artificial Intelligence, we can better appreciate how all-inclusive Allah's surveillance system is. The following verse cites some instances of His decrees which directly affect us yet we have no clue about these:

> **Allah alone has the knowledge of the Last Hour. It is He Who sends rain and knows what is in the wombs. No person knows what he will earn tomorrow. Nor does anyone know in which land he will die. Allah is All Knowing, All Aware.**
>
> **(Luqman 31: 34)**

All the above mentioned matters belong to the realm of the unseen, known to Allah alone. It is common knowledge that despite all tremendous advancements in technology we do not have any inkling about these issues. It must be clarified that the reference is not to the gender of the foetus, which can be easily determined. Rather, the allusion is to the fate or type or career of the baby in the womb. This verse highlights Allah's absolute power and majesty and boundless knowledge.

Allah's absolute power is correlated with His perfect knowledge of all things, major or minor. It points likewise to our helplessness and lack of knowledge of even such mundane matters of life: our fate and that of our children's, time and place of our death and our income. Allah decides these and all matters as it pleases Him. Mention is made here in particular of the life-giving rain, birth, fate, death and income which are matters of great importance for us. Yet we have no foreknowledge about these.

We should realise our limitations and acknowledge Allah's measureless power by praising and glorifying Him. Out of His immense knowledge, Allah decides what is best for us.

Points to ponder

- It is Allah alone Who knows what kind of a person would grow out of a body; the place where we would die, what we would accomplish tomorrow and when it would rain.
- In recognition of our total dependence on Almighty Allah we should submit ourselves wholly to Him.

Chapter 104

Allah's Power on the Day of Judgement

Throughout the Quran it is emphasised that Allah alone would exercise all power on the Day of Judgement. His decision would be marked by transparency and equity, contingent on our faith and actions. In Islam there is no concept of anyone acting as the redeemer or intercessor. With Allah's permission, prophets would plead for His clemency for someone. The Islamic doctrine of monotheism is reflected at its sharpest in Allah's dispensation of justice, as His discretion would be final and binding:

> **These Unbelievers do not recognize Allah as He should be. On the Day of Judgement the whole of earth will be under His control. The heavens will be rolled in His right hand. Glory be to Him! He is far above the partners they take with Him.**
>
> **(Al-Zumar 39: 67)**

Lost in worldliness, the disbelievers have no time or inclination to reflect on Allah's power and glory. They will see it only after their death. Presently they are blind to even self-evident truths about Allah and His excellent attributes. For awakening us out of our negligence, He sent down throughout history His books and messengers for our guidance. It is a great pity that we fail to recognise the all-powerful Allah. We all will witness first-hand His control over everything in the heavens and on earth. Worse, the disbelievers will not see even a trace of their false gods which will fill them with anguish and remorse.

However, it will be too late by then, for the truth will be very much before them.

As long as we are alive, we enjoy an excellent opportunity to mend our ways: accept true faith, do good actions and turn to almighty Allah, which is the only way out for our eternal joy.

Points to ponder

- Those who deny the Day of Judgement would be utter losers.
- Allah would recompense everyone. No deity, incarnation, saint or clergy would have any role on the Day of Judgement.

Chapter 105

Allah's Books

For the guidance of humankind down the millennia Allah has sent down many books through the agency of the archangel Jibrail to His messengers. Prior to the revelation of the Quran, the Torah and the Gospel had been in circulation. However, these had been corrupted by the clergy beyond recognition and are vitiated by even polytheism and depravity. Against this backdrop, Allah sent down His final, perfect book, the Quran, revealed piecemeal between 610 and 633, to Prophet Muhammad (peace be upon him), as specified in the following verse:

> **(O Prophet), tell them: "What! Shall I look for a judge other than Allah while He has sent to you the detailed Book?" Those given the Books earlier by God know well that the Quran is sent to you by your Lord in truth. So do not be among those who doubt (the truth).**
>
> **(Al-Anam 6: 114)**

The Prophet Muhammad's testimony of faith is worth reflecting. It pithily brings out Allah's greatness. Allah has done a huge favour to humanity by way of having sent down His extensive guidance, the Quran to the Prophet Muhammad (peace be upon him). No guidance other than the Quran is needed for our success in both the worlds. Allah had foretold in his earlier books, for example, the Bible, about the advent of the promised messenger,

Prophet Muhammad (peace be upon him) [Book of the Bible: Isaiah 42:1-13, and Deuteronomy 18:18-19].

For a variety of reasons – racial, theological, political and historical, the Jews and Christians of the day deliberately rejected Islam the Quran/ the Prophet Muhammad (peace be upon him).

We should accept the Quran, Allah's final scripture and lead our life by it. This is the way to eternal success.

Points to ponder

- Since the Quran is Allah's final guidance for humankind of all time and place, He has ensured its error-free preservation. Since the Prophet Muhammad's day to this day, millions of Muslims have memorised it from cover to cover.
- The Quran is in Arabic yet it is readily accessible in translation in all world languages.

Chapter 106

Allah's Reward for Our Charity

Amid all good actions, Islam places premium on charity. Allah exhorts us to give as much as we can in charity and promises manifold reward in the next life. In Islam the concept of charity has very wide connotations. Apart from providing financial help to the needy, treating others well also qualifies as charity, as it instils happiness into the social order. The Prophet Muhammad (peace be upon him) is on record, advising: "Meeting someone cheerfully, with a smile on your face is a kind of charity." The excellence of charity shines through this verse.

> **As to those men and women who give in charity a good loan to Allah, it will be increased many times for them. There is an honourable reward for them.**
>
> **(Al-Hadeed 57: 18)**

Allah asks men and women to spend in Allah's way. Islam presupposes that like men, women would have the means to give in charity. For, Islam grants equal economic rights and share in inheritance to women.

In Islam charity occupies pride of place. For testing our love of wealth and our concern or its lack for the underprivileged people, and our sense of answerability to Allah, Islam has prescribed the religious duty of zakah (paying 2.5% of our wealth) and generous charity. Out of His kindness towards the poor, Allah likens charity as a loan given to Him which He will return manifold in the next world to us if we give in charity in Allah's way. He has promised a high rank in the hereafter to those who cheerfully help the needy.

We should selflessly help the poor, without expecting anything in return. As charity earns Allah's pleasure, we should make it a point to donate as much as possible. We are only trustees of what Allah has kindly granted us.

Points to ponder

- Charity ensures a happy social order, in which no one suffers on account of poverty. Accordingly Islam accords it much importance.
- Charity reminds us that all that we have is a trust from Allah which should be spent in His way.

Chapter 107

Allah's Pardon

Allah introduces Himself as the oft-pardoning, most clement Lord. He warmly receives those who turn to Him in repentance. He has promised pardon even for die- hard sinners, provided they repent sincerely. Prophet Muhammad (peace be upon him) likened Allah's happiness on noting a repentant person to a camel owner who recovers his lost camel in a desert, while on a journey. As long as we are alive, the gates of Allah's pardon and mercy are wide open for us, as is clear from the following verse:

> **Do you not know that the kingdom of the heavens and the earth belongs to Allah? He punishes whom He wills. And He forgives whom He wills. He has power over everything.**
>
> **(Al-Maidah 5: 40)**

As the king, Allah will reward and punish us as He wills on the Day of Judgement. He is gracious enough to forgive even sinners, if they sincerely repent. As Allah is all-powerful, all-aware, He keeps a record of our actions. He may instantly punish us for our wrongdoing. However, this will defeat the whole purpose of our test in this life. He seeks to ascertain if we believe in Him and do good, as instructed by Him, while we have a choice, faculties and resources to act otherwise. That is why He keeps granting us opportunities upon opportunities in order to let us brighten or destroy our prospects in the next life. This manifests His discretion to punish or forgive us. However, throughout the Quran He has promised to pardon us if we repent sincerely.

Let us repose trust in Allah's mercy and forgiveness and look forward to our success in the next world.

Points to ponder

- The all-powerful Allah can punish us for our sins. However, He has ordained mercy for Himself.
- Let us make most of the opportunity available to us for seeking Allah's pardon which would ensure our felicity in the next life.

Chapter 108

Dwellers of Allah's Paradise

Allah has created paradise, embodying all joys imaginable. He has assured that those who profess and practise faith and good would be admitted to it. They would get there whatever they want, including the choicest food and drink and charming spouse. Islam does not feel shy of catering to the pleasures of the flesh which we naturally crave. A snippet of paradise features in this verse:

> **They will sit, facing one another. Ever-young youths will go around them, serving them with cups having drinks from a clear spring.**
>
> **(Al-Waqiah 56: 16-18)**

Allah is equally sensitive to the desires of women. As the pious men are promised beautiful, chaste women as companions in paradise, women too, will have ever-young male companions. That the dwellers of paradise will be sitting, face to face, points to their equal status and cheerful, friendly ambience there. Like men, women too, will have their choicest joys. Islam stands for gender justice and hence the particular mention of smart youths in paradise.

In the Quran, Allah juxtaposes the eternal joys of paradise with the transient life in this world. While discharging our obligations to Allah and human beings, which is a religious duty, we should always set our eyes on the hereafter. Our true faith, good actions and concern for the next life will take us to paradise. We should vigorously pursue this goal.

Points to ponder

- Enjoying all that is good is innate in our nature. Allah would satiate the pious in paradise.
- In Islam, lawful sex is celebrated. Accordingly, the joys of sex would also be available to the believers entering paradise.

Chapter 109

Demands of Faith

Out of His kindness Allah has very clearly spelled out for us the straight way. It is simple, easy to follow and has nothing metaphysical or something which is beyond our reach. Nor does it involve renouncing life and leading a life of only acts of worship and onerous spiritual exercises. As long as we have our Lord in our heart and mind, we worship Him, no matter if we are engaged in any worldly activity, including sleep or performing marital duty with our lawfully wedded spouse. The following verse instructs us in the requisites of faith:

> **Obey Allah and obey the Messenger and beware (of evil). If you turn away, know that it is the duty of Allah's Messenger to convey the message clearly.**
>
> **(Al-Maidah 5: 92)**

We must obey almighty Allah is to be obeyed by us. Since the Prophet Muhammad (peace be upon him) elucidates and demonstrates Allah's message, his teachings are to be followed as well. Accordingly, his sayings and conduct (*Hadith* and *Sunnah*) serve as a primary source of Islam.

Obeying Allah and His messenger should be our goal in life. In doing so, we should shun every evil and sin. Allah has sent down His messengers across the world. However, they did not compel anyone to accept faith. Islam stands for our choice to act as we will. However, it has, at the same time, eloquently guided us how to lead life to ensure our success, and warned us explicitly against the dire consequences, if we go astray.

Let us make most of the opportunity available to us now for our better future in the eternal next life.

Points to ponder

- Leading life in obedience to Allah and His messenger constitutes faith, irrespective of the action in which we are engaged.
- In Islam, faith is not some superstructure of dogma and rituals. We can easily practise faith while leading a normal life, having a career and its obligations.

Chapter 110

Allah's Plan for Us

Allah has sent each one of us to this world with a purpose. He has granted us a range of faculties, mental and physical. He seeks to ascertain how we lead life: in obedience to or our defiance of Him. He has ordained the eternal next life for us. Those of us who practise faith and good will be immensely rewarded. In contrast, those who fail this important test owing to their negligence would face its severe consequences. We should take this test in all seriousness as it will decide our success or loss in the next life, which is eternal. Allah's scheme of things is mentioned in this verse:

> **It is Allah Who created you (O mankind) from clay. Then He appointed a term (your life span). He has also fixed another term (the Last Day) which is known only to Him. Yet you are in doubt!**
>
> **(Al-Anam 6: 2)**

This throws light on Allah's scheme of things for us. We should bear in mind our lowly origin and our death, and our appearance before Allah for judgement.

Allah explains the purpose behind our creation. We are in this world for a brief period, to be followed by the everlasting hereafter. Only the all-powerful Allah knows when the last day will be. What is, nonetheless, certain and important for us is that we will have to render an account of our faith and actions to Allah on the Day of Judgement. He will decide our fate. The doctrine of life-after-death is logical. We are not rewarded or punished in full in this world for our actions. In many instances, evil flourishes while justice suffers. Allah has therefore devised the perfect mechanism of the next life to recompense us with perfect justice and fairness.

We should not harbour any doubt about the truth of the next life, which is inevitable. We should try our utmost to win Allah's pleasure on the Day of Judgement.

Points to ponder

- Allah has made the straight way distinct from the path of error and self-destruction. It is up to us to make the right choice.
- Our rejection of truth in the face of unmistakable pointers to the straight way would not harm Allah in the least. It will incur disaster only for us.

Chapter 111

Allah Alone Feeds Us

Viewed superficially, we may think that we support ourselves with our own hard earned money. On reflection, realise that it is Allah Who has gifted us the faculties to earn our bread. Moreover, all the natural resources on which we subsist are provided only by Him: the soil on which grain grows with rain and all that is conducive to harvest are favours from Allah. We could not attain anything on our own. How Allah provides for us is stated in the following verse:

> **Allah gives provision to every moving creature on earth. He knows where it lives and where it will finally rest. Everything is in the clear record.**
>
> **(Hud 11: 6)**

On reflection we may realise Allah's amazing arrangement for feeding everyone, including animals, birds, insects and all life forms. This has been in place since the time of creation and will continue until the last day. It is an overwhelming sign of Allah's power and wisdom. This underscores His lordship and forbearance. He grants sustenance even to those who do not believe in Him. Rather, they mock and condemn Him. At times, He bestows plenty of His bounties on disbelievers and they are seen prospering apparently. However, it is all part of our trial. Eventually the believers will be rewarded with paradise whereas disbelievers will roast in hellfire.

Another mind boggling attribute of Allah is His all-embracing knowledge. Nothing is hidden from Him. He will take His perfect record into account as He will reward and punish us on the Day of Judgement.

We should serve and worship all-powerful, all-knowing Allah.

Points to ponder

- We should constantly thank and praise Allah in our heart and mind for His vast beneficence to us.
- Lost in materialism we should not suffer from the delusion that we are self-sufficient. We thrive only because of Allah's mercy.

Chapter 112

Allah's Bestowal of Children upon Us

The procreation and perpetuity of our race is another amazing sign of Allah's creativity. He has put in place an elaborate, unfathomable arrangement for our multiplication and the replacement of one generation or community by another. Equally bewildering is His bestowal of sons, daughters or both or none upon us. In His wisdom He has devised this system over which we have little control. Allah speaks of this phenomenon in the following verse:

> **Allah's is the kingdom of the heavens and the earth. He creates what He wills. He grants females to whom He wills and males to whom He wills. Or He grants them both males and females. He leaves childless whom He wills. He is Almighty, the Wisest.**
>
> **(Al-Shura 42: 49-50)**

It is another pointer to Allah's power. So doing, the Quran removes a popular misconception in some communities about a childless couple whom they consider accursed. All this is part of Allah's design that He bestows a son or daughter or both on someone and does not bless some with either. As all-powerful, all-wise, He decides it as He wills. As His obedient servants we should reconcile to His will. In pre-Islamic Arabian society, the birth of a daughter was regarded as a stigma and some Arabs even buried their daughters alive. Islam eradicated this inhuman practice. In

Allah's eyes all are equal: whether we have a son, daughter or neither.

We cannot fathom Allah's grand plan. What is important is to repose faith in Him and turn to Him with full devotion.

Points to ponder

- Allah's immeasurable power is manifest in His granting children to us.
- Allah's arrangement of bestowal of sons and daughters on us since time immemorial has resulted in the consistent gender-ratio.

Chapter 113

Losers on the Day of Judgement

Allah is the best of judges. Since He embodies justice, He ensures that everyone is recompensed fully and fairly in the next world. His mercy demands that victims be redressed and their oppressors be punished. Generally speaking, the rich and powerful escape punishment in this world owing to loopholes in the legal and political system. Or, they are not punished in proportion to their heinous crimes. On the Day of Judgement, however, they would not have any help or support. They would end up as sheer losers, consigned forever to Hell:

> **Allah's is the kingdom of the heavens and the earth. On the Day of Judgement the followers of falsehood will be losers.**
>
> **(Al-Jathiyah 45: 27)**

The disbelievers will sorely regret their rejection of Allah on the Day of Judgement. We as humans are liable to neglect truth and turn a blind eye to even self-evident signs about Allah's oneness, power, knowledge, mercy and numerous other attributes. That is why Allah has put in place a comprehensive plan for our guidance: His books and messengers. We should draw on these divine sources for leading life. Otherwise, we will be utter losers on the Day of Judgement when all of us have to return to Him after our death.

Out of His kindness Allah has sent us reminders so that we are protected against punishment and destruction in the hereafter.

Points to ponder

- If we pay no heed to signs and Allah's elaborate arrangement for guidance, loss and ignominy would stare us in the face on the Day of Judgement.
- Since Allah is all-knowing, all-powerful, the evil ones cannot escape Him on the Day of Judgement.

Chapter 114

Allah Grants Us Control over the Earth

By giving us immense mental and physical faculties, Allah has done us a huge favour. We have been able to make the forces of nature subservient to us, something which no other creature on earth has been able to do. This has made life easy and comfortable. The Quran designates humankind as Allah's vicegerent on earth. Allah refers to this favour in this verse:

> **It is Allah Who has put the earth under your control. Go forth in its paths and eat of its produce. To Allah is the return.**
>
> **(Al-Mulk 67: 15)**

Allah has placed the entire earth at our disposal. We should be prudent as a trustee in our use of natural resources. We will have to render our account to Him.

Islam is an action-oriented religion. Allah does not ask us to retire to a cave and spend all our life remembering Him there. Far from it, Allah commands us to harness natural resources for our benefit, which He has so graciously and generously put at our disposal. In drawing on the produce of the earth we should be honest, fair and kind. We should not hoard or abuse what we get out of Allah's kindness. We should remember all along that we have to return to the real master of the earth, Allah and present our account.

This Allah-awareness will make this world a better place to live, in as it will be marked by mutual love, sympathy and fellow feeling.

Points to ponder

- Our privileged position on earth calls for our profuse thanks and praise for our Creator, Lord.
- It is our duty to be prudent in drawing on natural resources, shunning waste and greed.

Chapter 115

Allah's Warning to Us

As part of His guidance for us, which guarantees our success in both the worlds, Allah has graphically warned us against the horrible consequences of unbelief and committing evil. Several passages in the Quran describe at length agonizing punishment and hellfire to sensitise us to our eternal loss and suffering. Moreover, the spectacle of the destruction of the earlier unbelieving communities and their ruins found even today reiterate the same truth. While we are very particular about our loss and gain in worldly matters, we should be all the more serious about our end in the next life which is everlasting:

> **Do you feel secure that Allah Who is in the heavens will not cause you to be swallowed by the earth in an earthquake? Do you feel secure that Allah Who is in the heavens will not send against you a strong storm? Soon you will realize how (terrible) was Allah's warning. Those before them also rejected faith. How terrible was Allah's punishment!**
>
> **(Al-Mulk 67: 16-18)**

Allah is severe in punishment. We should not have any complacency. Earlier communities were destroyed by His devastating punishment. After Allah's final guidance in the form of the Quran and the Prophet Muhammad's example, which are fully preserved and easily accessible, Allah will not let loose in this world His scourge on any community, no matter how degenerate it might be. However, He keeps displaying glimpses of His absolute power as natural calamities (earthquake, flood, lightning and thunder, etc.) keep afflicting us.

We should seek Allah's refuge against His punishment and try our utmost to win His pleasure.

Points to ponder

- Dreading any loss is innate in our nature. Allah forewarns us about the terrible result of our misconduct, for which we should be grateful to Him.
- It is time for us to protect ourselves against Allah's punishment.
- Indulging in evil destroys both individual and social life. Allah's warnings should deter us from evil.

Chapter 116

Allah's Bounties

Allah asserts in the Quran that if we were to count His bounties which He has so graciously showered on all that exists, particularly human beings, we would not be able to reckon these. This astounding truth dawns upon us all the more as we reflect on His bounties which are numerous as well as aplenty. This should prompt us to thank and praise our beneficent and generous Lord. In the following verse only a few bounties, which are invaluable for us, are cited as an example:

> **(O Prophet), say: "It is Allah Who has created you and given you hearing, sight and hearts. Yet you thank (Him) little."**
>
> **(Al-Mulk 67: 23)**

We are reminded of the wonderful faculties of hearing, seeing and feeling, though we take these for granted and abuse these in disobeying Allah. Accordingly, the Quran comments that we hardly thank Allah for His numerous favours. These faculties, as mentioned above, are manifestations of Allah's creative power and His love and care. We cannot achieve anything if we do not have a sound, healthy body. We deeply realise their worth, if any of our body parts is in pain.

In view of Allah's numerous favours to us, particularly our body, we should turn gratefully to Him and lead life as commanded by Him. Though Allah does not need our thanks, He appreciates this gesture on our part.

Points to ponder

- For us life is unthinkable without the essential faculties of seeing, hearing and feeding. We however take these for granted and hardly appreciate our noble Lord Who has bestowed these on us.
- Using Allah's bounties for our own good and for others, and not abusing these in any way, constitutes the best thanksgiving for these, as these have boundless benefits for us.

Chapter 117

Plight of Sinners on the Day of Judgement

Allah has alerted us repeatedly and sincerely to the dire consequences of our committing wrongs, particularly ascribing partners to Allah. He has gifted us with conscience which keeps pricking us if we indulge in sins. Allah is not some wrathful, vindictive deity, deriving pleasure out of our pain and suffering. His mercy, nonetheless, demands that the guilty be punished and their victims get justice. A heart-rending scene of the misery of sinners on the Day of Judgement is recounted thus:

> **The record of their actions will be placed. You will see the sinners afraid of what is in the record. They will exclaim: "Ah! Woe to us! What a record is this! It does not leave out anything, small or big." They will find in it recorded all that they had done. Your Lord will not wrong anyone.**
>
> **(Al-Kahaf 18: 49)**

It underscores Allah's perfect justice and fairness. All of us will be rewarded and punished in the light of our own actions in this life. He will not treat anyone unfairly. In our era of DNA identification, biometrics and CCTVs and other effective surveillance gadgets, it is not at all hard to visualise how error-free and comprehensive the all-powerful, all-knowing Allah's recording system must be in place. That is why the Quran reproduces scenes of the utter bewilderment of disbelievers on the Day of

Judgment. They will be punished on the basis of the same irrefutable evidence.

Allah is the best judge and He will treat everyone fairly with regard to their record of deeds.

It is in our interest to mend our ways and avoid any disgrace and punishment on the Day of Judgement.

Points to ponder

- Allah's dispensation of justice, involving the award of severe punishment to culprits, is transparent and fair.
- Out of His boundless mercy Allah has forewarned us through His book and messenger against the horrid result of our wrongdoing in the next life.

Chapter 118

Ample Respite from Allah

Notwithstanding His absolute power, Allah does not seize us instantly for our wrongdoings. He is incredibly Forbearing in that He keeps heaping His bounties upon even His inveterate disbelievers who publicly revile Him. The apparent flourishing of sins and evil should not be misperceived. He lets everyone do what they choose. He has reserved His judgment after our death. The following verse explains this aspect of His dealing with us:

> **Your Lord is Most Forgiving, Most Merciful. Were He to punish them immediately for their actions, He would have immediately sent the punishment upon them. However, there is an appointed term for them. They will not find any respite beyond that.**
>
> **(Al-Kahaf 18: 58)**

Allah is most forbearing. He lets even the die-hard sinners do what they desire. However, He records all of their actions and will recompense them on the Day of Judgement. The all-wise, most merciful Allah has drawn up an elaborate scheme. We are granted ample opportunities to do good or evil as part of the same. Most graciously, He does not immediately punish us for our acts of omission and commission. Rather, He lets us pursue the course of action chosen by us. We will, nonetheless, have to bear the consequences of our actions. We cannot flee from the all-powerful Allah's grip. None of us can defer our death ordained by Him. Death is approaching each one of us fast.

We should take a lesson and follow the straight way in order to avoid almighty Allah's punishment, against which no one can save us.

Points to ponder

- Allah grants us numerous opportunities to do good and mend our ways if we have erred.
- As soon as we die, Allah's retribution comes into force. By then it is too late and pointless to avoid loss and suffering.

Chapter 119

Allah Has Ordained Stages of Our Life

Allah's creative ways are both innovative and inexhaustible. He has created us and lets us pass through several stages over which we have no control. In complete subservience to His will our own body, without our consent, undergoes amazing changes from a baby to a frail old person. Shakespeare underscores this human predicament when speaking of the seven stages of life. It is the constant change in us which manifests His total control, as indicated in this verse:

> **It is Allah Who causes your birth in a state of (helpless) weakness. Then after weakness He grants you strength and after strength He makes you weak and old. He creates as He wills. He is All Knowing, All Powerful.**
>
> **(Al-Rum 30: 54)**

Our attention is drawn to Allah's scheme of things as reflected in various stages of our life. It is an everyday sight how the young and the smart turn gradually into helpless, frail old people. Despite formidable advances in medicine and technology we all are vulnerable to decline and death.

Allah presents self-evident examples from our everyday life, which were as easy for the seventh-century illiterate Arabs to grasp as for us in the twenty first century. Attention is drawn to the universal, unavoidable natural law of getting old by the day. Out of His infinite wisdom He has paraded these telling spectacles before us. It is a great pity that we pass by these clear signs and warnings, lost in our lust for money, power and other worldly interests.

In view of the undeniable grim reality of old age and death, and our appearance before almighty Allah for judgement, we should take stock of our conduct and follow the straight way which will bring us peace and happiness.

Points to ponder

- Allah's creation is nothing mechanistic. He does not abandon us after having brought us into being.
- As the Supreme Lord, He oversees all that we do and induces major changes in our body constantly, which points unmistakably to His power and knowledge.

Chapter 120

Allah's Law of Inheritance

Allah is very keen that we should construct a happy, cordial social order. To achieve this, He has prescribed a range of laws which facilitate justice, fairness and equality in our life. Since money matters much, He has laid down an elaborate, egalitarian inheritance law, guaranteeing shares to our near and dear ones, especially women. It ensures a smooth transition of family belongings from one generation to another:

> **There is a share for men in what their parents and close relatives leave behind. Likewise there is a share for women in what their parents and close relatives leave behind. There is a share decided by Allah in what is left behind, be it little or much.**
>
> **(Al-Nisa 4: 7)**

Allah lays down the law of inheritance mandatory for believers. It is an egalitarian pronouncement. Prior to this, women were inherited like chattel. Islam granted women an equal share in inheritance. Allah makes it a point to describe women as inheritors in the same terms which are used for men.

In Islam, the husband is obliged to support his family. The wife does not have any financial responsibility. A woman gets her inheritance share from her parents, brother, sister, husband and children. This share is mandatory. Every Muslim is obliged to pay it. It points to woman's economic rights in Islam. Biased media, however, keeps projecting Muslim women as oppressed and victims of patriarchal Islam.

The all-wise Allah has prescribed such laws which are aimed at social cohesion, gender justice and economic empowerment.

Points to ponder

- Strikingly enough, the above quoted verse stands out for its gender parity. Along with men, women are specifically designated as heirs.
- In seventh-century Arabia in which woman was treated as a worthless commodity, Islam elevated her social and financial status by granting her a share in inheritance.

Chapter 121

Allah's Treatment of the Pious

Allah is most munificent. He rewards immensely those who are obedient to Him and lead life in accordance with His directives. He has prepared for them joys which no eye has ever seen or which no one has ever imagined. Generously enough, He rewards us for more than we deserve. We are granted His bounties for our intention to do some good, even if we are unable to execute it for some reason. A glimpse of the exalted position awaiting us in paradise is provided below:

> **However, for those who fear their Lord, there will be high chambers, with high chambers above them. There will be rivers beneath them. This is Allah's promise. Allah does not fail to fulfil His promise.**
>
> **(Al-Zumar 39: 20)**

The pious will abide in paradise forever. This should be read together with Allah's assertion that He never breaks His promise.

The most merciful and most affectionate Allah will lavishly reward the pious. If we profess and practise faith and take good care of our parents, family, the weak and the needy, particularly widows and orphans, Allah will bestow upon us magnificent palaces in paradise. The high chambers denote an exalted status in the hereafter. Allah is ever true to His word.

We should aim at grabbing this golden opportunity of entering paradise and getting a coveted place there.

Our true faith and good conduct can help us gain this distinction.

Points to ponder

- We should be grateful to Allah for promising huge incentives for our good conduct.
- Allah intends a social order for us in which each one of us is kind and nice to others and all enjoy a happy, peaceful social life.

Chapter 122

Allah As the Only Lord

The perfect functioning of and order in the universe unmistakably points to its oversight by the all-powerful one true God, Allah. He alone embodies all the attributes which are pre-requisites for managing immaculately affairs of the universe. There is no one like Him. In Islam there is no room for any flexibility on its central doctrine of Allah's oneness, to the exclusion of everyone else. All knowledge, power, sovereignty and all attributes belong in an absolute sense only to Him. To crown it all, He is eternal, without any beginning or end:

> **Never call upon any god besides Allah. There is no god other than Him. Everything will perish except He. His is the command. To Him all of you will be returned.**
>
> **(Al-Qasas 28: 88)**

Everyone other than Allah is mortal. In Him alone we should repose our trust. Islam is strictly monotheistic. It does not admit any partner/associate or incarnation with Allah Who is the only one true God. It is not therefore surprising that our belief in Allah being the only God features as the first and foremost article of Islamic faith.

Not only is Allah the only lord, He alone is imperishable. All would die except He, for He is eternal, who existed even before this universe and He would survive everyone. More importantly, He will revive the dead and call them to account. Only His command will reign supreme in the hereafter.

We should be concerned all along about our imminent appearance before Almighty Lord. For this we should have true faith and good actions to our credit.

Points to ponder

- The basic component of the Islamic concept of Allah is that He alone is the Lord.
- In view of Allah's absolute might, glory and mercy we should surrender ourselves wholly to Him.

Chapter 123

Allah Has Set Tests for Us

Allah has sent us to this world to ascertain who obeys or disobeys Him. He foreknows our conduct. However, He has granted us faculties and provided us ample opportunities to prove our mettle. He tests both believers and unbelievers in a variety of ways, ranging from adversity to prosperity, success and failure, and pain and happiness. He would take our response to these tests into stride in rewarding and punishing us on the Day of Judgement:

> **As some hurt touches you at sea, those whom you call besides Allah disappear. Allah alone helps you. When He brings you back to land, you again turn away from Him. Man is indeed thankless. Do you feel safe that He will not cause you to be swallowed up by earth when you are on land? Or He may not send against you a storm. Then you will not find any protector.**
>
> **(Al-Isra 17: 67-68)**

Allah is our only refuge, no matter where we may be: on land or sea. No one else can rescue us. It is our common weakness that in a crisis we fervently invoke Allah for help. However, after this incident we forget maintaining our link with our master Lord. Allah-awareness should permeate our consciousness. In all that we think or do, His pleasure should be uppermost in our mind and heart. For the all-powerful Allah may seize us any moment. We are too helpless to get any protection other than His.

Our life should be Allah-centric. In both good and bad times we should turn to Him and seek to win His pleasure.

Points to ponder

- Our main test consists in thanking our all-merciful Lord or disregarding His numerous favours.
- In Islam unbelievers are designated as *kafir* which denotes thanklessness and ingratitude. Far from being an offensive, obnoxious term, it points to their response to their Creator.

Chapter 124

Allah's Excellent Names

To Allah belong all excellent names, denoting His perfection and uniqueness. Of these, Allah (the one true God) and *Al-Rahman* (the most compassionate one) occupy pride of place. In the Quran, scores of His names and attributes feature, fitting in with the context. In the opening verses of the Quran He introduces Himself as the source of all mercy and kindness (*Al-Rahman* and *Al-Raheem*), the Nourisher Lord of the worlds (*Rabb Al-Alamiyyin*) and *Malik* (Master) of the Day of Judgement. The following verse deals with the issue of His names:

> **Whether you call Him Allah or Al-Rahman, you may call Him by any name. All of His names are excellent.**
>
> **(Al-Isra 17: 110)**

We are allowed to invoke Allah by any of His most beautiful names. What matters is our sincerity and devotion to Him. Many of His names denoting His perfect and unique attributes feature in the Quran and *Hadith* (the collection of the Prophet Muhammad's sayings). Islam does not attach any importance to ritualism, and does not insist on calling Allah by only one specific name. Our sincerity and devotion to Him, however, matter most.

We should focus on forging a strong emotional and spiritual bond with Allah, which, in turn, will infuse piety into us. This is the key to leading a peaceful, serene life in this world and getting Allah's immense bounties in the hereafter.

Points to ponder

- Since Allah transcends everything, addressing Him by any name which embraces His oneness and uniqueness suffices.
- We should show utmost respect and sanctity in taking any one of His several names. The Prophet Muhammad (peace be upon him) is on record having listed Allah's 99 names.

Chapter 125

Allah's Favourites?

In Islam the concept of God is not confined to any particular tribe, ethnicity or even belief. Allah is the universal Lord, heaping His favours alike on believers and unbelievers. He does not discriminate against anyone for any consideration. Needless to add, He has prescribed a way and wants us to follow it. However, He does not compel anyone into believing. Nor does He instantly punish those who reject Him. He facilitates the way which we choose, be it good or evil and would deliver His judgement at the end of time:

> **Allah does favours to everyone, these as well as those. The favours of your Lord are not denied to anyone.**
>
> **(Al-Isra 17: 20)**

This is illustrative of Allah's munificence. He showers His bounties upon one and all: the believers and disbelievers, without any regard for their caste, colour and ethnicity. We should turn gratefully to Him for His generous favours.

Allah's forbearance and generosity are boundless. Though He is all-powerful and may annihilate His enemies in no time, without any fear of consequences, He keeps granting them respite. He is so merciful that He may pardon all the excesses committed by a habitual sinner, provided that he turns to Him with sincerity and humility. We should not be surprised to see wrongdoers going unchecked in their crimes. Instant punishment to an offender is not the way of Allah.

We have the precious gift of life as an opportunity to improve our prospects in the hereafter. We should grab this opportunity with both the hands.

Points to ponder

- Allah is not the Lord of Muslims alone. He sustains everyone and enables them to accomplish what they prefer.
- Allah's reward and punishment is reserved for the hereafter. Those practising faith and good would be amply rewarded by Him on the Day of Judgement.

Chapter 126

Followers in Allah's Eyes

Out of His wisdom which we cannot fathom, Allah has granted various degrees of social, moral, spiritual and financial status to us. This is part of His test for our performance in different situations. In His bestowal He makes no discrimination between believers and unbelievers. One's standing in this life, however, does not carry His endorsement of their conduct. His reward and punishment will be manifest in the next life, contingent upon His judgment. The following verse indicates how Allah views us:

> **See, Allah has given more to some than others. In the Next Life some will have a higher position and excellence over others.**
>
> **(Al-Isra 17: 21)**

Allah disburses His provisions as it pleases Him. It is beyond us to fathom any rationale behind it. However, He has promised a better place for the believers in the next life. The distribution of wealth in the world strikes us as something beyond logic. Some of us have plenty of wealth, without having earned it by dint of any hard work. In contrast, there are many industrious, noble souls who are unable to meet even the basic necessities of life. The apparent inequality is part of the overall divine scheme. Allah seeks to ascertain our conduct as He places us in prosperous as well as adverse conditions.

The real, abiding reward is the next life. If we obey Allah in all circumstances, irrespective of being rich or poor, Allah will bestow His bounties on us, which is the real success.

Points to ponder

- Allah's perfect neutrality underscores His being most forbearing. Such kindness towards those who openly denounce Him is unimaginable for us.
- Allah closely watches our conduct. We would be soon subject to His recompense, something about which we should be seriously concerned.

Chapter 127

Allah Denounces Foeticide

In pre-Islamic Arabia and other parts of the world, foeticide was rampant. Fearing poverty callous parents killed their own children. In our time the same repugnant practice of foeticide persists, though the motives behind this are different: preference for a baby son and getting a baby daughter aborted or avoiding conception, or parents who may not be able to afford or maintain their standard of life after having a baby. Allah is the provider. He has been sustaining the poor also. Hence it is a heinous sin, not to have trust in Him. The following verse records Allah's revulsion towards it:

> **Do not kill your children, fearing poverty. Allah feeds you and will feed them as well. Killing them is a major sin.**
>
> **(Al-Isra 17: 31)**

We are asked not to kill our children out of the fear of poverty, including foeticide in our time. Allah's inexhaustible treasures suffice for all. Fear of poverty is innate in human nature. In pre-Islamic Arabia, people killed their children out of the fear of not being able to feed them. Today, owing to a preference for sons rather than daughters and for maintaining a high standard of life, foeticide still persists. Not having babies is fairly common in our society for a variety of reasons.

The all-wise Allah condemns such unnatural practices. He has been sustaining all living beings since time immemorial. With the latest advances in agricultural technology a higher yield has been able to meet our food needs, with the same area of land.

While recognising almighty Allah's perfect wisdom we must refrain from foeticide and pray to Him for blessing our resources.

Points to ponder

- Allah's commands are directed at correcting a social order in which good flourishes and all persons enjoy peace and happiness.
- Allah' resources should be harnessed for meeting needs, rather than curbing birth and enforcing strict population control.

Chapter 128

Allah's Advice for Us

The Quran, Allah's final book of guidance for all of humanity abounds in profound advice. These directives are for our own benefit. They seek to make us better human beings, responsible members of society and strengthen marital, familial and community ties. The Prophet Muhammad's illustrious life exemplifies how he practised these, as a result of which he stands out as a role model for everyone. Some pieces of invaluable advice mark the following verse:

> **Allah commands that you do justice and good to relatives, forbid shameful things, evil, and rebellion. He advises you so that you may take a lesson.**
>
> **(Al-Nahl 16: 90)**

For building a better world and cordial social relations Allah has promulgated the above commands. These do not benefit Him in any way; these are in our own interest. Allah being our Creator and intimately aware of our psyche which breeds discord, has urged us to shun these social evils. These destroy the social fabric and make our life miserable: injustice in any form, not restricted to only its legal sense; misbehavior towards others; indulging in sex outside marriage (be it consensual, adultery, rape, live-in relationship, or any form of LGTBQIA+). These strike at the foundations of our society and cordial relations.

It is in our interest to lead a peaceful, happy life, free from any friction. Allah's advice aims at constructing life-giving, positive social ethos.

Allah is not concerned only about our devotional worship to Him at the appointed hours. He is equally particular about our pleasant life and excellent conduct which augurs well for all of us.

Points to ponder

- The verse under discussion here is recited as part of the Friday prayer sermon which sensitises Muslims to excellent morals and manners.
- This set of directives aims at protecting the social fabric and ensuring social justice and morality.

Chapter 129

Allah's Directive Regarding Oaths

Allah urges us to lead a purposive life. Seriousness and goodness should mark all of our sayings and actions. Keeping true to one's word is a great virtue. It helps others in getting what is their due. Justice demands that we fulfil our obligations. Pledges and oaths are solemn promises which we should ensure to deliver. Apart from our acts of worship, Allah is equally concerned about our obligations to fellow human beings, as this comes out from the following verse:

> **Fulfil the pledge you have made to Allah. Do not break oaths after you have seriously taken these.**
>
> **(Al-Nahl 16: 91)**

We should be very sensitive about fulfilling the promises we make while taking Allah as a witness. As He is true to His promise, He asks us to deliver what we pledge. It will promote peace and happiness in society. Since Islam is an all-encompassing religion, it is not confined to some religious rituals and observances. Allah has guided us in every respect of our life. The reference here is in a very broad sense to all our obligations: to our Lord, to our body and soul, to our parents, family and friends, to our wider community and country, and to all human beings on the whole. Allah insists that we make it a point to fulfil all of these obligations to the best of our ability. This infuses a purpose and meaning into our life. Islam stands for a noble, productive life.

Our failure to keep our word which we have given to someone often leads to an ugly situation. It is equally sacrilegious to neglect any religious duty which we owe to our lord and master, Allah.

We should pay attention to our duties and discharge these as best as we can.

Points to ponder

- Allah asks us to discharge our duty to Him as well as to the wider community.
- In Islam, Allah/God is not some metaphysical or theological entity. He guides us extensively how to lead life, particularly in relation to our kith and kin, community, country, and the world at large.
- This set of directives aims at protecting the social fabric and ensuring social justice and morality.

Chapter 130

Objectives behind Allah's Commands

In Islam, Allah alone is the legislator. Apart from issuing some specific commands, recorded in the Quran, He has laid down broad parameters for ensuring our good conduct. Muslim jurists, over centuries, have applied the same divine criteria for resolving issues which keep cropping up with changing times. Prophet Muhammad (peace be upon him), sent down by Allah as mercy unto humankind, elucidated Allah's laws for our guidance. The following passage gives a fair idea of the thrust of Allah's commands:

> **Your Lord has given the following commands. A) Do not worship anyone besides the One True God. B). Be kind to parents, whether both or any of them turn old. C). Do not say to them any offensive word. D). Speak to them with respect. Be humble and kind to them. E). Keep praying: "O my Lord, have Your mercy on them as they brought me up when I was small." Your Lord knows well what is in your hearts. If you are pious, He is Most Forgiving to those who repent. Give to the relatives, the poor and the traveller their due. Do not waste your wealth.**
>
> **(Al-Isra 17: 23-26)**

These commands by Allah constitute the Islamic code of life, covering individual and community relationships, family obligations, morals and manners, and business dealings. In sum, these epitomise Allah's will regarding the kind of life we should lead. Apart from asking us to believe in monotheism which is a truth manifest in this universe, this divine directive lays premium on our being kind and affectionate towards our parents. Islam exhorts us to fulfil our obligations to them and express our gratitude to them. Allah who provides us with everything deserves our praise and thanks all the more. Being most merciful, He may condone our lapses if we repent to Him sincerely. Allah is very particular about our generous help to the poor and the needy. While we should liberally spend on all good causes, we must avoid any squandering or extravagance. This amounts to being ungrateful about a great bounty, wealth which is conferred upon us by Allah.

In sum, Allah is keen on our moral, social and economic well-being and instructs us thoroughly for our own good.

Points to ponder

- Affection and concern for parents is to the fore in the above commands. Parents are likewise asked to ensure excellent upbringing and moral training of their children.
- In Islam, the law has been a constantly evolving phenomenon. The spirit permeating Allah's commands lies at the heart of robust juristic activities of Muslim scholars.

Chapter 131

Purpose behind Allah's Creation

Some people take a superficial view of the world and think that it came into being owing to some natural factors and may disintegrate one day. Likewise, they hold that they are here in this world for enjoying life and their death will mark the end. The Quran, on the contrary, affirms a definite purpose behind creation and our life in this world. Allah has created everything with a purpose. He would take us to task for our conduct and our eternal life in the next world and it would be contingent on our faith and actions in this life. The following verse draws attention to this truth:

> **We have not created without a purpose the heavens, the earth and all that is between these two. This is the fancy of only the Unbelievers. Woe to the Unbelievers because of the Hellfire!**
>
> **(Saad 38: 27)**

Allah has created us in order to test us whether we believe in and obey Him unseen. We will be rewarded or punished on the basis of this trial. This rejects the silly notion held by some that our death is our final end and that the world would finish one day, without any follow up. Allah has brought this universe into being for a definite, serious purpose, of testing our faith and actions while providing so many bounties to us (our body, health, family, habitat, money and many faculties and resources). It is foolish to think that we will not be held accountable for all that we have got. Death is only a passing stage, to culminate into our resurrection, judgement, and reward and punishment.

The all-wise Allah has a grand design behind His creation which is explained to us through His book, the Quran and His messenger, Prophet Muhammad's teachings.

We should bear in mind the purpose behind our creation and follow the straight way shown to us by Allah and His messenger.

Points to ponder

- Allah has not created this world as a sport, without any objective.
- Those who refuse to understand the meaning of life and Allah's purpose behind creating everything deny a manifest truth. As a consequence, they would be consigned to hellfire.

Chapter 132

Spouses As Allah's Gift to Us

As Islam is a natural, complete way of life, it lays a premium on family life. Marital bliss, including the joys of sex and procreation within wedlock, is Allah's bounty which He has graciously bestowed on us. Islam opposes celibacy and monasticism as unnatural. Allah speaks of a good husband or wife as His gift to us. Needless to add, we truly enjoy life in the company of our spouse and family. The following verse highlights this blessing:

> **Allah has given you spouses of your own kind. He has granted you through your spouses children and grandchildren. He gives you pure things to eat. Do they still believe in falsehood and disbelieve in Allah's blessings?**
>
> **(Al-Nahl 16: 72)**

One of Allah's big favours to us is our family which gives us immense joy and makes life meaningful. In pre-Islamic Arabia and the rest of the world, women were treated as chattel, without any rights. The Quran proclaimed and implemented gender justice, granting women a share in inheritance. Our spouse is described as one of Allah's precious gifts to us. Apart from providing physical, emotional and psychological comfort and support, and companionship, spouses enable us to enjoy the blessing of having our children and grandchildren, who are invaluable for us. Allah thus urges us to be kind and considerate towards our soulmates.

Those given to falsehood and disbelief are blind to this and numerous other huge favours done to us by Allah. We should thank and glorify the all-wise, most merciful Allah for granting us life partners who are a source of immense joy to us.

Points to ponder

- Allah asks us to be thankful to Him for having blessed us with a wife in that she is pivotal to raising a family.
- Allah refers also to children and grandchildren as His blessing, underscoring the natural, family-centred life in Islam. Allah does not sanction unbridled sexual preferences, as manifest today in the wake of the LGBTQIA+ phenomenon.

Chapter 133

Allah's Countless Favours

For our existence, survival and enjoyment of life, we are wholly dependent, mostly on natural resources. These range from the constant free of charge supply of oxygen to rainwater, produce of the earth and our own bodily mechanism. It is Allah alone Who has granted everything. Even our own accomplishments are owing only to the physical, mental and other faculties bestowed upon us by Him. We are asked to reflect on this truth in this verse:

> **Allah gives you all that you ask. If you were to count Allah's favours, you will not be able to count these. Yet man is unjust and unthankful.**
>
> **(Ibraheem 14: 34)**

Allah's bounties to us are countless and embrace every aspect of our life: spiritual, emotional, mental and physical. Yet we hardly thank Him for His grace and kindness. Even on little reflection we can appreciate all kinds of bounties bestowed on us by Allah (our body, health, family and friends, social life and material resources and comforts). As it is, we have not earned most of these on our own. Even the earned ones are owing to the host of faculties and means heaped on us by our most compassionate, most generous lord. We stand naturally obliged to Him and should serve Him best by following the way of life He has prescribed. In so doing, we will earn success in both the worlds.

Disbelievers are condemned in Islam for being unthankful and unjust to their lord, for not even acknowledging the wealth of His favours which they keep drawing on all the time.

Points to ponder

- In recognition of Allah's numerous favours to us we should obey and glorify Him.
- Unbelievers are condemned for their ingratitude and their utter disregard for Allah's bestowal of countless bounties to them.

Chapter 134

Allah Is Omnipotent

Enjoying absolute power over everything that exists, Allah's is all-powerful. Take our own lives, for instance. Birth and death are the most important happenings in our lives. Yet we have no role whatsoever in these. We have no choice in the family, religion, country or era in which we are born. Likewise, we have no inkling about when, where and how we are going to die. Notwithstanding stupendous advancement in knowledge and skills, we realise all the more about our inadequacies. Some examples of Allah's power are adduced in the following verse:

> **Whatever mercy Allah grants to people, there is no one to stop it. Nor is there any to release what He stops, apart from Him alone. He is Almighty, the Wisest.**
>
> **(Fatir 35: 2)**

Allah being all-powerful bestows and withholds His mercy as it pleases Him. We should constantly pray to Him for His bestowal of bounties to us. Our belief in the one true God Who does what pleases Him gives us a valuable sense of tranquility and contentment. We are no longer dismayed by confusion and inconsolable trauma. We turn to Him for all our needs and wants, believing all the time that the most affectionate, most caring Allah will decide what is best for us. At times, we may have to undergo loss and crisis. However, it is so comforting and inspiring for us to realise that we will be eventually rewarded for our hardships. Out of His boundless mercy Allah will admit us to paradise, where we would enjoy bliss forever.

Our trust in our guardian lord, Allah enables us to bear with every problem in life.

Points to ponder

- No one however mighty they may be, can withhold what Allah grants to someone. He blesses whom He deems fit in His wisdom.
- We note on a regular basis the downfall of the so-called powerful ones. Power in its true sense, rests only with Allah. The recent Covid pandemic (2020–2021) was a manifestation of His might.

Chapter 135

Animals As Allah's Bounty

Of Allah's numerous bounties which He has generously placed at our disposal, animals stand out for their very many benefits to us since time immemorial. Our economy is dependent on them to some extent even today. Earlier, they were the only means of transport. People rode on horse and camel to undertake long, arduous journeys. To this day we draw on cattle for the amazing, fresh supply of meat, milk, poultry, dairy products, wool, tannery, etc. We should turn to Allah for having blessed us thus and be very sensitive to animal rights:

> **Allah created cattle. In these there are food, clothing and other benefits for you. In them there is pride and beauty as you drive them home in the evening, and as you lead them to fields in the morning. They carry your heavy loads to lands where you could not reach without much difficulty. Your Lord is Most Affectionate, Most Merciful to you. He created horses, mules and donkeys for you to ride and also for a show. He creates things which you do not even know.**
>
> **(Al-Nahl 16: 5-8)**

The reference here is to Allah's creation of cattle for our many benefits. This should fill our hearts with awe and gratitude. Even today our economy depends to an extent on cattle. Imagine the seventh-century pre-automobile world when we were totally dependent on animals for our basic need of transport. Allah spells out some of the major, self-evident benefits of only one of His numerous blessings. Cattle provide us milk, meat, leather, bones, means of transport, and help in our agricultural activities.

Allah's creative wonders are both countless and unique. This should fill our heart and mind with praise and glorification of Allah. This bright sign alone should convince us of Allah's absolute creative power, His ingenuity and His care and concern for our well-being.

Points to ponder

- Animals are cited here as Allah's creative wonder. The variety and beauty of animal life is indeed mind-blowing. Only the all-powerful Allah could bring them into being.
- As an activist of animal rights, the Prophet Muhammad (peace be upon him) on record instructed the seventh-century people to take good care of animals and shun any cruelty to them.

Chapter 136

The Way to Allah

Allah has done us a huge favour by showing us the straight way which leads to Him. As a result of following this way, we are blessed with success and happiness in both the worlds. His way is explicitly recorded for everyone, of all time and place, in His immaculately preserved book, the Quran and His final messenger Prophet Muhammad's life-giving teachings. It is in our own interest to adhere to this way for earning Allah's invaluable pleasure.

> **It is for Allah to show you the straight way. Some paths are not right. Had He willed, He could guide everyone.**
>
> **(Al-Nahl 16: 9)**

Allah's biggest favour to us is that He has shown us the way to win His pleasure. Otherwise, we would have been lost and incur His eternal punishment in the next life. Our top-most priority should be to find out and follow the straight way leading to Him. Allah being our lord, sustainer and guardian has provided for us in all respects: material resources for our survival and moral and spiritual guidance for our success and happiness in this world and the next. His guidance is available to all, as embodied in the Quran and the Prophet Muhammad's example. For testing our obedience to Him, He has also given us free will, which grants us freedom to choose any path, including that of sin and evil. Again, as part of His test, He does not compel any of us to follow the straight way. This would be against His grand plan of judgment.

As we see the disbelievers flourishing and the guilty not getting punished for their crimes, it should be understood as part of Allah's scheme of things. This is not any reflection on His absolute power.

Points to ponder

- Allah has not compelled us to follow only His way. Rather, He has granted us free will to choose what appeals to us most.
- As Allah's way is natural, logical, catering to our needs and aspirations we should be on our guard against any distraction or deviation from His way which would ruin our prospects in the eternal hereafter.

Chapter 137

Rain As Allah's Blessing

Life is unthinkable without water. It is nothing short of a miracle that Allah has been blessing us since day one with ample supply of water on a regular basis. It is amazing that billions of Allah's creatures get a constant, free of charge supply of such essentials as air, water, sunlight, fruits and produce of the earth, owing to His beneficence and generosity. We should be grateful to our most affectionate, most kind Lord. The following verse points to the pivotal role of rain in our life:

> **Allah sends down rain for you from the heavens. You drink this. And out of the same plants grow on which your cattle feed. With it He produces for you olives, date-palms, grapes and all kinds of fruits. In this are signs for those who think.**
>
> **(Al-Nahl 16: 10-11)**

Rain and its variety of yield are central to our life cycle. Out of His affection, Allah has provided it to us in plenty. Needless to add, water is essential to life. Out of His bountiful wisdom and affection for all living beings, Allah has put in place the amazing, regular supply of water which sustains us. Apart from drinking, the other main use of water is for the produce of the earth. The more we reflect on Allah's boundless mercy at work in this arrangement, the more we are persuaded of His power, knowledge and greatness. Rain stands out as an evident sign of Allah's creative marvels. As it revives the dead land after every summer, it brings to mind our resurrection after death for the final reckoning on the Day of Judgement.

As for other bounties, for the amazing gift of rain to us by Allah, we should serve, praise and glorify Him.

Points to ponder

- Rainwater is sent down by Allah for sustaining not only us, but also animals and all creatures. Truly, He is the sustainer of the entire universe.
- Our produce of the earth is also dependent on water. Allah thus caters to both our food and drink out of His generous mercy.

Chapter 138

The Sea As Allah's Sign

Allah's signs manifesting His power, ingenuity and mercy are numerous. Of these, the sea is visible to us. The wonders of sea life are too many to be described. The sheer size and vastness is awe-inspiring. It has tremendous benefits for us. Many communities settled along the coast subsist mainly on sea products. Allah has enabled us to sail on ships as well. The navy is an integral part of the defence system of many countries, concerned solely with sea. Out of His munificence Allah has made it subservient to us, as stated in the following verse:

> **Allah has subjected the sea so that you may eat fresh meat from it and also take out from it which you wear as ornament. You see the ships sailing through it in order that you may seek in it God's bounties. All this that you may thank Him.**
>
> **(Al-Nahl 16: 14)**

Our ability to draw upon something seemingly as uncontrollable as the turbulent sea represents another huge favour by Allah. The sea stands out as yet another sign of Allah's power and inexhaustible creativity. It is of tremendous value to us, as specified above. Not only has Allah graciously created the sea for us, He has also made it subservient to us. While drawing upon our mental and physical faculties granted to us by Allah, we have learnt, over the centuries, how to harness the sea for a host of purposes, accruing huge benefits. Only the all-powerful

Allah could create something so bewildering as the sea, with its own life system.

Our reflection on the sea should impel us to acknowledge our gratitude to Allah for having blessed us with it.

Points to ponder

- On our own we could not conquer the sea. We must thank and glorify Allah for having equipped us with the faculties and skills to subjugate it.
- The sea world with its flora and fauna represents yet another facet of Allah's creativity. We stand humbled to Him in view of both His grandeur and His kindness to us.

Chapter 139

Mountains and Stars As Allah's Signs

Allah does not thrust upon us belief in Him. Throughout the Quran He asks us to reflect on His self-evident signs in Nature. Generally speaking, we take these as routine matters and pay scant attention to their marvellous features, underscoring Allah's creativity and concern for us. He has created many objects of Nature which are of immense benefit to us, ranging from meeting our mundane immediate needs of sustenance to maintaining ecological balance. Mountains and stars are mentioned in this passage and we are asked to appreciate and delve deep into these bounties of Allah.

> **Allah has set firm mountains on earth so that it may not shake with you. He has made rivers and roads so that you may find your way. He has made other marks. People find their way by the stars also. Is the creator equal with one who cannot and does not create? Do you not take any lesson?**
>
> **(Al-Nahl 16: 15-17)**

Our attention is drawn to a host of Allah's bounties made available to us, which have made life easy and comfortable for us. These signs affirm Allah's oneness. We should draw this important lesson. Allah's creative power is reflected at its sharpest in the awe-inspiring mountains of all sorts, dotting the earth. Their benefits to us are too well-known to be elaborated. As they are markers, we should bring to mind their wonderful Creator, the one true God

Who brought these into being out of nothing and in no time. Moreover, He has taught us how to make the most of our natural resources, with our mental, physical and technological faculties, granted aplenty to us by Allah.

We should be concerned about identifying and pursuing Allah's way which guarantees our deliverance in the hereafter.

Points to ponder

- Allah urges us to use our faculties of observation, reason and inference for drawing fruitfully on His bounties which represent signs of His Lordship.
- It is a great pity that some credulous persons have taken to idolising even mountains and stars, though Allah has created these. As their sole Creator, Allah alone should be worshipped and praised.

Chapter 140

Allah's Food Cycle for Us

Allah has devised an elaborate, seemingly complex yet well-coordinated food chain for us, by subjecting the elements and forces of Nature to our service. He has appointed ways and means for us to draw upon the food system for our survival. It is common knowledge that any impediment to the system, for example, scarcity of water disturbs food production. We must thank Him for providing conducive conditions for food production.

> **Let man think about his food (how Allah provides it), Allah sends rain in plenty. And He splits the earth. Then He produces grain from it, and grapes and vegetables, and olives and palm trees, and gardens with tall trees, and fruits and fodder for your benefit and for your cattle.**
>
> **(Abasa 80: 24-32)**

This is another impressive list of Allah's precious favours to us and our cattle. All this should turn us into thankful servants of Allah. Food is yet another bewildering sign of Allah's magnificence, generosity and kindness towards us. We could not survive without the perfect food cycle (soil, rain and produce) devised by Allah. For millions of years, we have been subsisting on food resources provided for us and all life forms. We should make sure that we get food lawfully. Moreover, it should be wholesome, not one of the very few forbidden categories. Out of His affection,

Allah has permitted us to eat almost everything, barring a few, in order to test if we obey His command.

More importantly, we should profusely express our gratitude to Allah for such a fantastic gift as food granted by Him to us.

Points to ponder

- We, no doubt, grow and process our food. However, we should never lose sight of the fact that it is Allah alone Who feeds everyone, including even those who are His rebels.
- For catering to our basic need of food, we should turn humbly to Him and profusely thank Him for feeding us.

Chapter 141

Allah–the Most Affectionate

Notwithstanding His boundless power and grandeur Allah is most affectionate towards us. How reassuring are His assertions: "Your Lord has decreed mercy for Himself." (Al-Anam 6:164) and "Allah selects for His mercy whom He wills. He is full of bounties." (Al-Baqarah 2:105). Apart from providing everything to us, He listens to our prayers to Him and comforts us, saying that He is always near us, closer than our own jugular vein. Another manifestation of His kindness towards us is described in the following verse:

> **Has Allah not given him two eyes, and a tongue and two lips? Did Allah not show him the two highways (of good and evil)?**
>
> **(Al-Balad 90: 8-10)**

We are fortunate to have been blessed with mental and physical faculties and more importantly, Allah's guidance which may help us win His pleasure and our success in the next life.

Allah has blessed us not only with the physical faculties of sight and speech, but also with reason and thinking and discerning ability to distinguish between good and bad, or right and wrong. While we use our mind even in ordinary matters, we should reflect on these more important points: Who are we? Who has created us? What is the purpose of our life? Which way of life should we follow?

Allah has clearly shown the two ways of good and evil. Deep inside, each one of us knows what is good and what is not. It is our duty to utilise the faculties so kindly and generously granted to us by Allah for pursuing the straight way. We should not devote all our time to worldly activities, material loss and gain. Allah asks us to consider seriously the right way of life.

Points to ponder

- Allah has graciously made so much, specifically objects of Nature, subservient to us, underscoring His affection for us.
- Allah keeps overlooking our failings, grants us more and more opportunities and readily accepts our repentance, irrespective or the enormity of our sins.

Chapter 142

Rain As a Metaphor of Our Resurrection

The Islamic doctrine of our resurrection, that is, coming back to life after death, for Allah's judgement in the grand assembly at the end of time appeared intractable for the seventh-century unbelievers. They naively thought that once our body decomposes after death, how it can be brought back to life for Allah's reckoning. Allah cited the easy-to-understand, routine occurrence of rain: it revives dead land and plant life blossoms again in no time. This convinced them of the truth of Resurrection and they embraced Islam in large numbers in time. The same phenomenon is adduced here for our understanding:

> **Allah sends from the heavens blessed rain water. With this He causes gardens and crops to grow, and tall palm trees, with thick clusters. All this as provision for Allah's servants. Allah brings the dead land back to life with rain water. This is how (human beings) will come forth (from the earth on the Day of Judgement).**
>
> **(Qaf 50: 9-11)**

Apart from being an invaluable blessing, rain which revives the dead land should open our eyes to the imminent resurrection, as Allah will bring us back to life after our death to recompense us on the Day of Judgement. The metaphor of rain for explaining the phenomenon of resurrection and the afterlife, which belongs to the domain of the unseen, is very apt. Like the seventh-century Arabs, we too, see how rain revives dead land. By the same token, Allah will raise us after our death and question us about our faith and actions. He will judge accordingly and will send us to paradise or hell.

The all-wise, most compassionate Allah has explained the truth of the afterlife in a simple, easy to understand way. It is up to us to think seriously about our ultimate end and our eternal happiness in paradise or our eternal loss and punishment in hell. Our fate lies in our own hands. Allah's message is loud and clear.

Points to ponder

- It is easy for Allah, our Creator, Who brought us into being out of nothing to revive our dead body, irrespective of the lapse of a very long period of time.
- Our resurrection is essential for our appearance before Allah, with our record of faith and actions and Allah's judgement with reference to the same, followed by our eternal life in the next world.

Chapter 143

Features of Believers in Allah

Allah expects believers to possess certain distinctive features, which He has described, at places in the Quran. Believers should not only profess faith, their pious conduct should make them stand out. Islam represents an amalgam of faith and good actions. It asks believers to engage actively in doing good. This rules out monasticism or renunciation of life for believers. Allah spells out the features of believers and His reward for them in these verses:

> **The believing men and women are friends to one another. They command good and forbid evil. They regularly pray and pay Zakah. They obey Allah and His Messenger. Allah will have mercy on them. Allah is Almighty, the Wisest. Allah has promised the believing men and women the Gardens beneath which rivers flow. They will live in these, in delightful places of living in the eternal gardens. And Allah's pleasure is the greatest blessing. This is a great success.**
>
> **(Al-Tawbah 9: 71-72)**

In Allah's eyes, husband and wife are perfect soulmates. They protect each other from emotional distress, sexual misconduct and other pressures. More importantly, they help each other grow morally, as they exhort to praying and giving in charity. Such a bond pleases Allah. He has promised them excellent rewards in paradise.

Allah expects us to be sincere well-wishers of one another. By exhorting one another to do good we construct a happy, peaceful society marked by warm, cordial relations. We are supposed to not only pray but also fulfill our social obligations. As we note the poor and the needy, we must help them financially by paying them zakah (a religious duty in Islam of paying 2.5% of our wealth to the underprivileged)

Allah has promised us unimaginable joys in paradise as we discharge our duty to Allah (prayers) and human beings (charity and good treatment). The way to paradise is simple and easy.

Points to ponder

- Allah does not appreciate only lip service to faith. It asks believers to forge a strong community and work together towards good, apart from devotion to Him.
- Believers would enjoy Allah's majestic hospitality in paradise in recognition of their attainments.

Chapter 144

Reward for Believers

Since Allah has ordained kindness for Himself and is all-appreciative, He would shower heaps of His choicest rewards on believers. They would be recompensed generously for their adherence to faith in even adverse circumstances and their standing by truth and justice. A high rank in paradise awaits them. Allah appreciates even a minor good action on our part and often lavishes manifold rewards for those who discharge their obligations to Allah and fellow human beings.

> **Whoever does good—man or woman, and is a believer, Allah will give them a good life. He will certainly reward them for their good actions.**
>
> **(Al-Nahl 16: 97)**

Allah maintains total gender parity in His dealings, as He promises reward to both pious men and women alike.

The most affectionate Allah has prescribed an easy, simple way to our salvation and our eternal felicity in paradise. As long as we believe in the one true God and do good, both men and women, are promised immense rewards in the afterlife. Being almighty, Allah will keep His promise and show His mercy and generosity. Allah accords much importance to our good actions, as these contribute to constructing a happy society. Allah wants us to lead life in a cordial, positive ambience.

Points to ponder

- Allah, the best judge would generously reward us if we overcome the allure of this world and temptations to sin.
- Allah has promised both spiritual and physical pleasures for believers in paradise. Islam does not forbid joys of the body as long as they are within wedlock.

Chapter 145

Allah's Directive for Gender Relations

Islam does not admit the notion of the battle of the sexes. Allah has made men and women equal. Both can rise to great spiritual heights and win Allah's pleasure. Apart from prophets, Allah speaks highly of Maryam and Pharaoh's believing wife. He has granted the privilege of motherhood to woman. As women are naturally attractive to men, Allah has prescribed norms for their dress and privacy. This does not rob them of their economic rights. Khadijah (RA, the Arabic phrase is 'razi Allah tala anha' which means "May Allah be pleased with her"), the Prophet Muhammad's wife, was an affluent trader. The following verse instructs women to profess and practise chastity and modesty:

> **O Prophet, tell your wives and daughters and the believing women to draw a part of their outer garments around them. This is so that they be recognized (as such) and be not molested. Allah is Most Forgiving, Most Merciful.**
>
> **(Al-Ahzab 33: 59)**

This underscores the concern for protecting women's dignity. It also serves as the rationale behind the practice of hijab (headscarf) among Muslim women and girls.

Allah established the rights of women in seventh-century Arabia in which, as in other parts of the world, women were abused as a commodity. In pre-Islamic Arabia, stepsons after their father's death gained control over their stepmothers and exploited them. For conferring dignity upon women, Allah prescribed a dress code for them. Allah asks both men and women to cover certain parts of their body, as is the norm in any civilised society. Today, many women opt for hijab by choice. Even this has evoked hostile reactions among those given to Islam-bashing.

As in any walk of life, we should follow Allah's directive for wearing modest clothes.

Points to ponder

- Allah prescribes a dress code for both men and women, though it is more elaborate for the latter.
- Allah asks both men and women to guard their private parts and lower their gaze. (Al-Nur 24:30)

Chapter 146

Allah Forbids Sex outside Marriage

To protect the social fabric and practise self-restraint, Allah has prescribed the code of sexual conduct. In Islam sex is not something sinful or dirty, as misperceived by some. It celebrates healthy, meaningful sexual activity within wedlock. However, it forbids all forms of pre- or extra-marital sexual acts. Sexual permissiveness breeds many problems and evils: broken homes, plight of single parents and children, and disintegration of family life, etc. The following verse brands illicit sex as a ghastly sin:

> **Do not even go near sex outside marriage. It is shameful and an evil path.**
>
> **(Al-Isra 17: 32)**

Allah forbids any sexual act outside marriage. His command ensures peace, purity and order in our social life. Islam encourages marriage and regards sex as a natural, healthy activity. However, it should strictly be between husband and wife.

The Islamic sexual code laid down by the all-wise Allah protects social order against the chaos caused by permissive or unnatural sexual mores. Allah does not forbid sexual activity as it is both natural and essential for perpetuating the human race. However, sexual misconduct strikes at the roots of the social fabric and destroys family, the basic unit of life.

As Allah condemned sexual transgression strongly, we should be doubly careful about any lapse on our part.

Sex outside marriage is sheer lust which must be shunned. Allah has prescribed deterrent punishment against sex outside marriage.

Points to ponder

- Orderly sexual conduct is in the best interest of both individual and society at large and hence Allah's insistence on chastity and integrity.
- We should not indulge in anything obscene or immoral.

Chapter 147

Spouse in Paradise

Amid the delights of paradise, Allah mentions both beautiful women and ever-young youths. Islam does not prescribe celibacy as a virtue. So, along with other excellent rewards to be showered upon believers in paradise, they are also promised sexual pleasure and marital bliss there. Allah does not feel shy of catering to our innate sexual urges. The concept of paradise in Islam has been maliciously misconstrued by some as sensual:

> **This is a message (full of advice and lesson). There is an excellent end for the pious. The gates of the eternal gardens of Paradise will be wide open for them. They will sit there and ask for fruits in plenty and drinks. With them there will be chaste women of the same age.**
>
> **(Saad 38: 49-52)**

Allah promises chaste, beautiful women as companions as a reward for the pious in paradise. Since sexual urge is natural and joyful, Islam does not abhor it as something dirty or taboo. Some misguided persons criticise the Islamic concept of paradise as sensual and take exception to the mention of female companions there. The all-wise Allah has invested us with sexual urges and their satisfaction is a joy for us. Islam, therefore, does not treat sex as dirty or taboo. It only insists on participating in sexual activity only within wedlock. One of the rewards in paradise for pious believers is their companionship with charming females. We may be united there with our beloved spouses.

We should profess and practise true faith and good actions for gaining entry into paradise.

Points to ponder

- Reward and punishment is a basic plank of the Islamic scheme of the hereafter. All that we love to have is promised to us in paradise if we profess and practise faith and good behaviour.
- Garden, food, drink and beautiful spouse of the same age group are cited as some of the delights of paradise.

Chapter 148

The Earth As Allah's Sign

Allah's boundless power and amazing ingenuity are reflected at their sharpest in having provided us with the earth as our perfect habitat. Take landscape as an example: mountains, valley, rivers, lakes, forests, plains, marshes, coasts, and above all, soil which enables us to harvest grains, our staple food. With its flora and fauna and scenic beauty it presents wonderful spectacles, we should express our heartfelt gratitude to our Creator, Allah, for this great blessing. Some features of this blessing appear in the following verse:

> **Allah has created for you the earth like a carpet and made for you paths in it. He sends down water from the heavens and produces with it many different plants which you eat yourselves and give to your cattle. There are signs in it for the people of understanding. Allah created you from this earth and will return you to the same. And He will bring you out from it again.**
>
> **(Ta Ha 20: 53-55)**

We should be grateful to Allah for the earth as our habitat, signposts on the landscape, rain and the resultant vegetation, and grain and fodder for us and our cattle. However, we should remember it all along that we have to return to our Lord for His judgement. The earth with all of its variety, diversity and resources is an amazing spectacle of Allah's creative power. It serves as a suitable habitat for numerous life forms. Moreover, Allah has granted us the ability to draw upon it according to our needs. Since the first human couple, Adam's and Hawwa's advent on earth, it has sufficed our needs. On one hand, Allah draws our attention to its various benefits, which are essential to life. On the other, He reminds us of it as our burial ground. At His command on the Day of Judgement all of us will come out of it before Him for judgement.

We should remain cognizant of these truths and lead life, as dictated to us by our Lord and Creator, Allah.

Points to ponder

- Amazingly enough, the earth, apart from being our habit is also our burial site. It manifests history in an instructive manner as we witness ruins and the present-day sky scrapers side by side on it.
- The above passage speaks of cattle as a stakeholder of the planet earth. It is our duty to maintain ecological balance and protect the rights of other creatures on earth.

Chapter 149

Allah and False Gods

Notwithstanding the fact that Allah and false gods are incomparable in any respect, it is an audacious fact that many people, down the ages, have fallen prey to the latter. Allah asks us to use reason and answer some pertinent questions about their relevance and role. It is common knowledge that these are created from some material object and people themselves. They have nothing striking about themselves. At most, some people make their huge statues which are perishable. They have nothing to their credit: any creative wonder, benefit to devotees or spiritual blessing. Rather, they are wholly dependent on their votaries for their upkeep. The following Quranic passage deals a severe blow to the notion of idols:

> **(Are these false gods better) or Allah Who listens to the cry of those in distress, when they call upon Him? He removes their distress. He made (humankind) the inheritor of the earth. Is there a god associated with Allah? How little do you think! (Are these false gods better) or He Who guides you through darkness on land and sea, sends winds as bearers of good news, ahead of His mercy (rain)? Is there a god associated with Allah? He is above what they take as partners with Him. (Are these false gods better) or He Who created everyone in the first place and will create them again? He gives you sustenance from the heavens and the earth. Is there a god associated with**

Allah? (O Prophet) say: "Produce your evidence, if you are in the right."

(Al-Naml 27: 62-64)

Of the many favours of Allah listed in this passage, it is most comforting to note that He responds to our pleas and removes our misery. His absolute power is contrasted with the utter helplessness of false gods whom people foolishly associate with Him. It is common knowledge that we make idols with our own hands and these are incapable of doing anything. The above cogent account presses home the oneness of Allah, the Creator and the only lord and urges us to shun all forms of idolatry and polytheism on logical grounds.

Points to ponder

- Allah asks us to assess idols: what makes them eligible for worship – power, knowledge, mercy or any attribute at all?
- We should consider seriously the issue of godhead, and not be swayed by our ancestral ways or conformity.

Chapter 150

Ships As Allah's Gift to Us

Life is unthinkable without mobility and transport. We have been able to reach the present heights of progress on account of our ability to move and transport goods. Centuries before the aircraft industry brought about a dramatic advancement in travel, boats and ships were the means of transport. Up to this day ships meet our cargo movement needs—something crucial to our economy—particularly import and export of goods. We should thank and glorify Allah for enabling us to sail ships. The physical and mental faculties granted kindly by Him account for our control over the sea:

> **And Allah has created for them ships on which they ride. Had God willed so, He could drown them. Then they will not have any helper. Nor will they be saved. It is only Allah's mercy (that helps them survive). It enables them to enjoy life for a while.**
>
> **(Ya Sin 36: 42-44)**

Our ability to sail smoothly on ships is owing to Allah's mercy. However, we should not belost wholly in the joys of life. Transport is one of our basic needs. The most merciful Allah has equipped us with the mental and physical abilities to discover and invent things which improve the quality of our life. Shipping has been of tremendous value and help for us. While making most of this, we should bear in mind that on our own we could not sail on water. Our most affectionate lord has enabled us to achieve stupendous strides in transport and telecommunications. We should therefore turn to Him in all humility and gratitude, and while abiding by His directives we should seek His pleasure for our success in the hereafter.

Points to ponder

- The Quran recounts how Allah had instructed His messenger, Prophet Nuh (peace be upon him) in 3000 BC to build an ark for escaping floods.
- Notwithstanding our inventions, discoveries and technological feats, never forget that we have been able to accomplish these only owing to the abilities granted to us by Allah.

Chapter 151

Allah's Dispensation

Allah has created us all and given us a complete road map to show us how to lead our life. He has granted us freedom to act how we like. However, the mental faculty and conscience bestowed by Him constantly urge us to do good. Notwithstanding His mercy, Allah being the Lord would dispense justice perfectly on the Day of Judgement. Fairness demands that the persevering believers who suffered in this life in the cause of truth be suitably rewarded and the wicked who unleashed wrongdoings be punished. Allah's justice is highlighted in this verse:

> **Will Allah treat alike—those who believe and do good and those who spread corruption on earth? Will Allah treat them as equal—the pious and the wicked?"**
>
> **(Saad 38: 28)**

Perfect justice is another dominant trait of Allah. This is most satisfying for those of us who have faith and do good. Our Lord has put in place laws of nature which are applicable to all, believers and unbelievers alike. He does not intervene directly and instantly for rewarding the pious and punishing the culprits in this world. Even His messengers were mocked, wounded, persecuted and killed. We should therefore not be disheartened by the momentary prosperity or affluence of the wicked and disbelievers, and the plight of the righteous. All this is part of our test and trial by Allah. In the hereafter, however, Allah's perfect justice and power will prevail, as the evil ones would be consigned to horrible punishment and the virtuous believers would be blessed with the choicest reward and all that they wish. We should therefore not be confused over the state of affairs in the world.

Points to ponder

- The next life is essential for meeting justice, as the pious and the mischievous ones often go without any recompense in this world.
- Allah is not indifferent to our beliefs and actions. He keeps an error-free record of our conduct and would accordingly reward and punish us in the next life.

Chapter 152

Allah Does Not Overburden Us

Being our Creator, Allah knows our conditions best. Moreover, since He is most compassionate and most beneficent, He does not tax us beyond our capacity. We all have to face some tests and trials, ranging from financial to health and emotional issues. However, it is He Who grants us strength to bear these. Moreover, He would compensate us generously, if we rise to the occasion and resign to His will despite our best efforts to overcome the crises afflicting us:

> **Allah does not burden anyone beyond what He has given them. Allah will grant relief after hardship.**
>
> **(Al-Talaq 65: 7)**

Out of His boundless mercy Allah does not tax anyone beyond their capacity. In all Islamic religious commands, allowance is made for the sick, expecting and feeding mothers, and the old. Moreover, Allah blesses us after hardship which is part of our trial. While Allah's guidance, that is, the Quran and the Prophet Muhammad's teachings, are available to everyone, people vary in their mental, spiritual and other abilities. They have constraints of their circumstances too. The most merciful, all-aware Allah would take all factors into account while questioning us for our response to His call and our conduct. Since He is the best of judges and most compassionate, He may condone some of our lapses. However, we should try to keep our record straight and adhere to His message as much as possible. We should be grateful to Him for His promise of granting us ease after hardship.

Points to ponder

- In some Quranic verses Allah comforts us, assuring that hardship would be followed by ease.
- Reposing trust in the all-knowing, all-powerful Allah Who has always been so affectionate to us helps us resolve even a mountain of problems overwhelming us.

Chapter 153

Allah Has Decreed Our Lifespan

We have no clue how long we will live, though this information is of utmost importance to us. It belongs to the domain of *Al-Ghayb* (what lies outside the ken of our sense perception), known only to Allah. Out of His boundless wisdom He has decreed a certain lifespan for us, though we are totally at a loss to fathom its rationale. What is important is that we should make most of the opportunity granted to us and thus brighten our prospects in the next life which is eternal. Our faith and conduct in this life would determine our status in the next world.

> **Allah created you and then causes you to die. Some of you have your lives up to a weak old age. One then loses all knowledge after having had it. Allah is All Knowing, All Powerful.**
>
> **(Al-Nahl 16: 70)**

That we get old and frail with every passing day is common knowledge. Yet we usually disregard this manifest truth, forget about our impending death and make no preparation for the next life in which our fate will be decided on the basis of only our faith and good actions. For our lesson, the most wise, all-powerful Allah has placed the unmissable signs of decline and death around us. We are too helpless against this law of nature which overwhelms everyone, the rich and the poor and believers and unbelievers alike. We have no control over our lifespan or ageing. This is a wake-up call for all of us: to be ready for the unavoidable death, and the afterlife when we will appear before our Creator for answering regarding what we believed, what kind of life we led, our actions and the preparations we made for our success in the hereafter.

It is high time to mend our ways. In view of the all-pervading phenomenon of decay and death we should follow the right course of action, consisting true faith and good actions.

Points to ponder

- The secrecy about our date of death is a blessing in disguise. Had we known it, we would have suffered from acute depression and would have a death-in-life existence much before death overtook us.
- It is a great pity that even in the face of possessing such little knowledge about ourselves, we act arrogantly.

Chapter 154

Allah's Law of Success

In the following pithy verse, revealed some 1,500 years ago, Allah showed people a profound truth about attaining success. Our resolute will to change our condition is the key. Allah has blessed us with immense potentials and capacity. Our willpower to sort out problems, plan a better, happy future and devotion to the goals set by us guarantee our success. This holds true for individuals as well as communities:

> **Allah does not change the condition of people unless they change themselves.**
>
> (Al-Rad 13: 11)

Islam does not stand for fatalism. Allah facilitates the guidance and success of only those who are keen on self-development. Being the lord of everyone, irrespective of their belief and action, Allah is absolutely fair in providing equal opportunities to everyone, for example, the human body with marvellous physical and mental faculties, time, lifespan, natural resources, etc. Individuals and communities are subject to an identical law of nature: hard work and merit take them to great heights. Even if one decides to do evil and commit crimes, Allah does not interrupt them in the toils of their work. Being most forbearing, He lets each one of us pursue our preferred course of action.

We owe our debt of gratitude to Allah for being so objective and fair in His dealings with us, irrespective of our faith or any other label (ethnicity, colour, language, region, etc.). For our success in the afterlife too, He has laid down a simple yet comprehensive code of conduct for us. It is in our own interest to facilitate our success in the next life.

Points to ponder

- Generally speaking, Allah does not regularly intervene in our affairs. He has put in place laws of nature which work according to a certain pattern. Our sincere and meaningful alignment with these would bring about our success.
- Prophet Muhammad's life illustrates best how he induced transformation into the outlook and lives of early Muslims: as a result, they were the torch-bearers for centuries of learning innovation and skills (for documentation, see George Sarton's *Introduction to the History of Science*).

Chapter 155

Allah Would Cause Us to Die at the Appointed Hour

In His wisdom, Allah has preordained our lifespan, though we have no inkling. As part of His grand design, He has created us and provided us with an opportunity to purse the course of action which we choose. He does not compel us into doing anything. However, since He is all-powerful, all-resourceful, He facilitates what we opt for – good as well as evil. Eventually He would hold us to account for what we do or fail to do which we ought to have accomplished. The following verse declares this truth:

> **Were Allah to take people to task for their actions, He would not leave on earth a single living being. However, He grants them a chance until the appointed term. When their term expires, God will deal with His servants.**
>
> **(Fatir 35: 45)**

How forbearing and clement Allah is! He keeps on granting us chances upon chances for mending our ways. He does not instantly punish us for committing sins. Otherwise, we would have been annihilated a long time ago. As part of His meticulous and highly imaginative plan Allah grants us plenty of opportunities and abilities, and above all, free will to let us do what we wish. He does not stop any of us in the middle of our path, no matter how sinful it might be. He has provided us with His well-preserved guidance and warned us eloquently against the consequences of our violation of His directives.

Let us take stock of our conduct. We should not be misled by any of His punishment befalling us even in the face of our intransigence. As our respite will be over soon, we will have to face music.

Points to ponder

- We should not feel complacent about life and its numerous opportunities. All doors are, no doubt, wide open. However, our life is bound to end with death, followed by Allah's recompense.
- Allah has granted us a brief, limited respite. We should realise the true value of the gift of life. More importantly, we should constantly bear in mind that we would be eventually held answerable to Allah for our beliefs and actions.

Chapter 156

Allah's Self-Definition

Several passages in the Quran define and describe Allah. Since He is the all-in-all in the entire universe and we are entirely dependent on Him—from our life to provisions, fate, death and His final judgement—it is imperative for us to gain some idea about His being, attributes, will, and likes and dislikes. In Islam, Allah is not some quasi-philosophical, mysterious entity who is too intractable. The following Quranic passage cites Allah's self-definition:

> **All those in the heavens and on earth glorify Allah. He is Almighty, the Wisest. His is the kingdom of the heavens and the earth. He grants life and death. He has power over everything. He is the first and the last. He is the open and the hidden. He knows everything. He created the heavens and the earth in six days. He established Himself on the throne. He knows what enters and what comes out of the earth. Likewise He knows what comes down from and what goes up to the heavens. He is with you (O people) wherever you are. He is aware of all of your actions. His is the kingdom of the heavens and the earth. All matters are referred to Him (for decision). He merges night with day, and day with night. He knows even the secrets of all hearts.**
>
> **(Al-Hadid 57: 1-6)**

This is an awe-inspiring description of Allah's power, knowledge, and creative wonders. We should ensure our sound faith and good actions for winning His pleasure. The one true God, Allah, governs single handedly all aspects of our life, from creation to our death and our recompense on the Day of Judgement. His attributes, especially of power, knowledge, creativity and mercy are unique and absolute, having no peer even in the slightest. His will reigns supreme in the universe. Amazingly He watches each and every thing, including our actions and secrets of our hearts. No one has any say in His endless kingdom.

The Islamic concept of Allah stands out for its clarity and depth of coverage. We must surrender to such an almighty lord.

Points to ponder

- In Islam the concept of Allah is transparently clear. We can fathom some of His supreme attributes on reading the relevant passages in the Quran and Prophet Muhammad's elucidation.
- Although for the sake of comprehensible communication, some anthropomorphic images of Allah are used, it must be clarified at once that He transcends this description. He is too elevated to possess gender, body or form. Light upon light, in a very special sense, may be taken as an appropriate metaphor to describe Him.

Chapter 157

Allah's Plan Cannot Be Frustrated

In the whole universe Allah's word in final. He is too powerful to be thwarted by anyone. Since He is the Creator and master, they are at His beck and call. Objects of Nature, no matter how massive they might appear, unbelievers and inanimate entities obey Him as they are tied by the laws to which He has bound them. Who on earth can escape decay and death? Who can cross natural limitations placed on everything? The following verse asserts Allah's absolute power:

> **You cannot defeat (Allah's plan) on earth. You do not have any protector or supporter besides Allah.**
>
> **(Al-Shura 42: 31)**

Almighty Allah cannot be resisted by anyone, no matter how wealthy or powerful they might be. Illness and death overtaking us all is a telling evidence of our helplessness and mortality. So is our old age and the accompanying weakness and dementia. We should take refuge only with Allah. Allah throws an open challenge: No one can resist Him. We know well that death overtakes us, no matter how rich, powerful and famous we might be. It is Allah's will that prevails in the universe. On the last day, which has been approaching fast, He will bring to an end the present order. The catastrophe caused by His will, will kill and destroy everyone and everything. At an earlier stage He sniffed out many powerful communities that dominated the world. The laws of nature, our essential nature, properties of matter, decline and death, the last day and the Day of Judgement are the realities which none of us can disregard.

We should constantly seek Allah's mercy and forgiveness for our success in the afterlife.

Points to ponder

- As Allah is matchless, no one can take Him on. It goes without saying that creatures cannot overtake the Creator.
- Allah accomplishes whatever He wills. He does not have to think of consequences of His actions in that He is not answerable to anyone. It is an altogether different point that His actions being perfect do not betray any recklessness or wantonness.

Chapter 158

Death As Part of Allah's Scheme

Naturally, we all resent death. When we miss our near and dear ones, we tend to be more acutely critical of death. Some persons hastily and unthinkingly brand it as injustice and callousness on Allah's part. On little reflection, however, we realise death is not only natural, it is imperative as well. Take inheritance as a case in point. How can our own children get what is their due unless we die? More importantly, how can culprits who manage their non-apprehension, be punished for their serious crimes against humanity? How can the suffering pious be compensated for the wrongs inflicted upon them? How can we advance, if we do not make way for the young, energetic and enterprising ones?

> **Allah has decided death for all of you. (His plan) cannot be defeated. He may replace you with others like you. Or He may create you in (forms) that you do not know. You know well how you were created for the first time. Why then do you not take a lesson?**
>
> **(Al-Waqiah 56: 60-62)**

Apart from pronouncing the stark truth about death which is bound to overtake all of us, we are asked to ponder over the following points: we were created out of nothing; we will be created afresh for the Day of Judgement. We should take a lesson about Allah's absolute power and our helplessness. Death is an undeniable reality. We die at the time ordained for us by Allah, about which we have no clue. We are too helpless before Allah's absolute power. He might do whatever pleases Him, including the annihilation of the human race as a whole or the change of our form. We know that we were created out of nothing. We are in this world for a brief period of time, followed by our death and our appearance before Almighty Allah.

We should devote ourselves to brightening our prospects in the afterlife by obeying and glorifying Allah.

Points to ponder

- Allah has preordained our lifespan. Death cannot be advanced or delayed by anyone. We die at our appointed hour, irrespective of the best medical care.
- The idea of our ultimate death should always be at the back of our mind. It helps keep following the straight way and deters us from unbelief and evil actions.

Chapter 159

Allah Is Ever True to His Promise

Being most glorious and all-powerful Allah is always true to His promise. He has assured such delights which are even inconceivable to believers with good conduct and horrible punishment to those who deliberately reject His message. His promises and warnings will come true on the Day of Judgement, as He summons everyone. He would deal with everyone justly, with reference to their track record, particularly their faith and actions:

> **O people, Allah's promise is certainly true. Let the life of this world not deceive you. Let the great deceiver (Satan) not deceive you about Allah.**
>
> **(Fatir 35: 5)**

Allah's promises about our resurrection, reward and punishment and eternal life in the hereafter are bound to come true. Those engrossed in worldly activities, however, ignore these truths. They will pay dearly for their negligence. Lost in our hectic life schedule—workplace, family engagements and social commitments—we have little time to ponder on our Lord, His plan, His promise about our imminent death, our coming back to life on the Day of Judgement and our appearance before Allah Who will settle our account. Satan is exceptionally good at making us forgetful about these higher realities. Allah has sent down the Quran and the Prophet Muhammad (peace be upon him) as reminders to awaken us out of our slumber of worldliness and materialism.

We should be constantly on our guard against Satan's guile that keeps us away from Allah-awareness and the straight way. This would protect us against disaster in the afterlife.

Points to ponder

- Being faithful to His word is a natural corollary of being the Supreme Lord. It would be a contradiction in terms if the Almighty does not keep His word.
- Allah has promised His mercy for everyone. Everything that exists and flourishes in the universe is owing to His mercy, as He sustains everyone on such a massive scale.

Chapter 160

Winning Allah's Pleasure

Out of His overflowing affection and kindness for us, Allah has at length, described what pleases and displeases Him. Many Quranic passages detail this important truth, which is further explained by Prophet Muhammad (peace be upon him) in his advice to early Muslims who had been very keen on earning Allah's pleasure. This guarantees our success in both the worlds: a sense of purpose and meaning in this life and eternal joys in the next. The passage below recounts Allah's glory and identifies those who are destined to win His pleasure:

> **By the sun and its brightness, and the moon which follows it (the sun)! By the day which shows the brightness of the sun, and the night which hides (the sun light)! By the sky and by Allah Who built it! By the earth and by Allah Who spread it! By the soul and by Allah Who gave it proportion! Allah gave it (the sense) to know what is right and what is wrong. He who purifies his soul will be successful. But he who corrupts it will fail.**
>
> **(Al-Shams 91: 1-10)**

Among Allah's wondrous creations, listed above, the most important one for us is the moral faculty granted to us, which enables us to differentiate between good and evil. It is of immense help to us in both the worlds.

The opening part of the above quoted passage draws attention to some of the self-evident manifestations of

Allah's unique and immense power—the sun, moon and their movement in their respective orbits without any collision; the constant change of day and night, and brightness and darkness; the expansive earth as the habitat for billions of living beings, and the perfect proportion in all objects of Nature. More importantly, Allah has invested us with conscience, a strong, innate moral sense which instinctively tells us what is right and wrong. We should act on it in shunning polytheism and evil acts. Moreover, we should imbibe constancy, obedience and being beneficial from Nature.

To attain true faith and self-development, natural signs and conscience suffice for us.

Points to ponder

- Allah is not inaccessible. Nor is He, notwithstanding His transcendence, detached from us.
- In Islam there is no clergy. Without the role of clergy, we can directly invoke Allah and get rewarded by Him in this world or the next.

Chapter 161

Allah's Numerous Bounties

It is simply beyond our reckoning to count Allah's bounties which are both numerous and varied. Take a garden as an example. The range of trees, and their shapes, sizes, branches, leaves, fruits, flowers, textures, colours and fragrances are fascinatingly diverse. Then there are plants, birds, insects, landscape and skyscape that are of various hues and colours. The same holds true for every aspect of the universe, from the cosmos to our body. Not only are these bounties splendid and original, these are immensely beneficial to us as well. The following verse urges us to reflect on this truth:

> **Allah has spread out the earth for all beings. In it are fruits and palm trees with dates. In it are different types of corn, with husk and grain. Then which of the favours of your Lord will you (human beings and Jinn) deny?**
>
> **(Al-Rahman 55: 10-13)**

There is a mind-boggling catalogue of Allah's bounties which He has so graciously placed at our disposal. These divine favours are available in an equal measure to believers and disbelievers alike. This underscores Allah's perfect justice, grace and forbearance. He keeps on sustaining generously even die-hard atheists and polytheists. As we consider the amazing ability of soil to produce such a wide variety of plants, fruits, flowers, herbs, vines, trees, and most importantly, grain, we realise Allah's power and mercy unto us. Without this perfect arrangement in place for our sustenance, we could not survive.

Allah's favours to us are countless, particularly the natural resources provided by Him. With the help of Allah's gifts to us, our mental and physical faculties, we should make the most of His favours for leading a life marked by justice, fairness and fellow feeling which will bring us happiness.

In the face of numerous wondrous favours of Allah, on which we depend for our life, we cannot and should not deny the existence and glory of the one true God.

Points to ponder

- Creation with its stupendous variety should bring to our mind the power and glory of its amazing Creator. The spectacles around us persuade us all the more about the existence and oneness of the Creator and Lord, Allah.
- We draw constantly on Allah's bounties. This calls for our devotion and thanksgiving to Allah by way of worship and obedience to Him.

Chapter 162

Mates As Allah's Blessing to Us

Amid Allah's countless blessings, the husband-wife relationship deserves a special mention. First, He has created both of them from the same species. It facilitates a better bond. Had either one been from any other species, we could not fully enjoy marital bliss. Moreover, apart from satisfying our strong, natural sexual urges, they are excellent soulmates, standing by us all the time, particularly in old age, when children have left the nest. The following verse makes a pointed reference to this special blessing bestowed upon us by our loving and caring Lord:

> **It is one of Allah's signs that He created for you mates from your own kind so that you may find comfort in them. He has put love and mercy between you (man and wife). In this are signs for those who reflect.**
>
> **(Al-Rum 30: 21)**

Love between husband and wife has been infused by Allah out of His kindness. This makes our family life a source of comfort and joy. We should be grateful to Allah for helping us overcome the false notion of the "battle of sexes." The Prophet Muhammad (peace be upon him) loved his wives very much and they were devoted in equal measure to him. The Prophet Muhammad (peace be upon him) stands out as a role model for Muslims.

The conjugal relationship is very intimate. As life partners we spend a major part of our life in close, rather inseparable company of our spouse. Apart from meeting biological needs, spouses turn out to be soulmates, standing by each other in health and sickness, and in raising family. Such a close bond between two strangers, belonging to two different genders—male and female, with divergent personalities, is a gift from Allah, our most compassionate and caring Creator. He has placed such love and tender feelings in the couple that they sacrifice all that they have for each other.

We should thank Allah from the depths of our heart for forging such a wonderful arrangement for our mutual help, comfort and satisfaction.

Points to ponder

- Allah employs the metaphor of a garment for spouses: "They (wives) are your garments and you theirs" (Al-Baqarah 2:187). This connotes mutual protection, intimacy, beauty, comfort and adornment.
- As Allah has instilled mutual love and affection between a married couple, it contributes significantly to making a happy family and children grow up in a positive, healthy ambience.

Chapter 163

Allah's Creative Wonders

As we look around, we are struck by Allah's creative wonders, from gigantic galaxies to nano particles. These are splendid in both quality and quantity. All of human accomplishments are, at best mimetic whereas all of His creation is original and free from repetition. Take for example, any two human beings. Notwithstanding their belonging to the same species, they are markedly different, rather unique in numerous respects. On noting His creative genius, we can only praise His glory:

> **Allah has created the heavens, without a pillar. You can see this. And He has placed mountains on earth so that it may not shake with you. He has spread on earth all kinds of animals. And He sends water from the sky and lets all kinds of wonderful plants grow on it. This is Allah's creation. Now show me what is created by those (i.e. false gods) besides Him? The wrongdoers are clearly in error.**
>
> **(Luqman 31: 10-11)**

Another impressive catalogue exhibiting Allah's creative wonders: the endless sky as a canopy without any supporting pillar, huge mountains maintaining geo-equilibrium, a dazzling variety of animals spread across the world, and rain facilitating produce of all types. No one other than Allah has any share in creation. This also underscores Allah's power, ingenuity and inexhaustible treasures. He has been sustaining, governing and maintaining our vast universe since time immemorial. In comparison, we cannot think of anyone with such accomplishments to his credit. We know well how worthless idols are. Likewise, atheists have no answer to the perfect, consistent functioning of the universe and numerous creative wonders around us without a creator.

Let us devote ourselves fully to serving and glorifying almighty Allah. He does not need our worship. It is in our interest to adhere to the way of life laid down by Him.

Points to ponder

- Allah is unique as the Creator. He has brought into being everything out of nothing, and without a pre-existing model.
- His creative wonders are not exquisite and exotic, these are of tremendous benefit to us. Rather, there is no life without these—the sun, air, rainwater and planet earth.

Chapter 164

Appreciation of Allah's Glory

That Allah is most glorious is readily observable. His bounties help us survive and flourish. No one can be blind to His ingenuity and power. One need not be a scientist or even a literate person to perceive His glory. The Quran was initially addressed to the seventh-century illiterate Arabs. It drew their attention to the self-evident signs in Nature. For example, Allah asks them to reflect on the creation of the following with which they are familiar—camel, sky, mountain and earth (Al-Ghashiyya 88:17-20). Another Quranic passage asking us to reflect on creation is as follows:

> **Do they not reflect over themselves? Allah has created the heavens and the earth and all that is between these with a purpose and for an appointed term. Yet most of the people deny their meeting with their Lord. Do they not travel through the earth? (If they do), they will observe the end of those before them. They were even stronger and had tilled and populated the land more than they have. Messengers had been sent to them with clear signs. It was not Allah Who wronged them. Rather, they wronged themselves.**
>
> **(Al-Rum 30: 8-9)**

We are asked to reflect on these serious issues: ruins of earlier mighty communities who perished, the purpose of life, our brief lifespan and messengers' clear guidance. It is a great pity that we disregard altogether Allah's numerous signs pointing to His oneness, His power, and His grand plan of life, death and the afterlife. We are so preoccupied with our material pursuits and petty matters that we lose sight of the most serious and evident reality – death, followed by our accountability to Allah and the consequent reward and punishment for ever in the eternal life-to-come.

We do not learn any lesson from the tragic, catastrophic end of mighty empires and civilisations. We would end up as utter losers like them if we do not recognise the ultimate truth about Allah, our obedience to Him and our fate in the hereafter. Let us act soon before it is too late.

Points to ponder

- For embracing and strengthening faith there are multitudes of signs around us. We need the right frame of mind and willingness to accept truth.
- Faith infuses into us the sense of a purpose of life and seriousness. This is essential for developing individual, family and community life.

Chapter 165

The Day of Judgement Is Inevitable

We tend to get so engrossed in our material pursuits, particularly family and money matters that we disregard the fast-approaching reality of our death, to be followed by the Day of Judgement. Allah would interrogate us, particularly how we spent our time, money and energy. If we do not prepare ourselves adequately for this unavoidable reality, we will regret it forever. Our poor record of faith and actions would land us into hellfire to roast forever. What an agonizing thought! Often does Allah pose these questions, as in this verse:

> **By the wind that scatters dust, by the clouds full of rain water, by the ships that move with ease! By the angels who distribute things according to Allah's command. What you are promised (i.e. the Day of Judgement) is true. The Judgement will certainly happen.**
>
> **(Al-Dhariyat 51: 1-6)**

Another bewildering catalogue of a wide range of Allah's stupendous creations, notably winds, clouds, and angels, which point to the ultimate truth: Allah's omnipotence and the approaching Day of Judgement. The afterlife is as certain and natural as winds raising dust and clouds bringing rain. Those who do not use reason or are lost in shallow trivia do not recognise the inevitability of the Day of Judgement. Every action, good or bad, has its consequences. In this brief life with a limited time span and no error-free follow-up mechanism, the consequences of our actions are not rewarded or punished in full. For example, if a serial killer or those responsible for war crimes or for causing holocaust may get the death sentence only once. Likewise, a martyr dies before he is rewarded for his heroic action. Moreover, the justice system in this world can be easily manipulated by the rich and the powerful. They may go scot free.

Common sense demands that the Day of Judgment with the all-powerful and the best judge, Allah in the chair for recompensing us in full for our good and bad actions.

Points to ponder

- As long as we are alive, we have a chance to mend our ways. Once we die, we would be absolutely helpless. Allah gives us this wake-up call.
- As we store provisions for a rainy day, faith and good actions would guarantee our eternal felicity in the next world. It is high time to think about this inevitable eventuality which would affect each one of us.

Chapter 166

The Successful in Allah's Eyes

For our guidance, Allah has foretold who would attain success in the hereafter and be admitted to paradise. Surah Al-Mumunin (23) opens with the declaration: "The believers have achieved success" in Allah's eyes. This gives us an excellent opportunity to take stock of our worldview and ways of life and carry out a reality check to see if we are on the way prescribed by Allah. It has two main component:

i. Sound faith, free of all accretion, and

ii. Noble actions which satisfy us.

> **Allah will accept your actions and forgive your sins. He who obeys God and His Messenger attains the highest achievement.**
>
> **(Al-Ahzab 33: 71)**

Allah is gracious enough to appreciate our good actions and reward us. It is He Who has granted us all wealth. However, when we give a part of it in charity, He is pleased. Likewise, when we repent, He forgives us magnanimously. He has promised us the highest reward imaginable. He is not vindictive, sadist or tyrannical in gloating over our pain and suffering.

Foolishly we have set false, empty standards of achievements: wealth, political power and social standing. We know how temporary and unreal they are. A celebrity of today is without a trace tomorrow. Those in power may be ousted in no time. Our conduct and faith, however, have a lasting impact. These benefit those around us in a real sense. More importantly, these carry weight in the eyes of our Lord. As He summons us on the Day of Judgment, He will rate only our true faith and good actions highly. This in turn, would decide our eternal fate of reward or punishment in the hereafter.

As Allah reckons only true faith and good action, we should first seek His forgiveness for our past lapses and henceforth engage in winning Allah's pleasure which alone matters.

Points to ponder

- Be grateful to Allah for providing an extensive road map, embracing all gamuts of life, from our belief system to social, political, moral and economic order.
- Since Islam and Prophet Muhammad (peace be upon him) represent Allah's final guidance valid until the last day, Allah has ensured the preservation and dissemination of His final message across the world. In the last 1,500 years, since its first appearance, Islam has now reached every part of the world in all languages and the internet.

Chapter 167

Allah Is the Everlasting

Being the Supreme Lord of the universe, Allah is eternal. He has been there, without a beginning or end. To a naïve person this proposition may sound somewhat strange. However, logically speaking, if we do not take Him as the everlasting one, it gives rise to many questions about His omnipotence and uniqueness. Without being eternal, He would appear as a flawed entity which is inconsistent with the concept of the supreme lord. As a matter of fact, we have to accept this important requisite of the lord:

> **What is with you will end. But what is with Allah will last forever. Allah will certainly reward those who are patient and do good.**
>
> **(Al-Nahl 16: 96)**

Allah's treasure is inexhaustible. His ample rewards to us will not diminish His resources. We see only an infinitesimal part of His treasure around us as natural resources in the universe. We are told the worth of this worldly life clearly in the above lines. Its duration and glitter are only for now. Many of us experience the loss of what we thought to be something precious during our life. For instance, take old age. We take great pride in our sound body, mental prowess, ability to earn huge sums of money, a wide circle of friends, and even admirers. And we note a marked decline in all of these as we grow old. We watch helplessly as all sorts of losses are inflicted upon us.

We should always remember that worldly joys are short-lived. The ultimate truth is our faith, coupled with noble actions and our devotion to Allah. This alone would bestow on us eternal happiness in the everlasting afterlife.

Points to ponder

- Allah denotes perfection and uniqueness. His eternality should not pose any difficulty for us as believers.
- In the Quran, Allah is described as someone whom fatigue, sleep or any shortcoming does not touch. As the everlasting one, He has been perfectly managing all the affairs of the universe and would deliver His Judgement on the Day of Retribution at the end of time.

Chapter 168

Allah's Wrath

Notwithstanding His immeasurable kindness and mercy, Allah is also the Lord of Retribution. As He has put all of us to tests and trials, He is bound to act as the judge and recompense us what we deserve. Being the best judge, He enforces retribution and His justice system is marked by utmost fairness and transparency. Retribution is one of His essential attributes which is integral to His lordship:

> **Do not cross the limits. Otherwise, My wrath will be upon you. He who incurs My wrath upon him is destroyed.**
>
> **(Ta Ha 20: 81)**

Notwithstanding His overflowing kindness and forbearance, Allah punishes vehemently those who defy Him. His wrath stems from justice which demands that the guilty be punished. Allah's ways are not whimsical or arbitrary. Unlike us he does not act on the spur of moment, subject to any fit of anger or temperamental issues. The most forbearing, the all-wise and perfect Allah has clearly stated what pleases and angers Him. Hundreds of passages in the Quran and the Prophet Muhammad's Hadith (the well-documented record of his sayings) instruct us eloquently that true faith and good actions are dear to Allah and that He does not put up with polytheism and evil. So everything appears in black and white, without any grey area.

Allah has laid down the limits regarding our behavior (popularly known as shariah). If we make it our priority to promote and strengthen our sincerity to Allah, success awaits us in the next life.

Points to ponder

- As Allah has clearly explained what He likes most and what incurs His wrath, His attribute of retribution should not come as a surprise.
- Allah's wrath is not whimsical or temperamental. His book, the Quran and His final messenger, Prophet Muhammad's statements spell out our actions which evoke His anger and punishment: polytheism, social, sexual, economic, and moral misconduct, injustice, exploitation of the weak, corruption, and all that weakens the socio-moral fabric are detested by Him.

Chapter 169

Our Ultimate Return to Allah

Throughout His book of guidance, the Quran, Allah presses home the truth: this life is ephemeral and all of us have to return eventually to our Creator and Lord. He has granted us opportunities to pay heed to His message. Regrettably, we are so lost in the din and glitter of materialism and worldliness that we neglect the crucial truth: our ultimate return to our Lord Who would judge the record of our actions and faith and award us paradise or hell as our abode, as stressed in the following verse:

> **(O Prophet), tell them: "The angel of death seizes your soul. He is assigned for you. Then you will be returned to your Lord."**
>
> **(Al-Sajdah 32: 11)**

Allah has ordained death for all of us, including His beloved, chosen servants known as prophets. Allah alone is immortal. He will judge us all. Our attention is drawn to death, a grim reality which each one of us has to face sooner or later. We are absolutely helpless with regard to death despite our best possible medication and preventive measures.

Believers do not fear death. Allah has assured them that it is only a stage, leading to the afterlife. They will enjoy perfect bliss there if they profess and practise true faith and good action.

So believers are ever ready to greet death and look forward to their Lord's mercy which will bring to them eternal happiness in the next life.

Points to ponder

- The afterlife is inseparable from the present life. Generally speaking, we disregard this connection and focus only on material objects of the world, particularly money, power and higher standard of life.
- Our belief in the hereafter and our constant oversight and judgement by Allah helps us follow steadily the straight way, which, in turn, makes our life in this world happy and peaceful.

Chapter 170

Allah's Self-Description

As Allah is too transcendent and absolutely invisible to us, He has done us a big favour in having described His self to us in the Quran: Who is He, His approval and disapproval of certain things, His criteria for judgement and His scheme of things, including the purpose of our life. His guidance had not reached the pre-Islamic seventh-century Arabia and the rest of the world in its pristine purity for centuries. Its extensive exposition in the Quran helped many form a better idea of their Creator, His attributes and His plan for human beings. His oneness is the main plank of His self-definition, as it comes out from the following verse:

> **Say: "Allah is One. Allah is the Ever-Living, the Unique. He does not give birth. He was not born. There is no one (at all) like Him"**
>
> **(Al-Ikhlas 112: 1-4)**

It summarises the essence of Allah's attributes: His oneness and uniqueness. There is nothing like Him. This passage strikes at the root of anthropomorphism: Allah is not some created being, having parents, spouse or child. He is far above human attributes. Equally forthright is the repudiation of any notion of His partner or equal. He is absolutely unique and hence the lord Who commands worship and obedience by all creatures. In His nature, person and features, no one is like Him. Being eternal, without any beginning or end is special to Allah. That He does not have parents, spouse or child, once again, underscores the truth that He is unique, and independent of all else. In every respect, His being and attributes, and accomplishments, no one is even remotely similar to Him. Being all-powerful and unique, He alone deserves to be worshipped and glorified.

In view of His excellence, Islam is strictly monotheistic and Muslims lead a consistently Allah-centric life. For them Allah is all in all. They rule out any partner or associate with Him. Prophets, angels, jinn (an invisible creature) saints and all creatures are at His beck and call, having no power whatsoever.

Points to ponder

- Allah has not left his description to the speculation of theologians. Several Quranic passages identify His names, attributes, and relationship with us.
- Since there can logically be only one master, king and lord of the universe, Allah makes it abundantly clear that He alone is the one true God, Who deserves to be worshipped and obeyed.

Chapter 171

Allah's Attributes

In Islam the concept of Allah is not a mystery. Obviously, His book, the Quran provides no physical or corporal details as He transcends any form, shape or physical dimension. Yet His names, attributes, like and dislikes and His plan for us, which concern us directly, are related at length in both the Quran and *Hadith* (Prophet Muhammad's sayings). Although Islam forbids anthropomorphism, for the ease of communication His eyes, hands and face, etc. are mentioned figuratively in the Quran. We have, however, no clue about their exact form. The following verse vividly depicts some of His prominent attributes:

> **Allah is the Ever Living, the Self-Subsisting. There is no god besides Him. Neither slumber nor sleep overtakes Him. His is all that is in the heavens and all that is on earth. Who can recommend (anyone's case) to Him, except with His permission? He knows what lies before and behind His creatures. They cannot encompass anything of His knowledge, except what He wills. His throne extends over the heavens and the earth. He feels no fatigue in guarding them. He is All High, Most Glorious.**
>
> **(Al-Baqarah 2: 255)**

We get here a graphic picture of Allah's all-encompassing power and knowledge. His eternal nature, without any beginning or end, makes Him the supreme lord. No one can dare recommend anyone's case to Him. He is so unique that He does not need any rest or sleep. This point assumes significance in view of the Jewish or Christian tradition that God had "rested" on the seventh day after His exertion in having created the universe in six days. (Genesis 2: 2-3)

The above account underscores Allah's unquestioning, limitless power. His is the last word related to all affairs in the heavens and on earth. The same holds true for His Judgement on the last day. Unless authorised by Him, no messenger can plead mercy for anyone. His kingdom is both unique and measureless, extending everywhere. More strikingly, as the ever-living, ever-alert one, He constantly oversees all that happens. He will decide our fate, marked by His justice, fairness and mercy.

In view of such splendour and glory of Allah, we must surrender ourselves body and soul to Him and strive to earn His pleasure.

Points to ponder

- The extensive profile of Allah in the human language facilitates our connect with Him. That He listens to us particularly our supplications, watches our actions and issues commands is very reassuring for us. We feel confident and comfortable in turning to Him.

- The detailed description of Allah, especially of His excellent names and awe-inspiring attributes leaves a distinct impression of His glory and majesty on our mind and heart.

Chapter 172

Some of Allah's Favours to Us

Allah is most munificent and most beneficent. He has showered upon us His countless blessings which we cannot even encompass. His sustenance is an instance in point. Even in our pre-natal phase, He provides so much for us: in the comfort and safety of our mother's womb we are constantly nourished, without any effort on our part. He infuses such love and affection for us that for our parents and near and dear ones, as a baby, we are a bundle of joy. At a later stage He enables us to earn our bread and reinforces us with the support of our family, friends, community and countrymen. On our own we could not achieve all this.

> **Allah has spread out the earth and set firm mountains on it. He lets everything grow in due balance. He has provided means of support for you (O people) and also for those whom you do not feed. He has treasures upon treasures of everything. He sends down things in due proportion. He sends fertilizing winds and then causes rain to fall from the sky. He thus provides you with plenty of water to drink. You could not otherwise store it for yourselves.**
>
> **(Al-Hjir 15: 19-22)**

This is another assertion of Allah's greatness. He provides sustenance to all, including those whom we cannot even imagine. Yet His treasure is never exhausted. A perfect sense of balance, interconnection and proportion permeates His creation, ensuring the smooth functioning of the universe, ranging from the gigantic galaxies and the sun to nano particles which have come to our knowledge fairly recently.

He has done immense favours to all living beings, as He feeds them. The natural water conservation system is another pointer to His matchless role as the sustainer *par excellence:* His amazing wisdom is on display in each and every natural phenomenon—the earth as our habitat, mountains for the geo-ecological balance, a sense of proportion marking every creation, as any tampering with it would incur disaster, the pollination system for the blossoming of all vegetation and rain which serves as the lifeline for all living beings.

How ironic it is that we pay no heed to these natural marvels and take these for granted, as routine matters. We should ponder over these signs of almighty Allah and turn to Him earnestly, seeking His mercy.

Points to ponder

- In physical, mental, emotional, social and spiritual domains we stand indebted to Allah's favours. Without these we could not get anything.
- In view of Allah's numerous favours, we owe Him absolute surrender and unquestioning obedience.

Chapter 173

Pointers to Allah's Creative Power

We cannot possibly turn a blind eye to Allah's creative power. Some people may not believe in God. However, even an atheist cannot deny the marvels of Nature, their variety and sheer volume. It is plain common sense that these could not come up on their own; they exhibit adherence to certain laws and display regularity and uniformity. They do not deviate even an inch from their orbit, properties and other features. Allah creates, governs and increases His favours, as indicated in this verse:

> **Allah sends down rain from the heavens and revives the dead land with it. In this there is a sign for those who listen. There is a lesson for you in cattle. Allah gives you milk for your drink, out of that which is in their bellies between excreta and blood. It is a pure and delightful drink for those who take it. (There is a lesson for you) in the fruit of date palm and grapes. You get intoxicants and wholesome drink and food from these. In this is a sign for the wise. Your Lord taught the bee to build its hives in the mountain, trees and in what people build. Then bees suck the juice of every kind of fruit and keep following the paths of your Lord. There comes from their bodies a drink (honey) of various colours. There is healing for people in it. In this is a sign for the thinking people.**
>
> **(Al-Nahl 16: 65-69)**

Rainwater and cattle are, in particular, paraded here as the pointers to Allah's unmistakable creative power. We all know how important water is as a source of our life. Equally baffling is the phenomenon of the provision of the life-giving milk which we get from the body of cattle, between their excreta and blood. Fruits, honeybee and honey are also cited as evidence of His amazing creativity, on which we should reflect.

Keeping in mind the mental level of its immediate addressees, the illiterate, primitive seventh-century Arabs, Allah mentions some of His favours with which they could relate easily and appreciate His power. It is for us, in the technologically advanced twenty-first century, to explore and harness further the natural resources placed by Him at our disposal, with the help of the mental faculties bestowed, once again, by Him on us.

More importantly, this study should lead us to serving, worshipping and exalting the most merciful lord, Allah, Who has done so much for us.

Points to ponder

- The illustrative list in the above passage gives us some idea of the depth and breadth of Allah's favours to us.
- Cattle—seemingly ordinary creatures, stand out as a telling example of Allah's creative wonder. How striking is the point that milk, a pure, wholesome drink of tremendous benefit to us, comes out from their belly, between excreta and blood.

Chapter 174

Allah's Law of Rise and Fall of Communities

History bears out vicissitudes in the fate of communities down the ages. This phenomenon of the success and failure of nations has been brilliantly analysed in the works of Edward Gibbon and Arnold Toynbee in *The Decline and Fall of the Roman Empire* and *History of Civilizations,* respectively. In the Quran, Allah discusses this phenomenon, asserting that it is not something haphazard. As a community gradually deviates from and abandons the straight way, they are doomed for destruction. Allah's intervention is indicated in this verse:

> **(O Prophet), say: "O Allah, Lord of power! You grant power to whom You will and You take away power from whom You will. You raise whom You will and degrade whom You will. All good is in Your hand. You have power over everything."**
>
> **(Ali Imran 3: 26)**

Allah is the only sovereign. Worldly emperors are ephemeral, subject to their humiliating ouster, coups, decline and inescapable death. Allah confers and withdraws honour at His will, a spectacle which we frequently witness in the downfall of the so-called powerful and mighty persons among us. Allah's power is at work in this world in the decline of those who deem themselves to be superior. Most of them enjoy glory for a brief period and eventually they face death–the leveller which reduces them to dust and ashes.

More importantly, Allah will confer on us the abiding status of honour or disgrace on the Day of Judgment. The all-powerful, the all-knowing Allah will weigh our faith and actions and will justly reward or punish us.

Far from running after the brief, transient fame and wealth in this world, we should focus on pleasing Allah, obeying Him and His messenger, Prophet Muhammad (peace be upon him) and following the straight way, which alone would accrue to us the everlasting honour and glory in the next life.

Points to ponder

- Allah's bestowal of power and success on us and His debasement are contingent upon our moral fibre. Our debauchery results in loss and destruction.
- Equally instructive is the phenomenon of the replacement of one community by another as leaders. In fairly recent times we have witnessed the downfall of Imperialism, Fascism and Communism. We should adhere to the divine guidance for success in both the worlds.

Chapter 175

Allah's Insistence on Belief in the Hereafter

Apart from Allah's recurrent command to affirm His oneness as the only true God, He repeatedly asks us to believe in the doctrine of the hereafter, particularly the Day of Judgment and our eternal reward and punishment in the next life. This belief is the most effective deterrent against base desires and the resultant misconduct. Our inner voice, our conscience can stop what law and state cannot achieve despite all their efforts. Our notion of being self-sufficient, or arrogance impels us to deny the hereafter, as stated in the following verse:

> **Your God is the One True God. Those who deny the Hereafter, their hearts are full of rejecting the truth. They are arrogant people**
>
> **(Al-Nahl 16: 22)**

The three main pillars of faith in Islam are: 1) Belief in the one true God, 2) Belief in Prophet Muhammad (peace be upon him) as Allah's final messenger, and 3) Belief in the afterlife in which Allah will reward and punish us, in relation to our faith and actions in this world.

All three beliefs are logically inter-related. Allah, our Lord sent down a series of messengers in all time and place, with the Prophet Muhammad (peace be upon him) (570–633 CE) as the final messenger until the last day for the guidance of humankind. Allah's guidance is recorded in its pristine purity in the form of the Quran and the Prophet Muhammad's example (his conduct and sayings known respectively as Sirah and Hadith) as role models. All of us will be judged after our death on the Day of Judgement and we will be rewarded and punished on the basis of our faith and actions during our lifetime.

It is worth remembering that the one true God, Allah, alone will end the present order as and when He wills it, will resurrect us and pass judgement on us. No one, including His messenger, has any say in the matters of the last day, our reckoning and our fate in the eternal next life.

We should pray fervently to Allah for turning us into His sincere, obedient servants and for our success in the next life.

Points to ponder

- Allah keeps reminding us of our ultimate end in the hereafter. Our negligence may cost us dearly as we would have to face suffering and agonizing pain and humiliation forever in the next life.

- As a highway is profusely signposted, directing us to our destination, Allah constantly depicts scenes of the hereafter in the Quran so that we behave well in this life in order to earn eternal felicity.

Chapter 176

Allah's Command to Us

Allah's command to us is simple and straightforward: To believe in Him and follow the straight way prescribed by Him. Islam does not admit any mythology or superstructure of dogma. Our belief in one God makes us feel confident and strong and boosts our self-respect. Likewise, doing good instills inner happiness and satisfaction in us. Thus, belief and good actions are to our own benefit and joy. Allah declares:

> **I am Allah. There is no god besides Me. So worship Me. Pray regularly to remember Me.**
>
> **(Ta Ha 20: 14)**

Constant thoughts of Allah should occupy us in all that we do or say. So our engagement in earning our bread lawfully is as good as prayer. So is sleep, with the intention to pray and serve the cause of Allah and earn bread lawfully the next day. Allah-awareness is the most effective means for shunning any sin. Islam represents the natural way. It does not involve a superstructure of rituals, offerings or renouncing life. Our duty as believers is simple and easy to perform. Apart from observing only a few religious duties (5 mandatory prayers, one month fasting, 2.5% charity on wealth and Hajj (pilgrimage to Makkah, Saudi Arabia) once a lifetime if we have the financial means to do so). Islam regards our entire life and all our routine activities as acts of worship, provided that we remember Allah in our heart and mind and do everything with the intention of pleasing Him. On this count, Allah's messenger, the Prophet Muhammad's well-documented illustrious life is instructive: he was the head of state, army general, statesman, a loving and caring husband, an affectionate father and a considerate leader, mentor and companion of thousands of those who had accepted Islam at his hands, and above all, a humble servant of Allah and a devout worshipper who was a paragon of virtues.

Allah-awareness is the key to our success in both the worlds. Let us imbibe it as much as we can.

Points to ponder

- Allah's demands are not very taxing. He does not ask us to give Him all our hard-earned money or renounce life for worshipping Him all the time.
- Monotheism is at the heart of the Islamic belief system. It is the height of ingratitude to associate someone with Allah Who alone is our Creator and benefactor. We see for ourselves the abject helplessness of false gods made by devotees themselves of stone and wood. How can they command any respect? They are incapable of providing any guidance.

Chapter 177

Allah's Arrangements for Us

Allah's creation is systematic and highly organised. From the rotation of the gigantic earth around the sun to the micro-level cells in our body, everything is bound by certain laws of nature and a well-defined course of action. Take the alternation of day and night and the creation of male and female—they supplement and complement one another. Had our Lord not been so considerate and all-wise, there would have been chaos. The smooth, error-free functioning of the universe speaks volumes about its Creator, Allah's greatness:

> **Allah causes the dawn break and made the night for rest, and the sun and the moon for calculating time. All this is the arrangement of Allah the Almighty, All Knowing.**
>
> **(Al-Anam 6: 96)**

The alternation of day and night is another recurrent manifestation of Allah's power and creativity. Since we take it for granted, we fail to perceive or appreciate this amazing feat of Allah's power and wisdom. The same holds true for the sun and the moon and their tremendous benefits for us. We should turn humbly and thankfully to Him for these precious gifts.

Allah urges us to embrace Islam on rational, logical grounds. He asks us to reflect on the natural phenomena around to us, as visible and comprehensible to us today as these were to the illiterate seventh-century Arabs, among whom Allah's last messenger, Prophet Muhammad (peace be upon him) was born. On studying these, we realise the perfect, consistent functioning of the universe, with everything in place, in the most befitting way and accruing numerous benefits to all living beings. This unmistakably points to the all-wise, all-powerful Creator behind these, Who is one, without any partner. The life, death and resurrection cycle is unmissable.

We should therefore believe in one true God, follow His guidance and prepare ourselves better for the eternal afterlife.

Points to ponder

- Notwithstanding being massive, Allah's scheme of things is easy to follow. The birth-death-rebirth cycle, to be concluded with Allah's judgment may be easily grasped by all of us.
- The working of the hereafter is also logical and understandable. We would be adjudged solely, to the exclusion of any external factor, on the basis of our own faith and actions.

Chapter 178

Allah Has Devised the Unity of Mankind

Allah is the universal God, not only of believers in Him. He has created everyone alike. He has provided everything to everyone, be they believers or unbelievers. Allah emphasises this truth at places in the Quran that all of humankind represents a single family, born of the first pair of human beings on earth: Adam and Eve. Allah does not discriminate against anyone on the labels of ethnicity, colour, gender, etc. He is nonetheless, particular about our belief system. For our own good He urges us to profess and practise faith and good:

> **It is Allah Who created you all from a single person (Adam) and appointed for you a place of stay (this world) and a resting place (the Next world). He has explained His signs for those who realize (the truth).**
>
> **(Al-Anam 6: 98)**

Our common ancestry and the same ultimate end should evoke our attention and this should result in our submission to our Creator, Allah. Islam stands for peaceful coexistence and pluralism. Allah has, no doubt, prescribed Islam as the only true religion for us and promised reward and punishment for our obedience or otherwise to Him. At the same time, Allah declares that there is no compulsion in matters of faith. The Prophet Muhammad (peace be upon him) won over the heart and mind of people and they embraced Islam. He never resorted to coercion. Jews and Christians flourished in Arabia when for centuries

Muslims were the rulers there. It is again Allah Who has invested us with free will and we may choose a way we prefer. However, as the most affectionate patron and guardian, Allah, has clearly explained the great benefits of belief and the eternal loss and damnation on account of our disbelief.

Let us choose the straight way which will earn Allah's pleasure and our eternal success.

Points to ponder

- In one of his profound sayings, the Prophet Muhammad (peace be upon him) tells people: "Allah does not look at your appearance (race, gender, colour, etc., He takes into account your heart."
- It is ironical that despite the unity of mankind devised by Allah, we have degraded religion to a divisive force, which is largely responsible for discord in our polity across the world.

Chapter 179

Plant Life As Allah's Sign

The plant kingdom is another unmissable sign of Allah's creative genius. Their variety, beauty and benefits for us as food, drink, fuel, medicine, timber and oxygen supply are too well-known to be elaborated. The evolution of a sprawling oak tree from a tiny seed is a spectacle which only the all-powerful and ever-innovative Allah could accomplish. The plant kingdom is pivotal to the life cycle involving all living beings, rain and ecology. The following verse underscores this amazing bounty from the most generous, most compassionate Lord to us:

> **It is Allah Who sends water from the heavens and with it produces all kinds of plants. From it He produces green crops, grain, olives and pomegranates. All of these look alike yet these differ so much. When they begin to bear fruits, observe their fruits—how they become ripe. In all this there are signs for those who have faith.**
>
> **(Al-Anam 6: 99)**

Plant life, particularly fruits, represent Allah's big favour to us. Their variety in both quality and quantity is something amazing. Only Allah, the Supreme Creator could accomplish all this. This evident sign, the growth of a tiny seed into a huge fruit-bearing tree should make us think about our Creator Who has blessed us with this and many more bounties. This, in turn, impels us to obey and thank Him for His kind sustenance. In doing so, we will enjoy a spiritually and morally satisfying, tranquil life in this world and a life of eternal joys in the hereafter.

Points to ponder

- It is a pity that we take plants for granted, without reflecting on Allah's ingenuity that has brought them into being.
- Plants have been of tremendous benefit to us. More importantly, these are a constant reminder of Allah's creativity and beneficence.

Chapter 180

Allah's Oneness

Pure, unadulterated monotheism is the central belief in Islam. It does not entertain even a streak of deism, pantheism or polytheism. He embodies all excellent attributes and enjoys knowledge and power in an absolute sense. The issue of any partner or equal or associate or family does not arise in His case – He is eternal and unique. All power rests solely with Him and He accomplishes what He wills, without any consideration of consequences. He is not answerable to anyone. The logic behind this Islamic cardinal belief is adduced in the following verse:

> **Have they taken such gods on earth who can bring the dead to life? Had there been a god other than the One True God, Allah in the heavens and on earth, there would have been confusion. Glory be to Allah, the Lord of the throne! He is far above what they say about Him.**
>
> **(Al-Anbiya 21: 21-22)**

This affirms Allah's oneness and rules out any plurality of gods which would have resulted in chaos. The seamless order and coordination amid all the components of the universe underscore the rule of only one true God, Allah. Since Allah is all-powerful, He brought this universe into being out of nothing, and without any help or support from anyone. He alone causes life and death. More importantly, He will put an end to this world when it pleases Him, will bring all the dead back to life and adjudge their faith and actions. His objective behind our creation is to test if we believe in Him the unseen, in view of His signs which we can easily comprehend with our mental faculties which are granted to us by Him.

Allah rejects any notion of more than one god on purely logical grounds. Had there been more than one all-powerful lord, it would have resulted in their clash and the consequent chaos in the universe.

The belief in one true God is highly plausible and logical. This alone can bring about our deliverance in the hereafter.

Points to ponder

- In Islam Allah is all-in-all; all others are His creatures and subservient to Him in an absolute sense. Angels are an automated, robot or AI-type species, who execute unquestioningly in no time what Allah commands them. Messengers or prophets are His chosen servants who faithfully carry out His assignment of transmitting and elucidating His message.

- In Islam there is a direct, one-to-one relationship between Allah and man, to the exclusion of any clergy or intermediary. Muslim religious scholars (*ulema*) only explain or adapt Allah's message according to changing times.

Chapter 181

Allah's Universal Message

Though initially delivered through Allah's final book of guidance, the Quran, revealed piecemeal between 610 and 633 CE through the agency of the archangel Jibrail in Arabic, to the last messenger, Prophet Muhammad (peace be upon him), the message is for all time. It does take up local issues and helped the nascent Muslim community evolve and grow. Its thrust is directed at everyone, regardless of their time, place, ethnicity and colour. Its universal appeal made Islam the fastest growing religion and within 100 years of its emergence, it was accepted by a large number of people all over the world, including those in Europe and Africa.

> **Allah sent this message to the Messengers before you and sent the same to you: "There is no god besides Me. So worship Me."**
>
> **(Al-Anbiya 21: 25)**

Common to all the books revealed by Allah is the message of monotheism: serving and worshipping Allah. Islam and the Quran represent the final sequel of Allah's guidance to humankind down the ages. Islam has been the universal religion from the beginning of time when Prophet Adam (peace be upon him), the first man along with his wife, Hawwa (Eve) descended to the earth. Since then the human race has multiplied in all parts of the world through Prophets Noah, Abraham, Moses and Jesus (peace be upon them). They were prominent among a long series of Allah's prophets in various eras and regions. Prophet Muhammad (peace be upon him) is the final messenger.

All messengers always preached: belief in the one true God, and doing good. This has been Allah's message in all time and place. Let us greet it for our eternal success in the hereafter.

Points to ponder

- Notwithstanding its origin in seventh-century Arabia, Islam turned out to be a major world force, outside the confines of the Arab world. Throughout history, non-Arab Muslims have heavily outnumbered Arab Muslims.
- Among the Prophet Muhammad's close companions were the black African, Bilal (RA), the Persian Salman, and the Copt Mary was his wife. Today millions of Muslims live in the West, pointing as it does to the global profile of Islam.

Chapter 182

Our Supplications to Allah

Allah encourages us to invoke Him, present our supplications to Him and forge a direct relationship with Him. He has made it perfectly clear that He listens to our supplication and responds in the way He deems fit. Even if our supplications are not granted for considerations known only to Him, He would compensate it in this or, definitely in the next world. In sum, our supplication does not go unheard. This sincere communication with Allah imparts inner strength and tranquillity, which we cannot attain in any other way. The following passage stands out as a model supplication taught to us by Allah. Muslims recite it in every daily prayer:

> **In the name of Allah, Most Compassionate, Most Merciful. All praise is for Allah Who is the Lord of the universe. He is Most Compassionate, Most Merciful. He is the Master of the Day of Judgement. (O Allah), We worship only You and we seek help only from You. Guide us to the straight way. The way of those whom You blessed; those who did not draw Your wrath (upon themselves because of their evil actions), and those who did not lose the way.**
>
> **(Al-Fatihah1: 1-7)**

The Quran opens with mentioning Allah's most striking attribute: His mercy and kindness to us. He is the lord of both this world and the next. Therefore we should turn only to Him for seeking guidance which will ensure our success in the hereafter. We should shun sin which displeases Him and try our level best to win His pleasure.

Significantly enough, this supplication appears at the beginning of the Quran. Allah asks us to pray to Him for showing us the straight way. The Quran, in a nutshell, describes what this straight way is; how it helps in constructing a happy, cordial social order and how its adherence guarantees our success in the next world by taking us to paradise and defending us against hell.

Points to ponder

- Prior to submitting our supplication, we should praise and glorify Allah and ask for His kind, merciful response to our personal or collective problems. He would respond affectionately to our supplications as He is most compassionate.
- The Prophet Muhammad (peace be upon him) remarked that supplication is the essence of worship. It underscores our total devotion to and dependence upon Him.

Chapter 183

Unbelievers' Rejection of Allah

Allah expresses dismay over the unbelievers' rejection of truth. First, they refuse to act on reason to reflect on the amazing creative wonders and numerous signs which are around them. They stubbornly cling to their ancestral notions and superstitions. Prophet Muhammad (peace be upon him) was a prominent member of their own community. Prior to his assuming prophethood he had spent 40 years of his unblemished life in their midst. In recognition of his many virtues, they had bestowed upon him the laudatory epithets of *Al-Ameen* (the trustworthy) and *Al-Sadiq* (the truthful). However, as he invited them to the call to truth, they turned hostile to him and took to persecuting them. The following verse lays bare their irrational outlook:

> **It is Allah Who causes life and death. He brings about the change of night and day. Will you not think over all this? No, they say what the earlier (Unbelievers) said. They ask: "Will we be brought back to life after our death when we are reduced to dust and bones? This is only a promise made to us and also to our fathers before. All these are no more than the tales of the past."**
>
> **(Al-Muminun 23: 80-83)**

Life-after-death seems improbable to some people. Throughout, the Quran employs the analogy of the dry, parched land in summer which returns to life after rainfall.

By the same token Allah will bring us back to life on the Day of Judgement for rewarding and punishing us. Polytheists of the Prophet Muhammad's day and atheists of our time dismiss sneeringly the idea of the afterlife. First, our coming back to life after death is neither difficult nor implausible. The all-powerful Allah Who created us out of nothing in the first place may easily accomplish our resurrection in no time. The rebirth of vegetation contingent upon rain following a scorching summer is common knowledge. Moreover, the very objective behind Allah creating us is our test: its result will appear only when we die and cease to act. To recompense us for our test, the afterlife and Judgement by the best of judges, Allah, is essential. This world is not an ideal place in which only the good thrive and the evil are punished instantly and suitably. The afterlife is a natural corollary to the present life.

Points to ponder

- Belief in the hereafter was the main stumbling block. Humans foolishly thought that after death once their bodies were decomposed, they could not be brought back to life. They disregarded the manifest truth that the all-powerful Allah Who created them in the first place could easily regenerate them.
- Unbelievers stand condemned for supressing truth and their ingratitude to Allah for His numerous bounties.

Chapter 184

Allah's Guided Servants

In contrast to the diffident unbelievers who disregard Allah's signs and miracles, there are some noble souls, who, guided by reason and good sense readily accept faith. Moreover, they consistently adhere to faith in the face of trials and tribulations. The Prophet Muhammad's family and friends who had embraced faith were killed, tortured, exiled and subjected to socio-economic boycott for years. Yet their persecution did not dent, in the least, their devotion to Allah or Islam. They led an exemplary life, markedly different from their sinful ways in the pre-Islamic era:

> **(The guided ones are) in houses (mosques) which Allah has allowed to be raised for mentioning His name. In them people give glory to Him in mornings and evenings. Neither business nor trade keeps them away from mentioning God, offering Prayer regularly and paying Zakah. They fear the Day of Judgement when the hearts and eyes will be upset. Allah will pay them back for their best actions and will give more out of His grace. Allah gives whom He wills without any measure.**
>
> **(Al-Nur 24: 36-38)**

Allah will lavishly reward believers, with true faith, good actions to their credit and devotion to Him. Apart from praying single-mindedly to Allah, believers generously give in charity (zakah) to underprivileged fellow human beings.

Islam strikes an amazing balance between acts of worship and lawful worldly pursuits which are essential for our survival and for the progress of humanity in every domain, particularly in such fields which accrue relief and benefits to everyone (medical technology, agricultural yield, social welfare measures, etc.).

Allah expects us to perform our religious duties (prayer and zakah for financially helping the needy) sincerely and to be imbued with Allah-awareness and concern for the Day of Judgement, along with our engagement in trade and business.

We should come up to this amalgam of imbibing Allah-awareness in all that we do. This will fetch us eternal rewards.

Points to ponder

- Allah has promised immense rewards for the pious in view of their withstanding temptations and self-restraint. They put up resolutely with adversity but protect their honesty and integrity.
- The pious exercise positive impact on community. In deference to them, many persons give up evil and revert to the straight way. Their halo reinforces the spread of divine guidance in society.

Chapter 185

Allah's Treatment of Unbelievers

As opposed to believers, Allah would deal sternly with unbelievers. He has granted them all bounties, without any discrimination. He has invested them with mental faculty and discernment. While drawing upon the same they excel in worldly matters. However, they deliberately turn a blind eye to Allah's signs, guidance, book and messengers. They display no shrewdness regarding the purpose of their life, their Creator, and their ultimate end. Some of them are brazen enough even to mock and denounce their lord. It is a sordid instance of a creature rebelling against their Creator.

> **The Unbelievers' actions are like a mirage in a desert. A thirsty person mistakes it for water until he comes to it and finds it to be nothing. He only finds Allah with himself. Allah will pay him his account. Allah is quick in taking account. (The Unbelievers' condition) is like that of the depths of darkness in a vast, deep sea. A wave from above covers him, above which is the cloud. All this creates layers upon layers of darkness. As he puts out his hand, he can hardly see it. He whom Allah does not give light, there is no light for him.**
>
> **(Al-Nur 24: 39-40)**

It relates the plight of disbelievers. They will be punished for their error. They cannot escape Him at all. The unbelievers deliberately reject and suppress truth. As a result, they get lost in error and confusion. Allah describes their plight in a figurative language in the above quote. They harbour false notions as a mirage, aimless pursuits which do not bless them with the peace of mind and spiritual fulfillment. They suffer from the delusion that there is no one to stop them from doing wrong. True, they are not seized then and there. However, this fleeting life will come to an end soon. Then they will undergo terrible consequences for their rejection and their preference for the darkness of disbelief.

May Allah save us against such blindness which keeps us away from light and the way to our Creator, Allah.

Points to ponder

- Allah is not unjust in punishing unbelievers in the hereafter. They drew wholly upon His bounties yet abused His kindness in rejecting Him. By every canon of justice and fairness they deserve to be paid back for their intransigence.
- Unbelievers should be punished also for misleading unsuspecting people. They corrupt the moral and social order. Their abuse of divine favours prompts others also to go astray. Their evil influence is their other major sin.

Chapter 186

Water: Allah's Life-Giving Gift

Although some of us take water as something ordinary, it is a life-giving gift from the most bountiful, most kind Lord, Allah. Those living in arid regions know how precious it is and how hard it is to get it. Water is both pure and an excellent cleaning agent and its intake is essential for our body. Allah has devised an amazingly constant supply of water through rain and its equally wonderful storage system in the form of seas, rivers, lakes, ponds, etc. Its pivotal role in cultivation of food items does not call for any elaboration.

> **It is Allah Who sends winds as good news announcing His mercy. He sends pure water from the sky. He brings back with it the dead land to life. He gives it as a drink to cattle and human beings created by Him in great numbers. He presents this (sign) again and again before them so that they may take a lesson. However, most of the people reject the truth and do not thank Him.**
>
> **(Al-Furqan 25: 48-50)**

What is noteworthy in this account of Allah's munificent bounties is that He caters in equal measure to the needs of both human beings and animals. Islam sensitised people to animal rights as far back as early seventh century when even the concept of human rights was hardly professed and practised. The all-wise Allah presents before us rain as His major sign: its life-giving role and its spectacle of re-enacting our resurrection after death, to be followed by our appearance before Allah in the grand assembly for our reckoning.

The Quran draws our attention repeatedly to the lesson emerging from the fairly common phenomenon of rain: to appreciate Allah as the Lord for having arranged for such a blessing as water for us and for all living beings, and to realise that in the same manner He will gather all of us together on the Day of Judgement. Glorify and thank Allah for the precious gift of water.

Points to ponder

- While speaking of water as His bounty, Allah makes it a point to send it down for all living beings. We should consider animals as stakeholders and take good care of them.
- Rainwater is another pointer to Allah's immense glory. The whole cycle is stunning: how vapour forms and rises, how clouds are formed and scattered, how it rains across the world in a particular measure and how rainwater contributes to water storage in various forms.

Chapter 187

Allah's Uniqueness

Allah is unique in every respect. His being without a peer is special to Him. Some misguided people have set up certain entities as equal; some ascribe a son to him and some take certain beings as His associates, without whose assistance He cannot proceed. Islam rules out all these assumptions and insists firmly on His oneness. The idolatrous, polytheistic Arabs of Prophet Muhammad's era tried hard to convince him to strike a deal according to which their idols would have parity with Allah. They promised their allegiance to him, if he agreed on this compromise. However, he rejected it outright, ruling out any partner with Allah.

> **(O Prophet), say: "All praise is for Allah. Peace be on His servants chosen by Him." (Ask them): "Who is better—Allah or those whom they take with Him as His partners?" (Are these false gods better) or He who created the heavens and the earth and sends down for you water from the sky? He causes beautiful orchards to grow with water. You could not grow those trees. Is there a god associated with Allah? No, they are given to straying from the straight way.**
>
> **(Al-Naml 27: 59-60)**

Islam is very particular about the doctrine of Allah's oneness, as the only true God. It rejects outright even the slightest notion of polytheism. In a comparative streak, the above passage contrasts Allah's absolute power with the utter helplessness and worthlessness of false gods. We are asked to contemplate: Is this universe the creation of the one true God or of a pantheon of deities? Could multiple gods achieve the perfect, smooth sailing of the universe? Are man-made idols of wood, clay, marble or any material provided by Allah capable of doing anything, even removing a fly sitting on them? How can they rescue us, or even create and sustain us? There is absolutely nothing to suggest the role of any partner or associate in any of Allah's accomplishments.

Monotheism is the natural, logical rationale behind our creation, sustenance and final accountability on the Day of Judgement.

Points to ponder

- Islam is strictly monotheistic. It no doubt upholds the principle of peaceful co-existence, but it draws a clear line regarding godhead: Only one true God is to be worshipped and obeyed.
- Since Allah is the Creator, Master and Sovereign in an absolute sense, there is no room in Islam for anyone else. Even angels and prophets, who enjoy an exalted position in their own right, do not have even an iota of godhead.

Chapter 188

Glorifying Allah

It is innate in our nature to appreciate and praise something impressive, beneficial and powerful. Acclaiming things or persons is a fairly common, natural human response. Given this, we can never adequately applaud and exalt Allah in view of His matchless grandeur and splendour. The Quran sums it up, asserting that if all the seas were ink and all the trees pen, these would be insufficient for glorifying Allah, the exalted. (Al-Kahf 18:109 and Luqman 31:27).

> **Your Lord creates and chooses what He wills and they (false gods) have no choice. Glory be to Allah! He is far above the partners they take with Him. Your Lord knows what is hidden in the Unbelievers' hearts and what they declare. He is Allah; there is no god other than Him. For Him is the praise in this world and in the Hereafter. His is the command. To Him all of you will be returned.**
>
> **(Al-Qasas 28: 68-70)**

Here is another passage proclaiming Allah's abundant knowledge, power, creativity and position. No one can vie with Him in any respect. He deserves every praise and glorification. The all-powerful, self-sufficient Allah does not ask us to give Him anything (money, offering, etc.). The charity and animal sacrifice prescribed by Him are meant solely for the needy and the underprivileged. As for religious duties, these, once again, are for our self-discipline, self-development, spiritual satisfaction and cordial social interaction. These help construct a better society characterised by a strong bond of fraternity. Take prayer as an instance in point. Believers in each and every locality meet one another five times a day in congregational prayer and a larger assembly gathers every week and twice a year for Friday and Eid prayers respectively. This helps foster cordial social relations. These gatherings also serve as an excellent platform for orienting and sensitising people to good causes, including charity and civic sense.

The all-wise Allah has devised the Islamic faith and practices in our best interest.

Points to ponder

- Allah does not stand in need of our praise or even worship. He is eternally most praiseworthy. For testing our mettle, however, He has asked us to appreciate His greatness.
- Glorifying Allah fills our heart and mind with innermost spiritual and emotional ecstasy and tranquillity. We would earn His pleasure for displaying our humility and submission to Him.

Chapter 189

Allah Condemns Misers

Allah's directives for us are all-inclusive. Money matters occupy an important place in our life. We all devote considerable time and energy to earning money. Allah advises us extensively on this vital aspect of our behaviour and life. Out of His generosity and kindness He has blessed us with wealth in varying degrees. At the same time, He has instructed us how to take up money matters. In the following verse, He asks us not to be miserly and threatens misers with punishment in the hereafter:

> **Those who are miserly about what Allah has given them out of His grace should not think that it (being miserly) is good for them. No, it is bad for them. On the Day of Judgement the things they refuse to spend will be tied round their necks like a collar. Allah's is the inheritance of the heavens and the earth. Allah is aware of all that you do.**
>
> **(Ali Imran 3: 180)**

Apart from the articles of faith, on the Day of Judgement we will also be interrogated about our conduct. Allah urges us to give generously in charity and condemns miserliness. He will severely punish those who do not help the weak and needy and hoard wealth. Allah wants us to construct a happy social order characterised by warm feelings of fraternity, sympathy and large-heartedness. The all-wise guardian, Allah, has made us a trustee, not the owner or master of the material resources (land, wealth, etc.)

granted to us. He has graciously guided us how to spend our money. The Prophet Muhammad (peace be upon him) demonstrated Allah's directives in practice. He gave almost all that he had in charity. He was exceptionally generous, yet not extravagant, in spending the little money he had for good causes.

By this definition, believers cannot be misers. A miser considers himself as the master of his belongings. Moreover, he does not act on frequent exhortations in the Quran and *Hadith* for helping those in need. The all-wise, most munificent Allah roots out the loathsome act of miserliness.

Points to ponder

- Always keep in mind that we are only trustees of all that we have, including money. We should therefore abide by the directives issued by its real owner, Allah.
- Allah places premium on charity and exhorts us to give as much as possible to the poor. Allah has prescribed zakah (welfare tax) on the affluent in order to ensure fair distribution of wealth.

Chapter 190

Allah Disapproves of Boasting

As part of our moral training, Allah has directed us to shun certain vices. Amid these, He warns us against showing off. This particular vice badly damages the social fabric. Take the reprehensible trend of extravagant wedding parties in our society. It places an unnecessary and intolerable burden on parents. They repay interest-based loans throughout their lives for the huge money spent by them on sheer show off—from flowers, decoration, a large variety of food items, etc. For facilitating our carefree, simple life Allah cautions us:

> **Allah does not love those who spend their wealth to make a show of it before people. They do not believe in Allah and the Day of Judgement. He who takes Satan as a companion takes a very bad companion.**
>
> **(Al-Nisa 4: 38)**

We should lead a simple life, free from boasting, pretension and affectation. We are exhorted to guard ourselves against Satan who impels us to commit evil. While Allah does not recommend monasticism as a way of life for believers, he does urge us to lead a simple, modest life. Materialism, lust for wealth, greed, and craze for a higher standard of life and luxurious lifestyle have no room in Islam. Although the Prophet Muhammad (peace be upon him) was the head of the sprawling, ever increasing state of Madina, and some of his companions, namely, Abu Bakr (RA) and

Uthman (RA) were prosperous traders, who led a frugal life and generously spent on charity.

As showing off and boasting about one's wealth corrupts the social order and drives people to crass materialism while forgetting all noble ideas and spirituality, Allah asks believers to shun these vices. In doing so, His concern is to preserve the purity and simplicity of the social fabric.

Points to ponder

- In the Quran Allah condemns those who pray to show off and refuse to lend items of daily use to their friends and neighbours (Surah Al-Maun). It underscores Allah's concern for protecting and maintain a cordial social fabric.
- According to the Islamic tradition, Satan, a jinn, was expelled from paradise for boasting about his piety, and his arrogance in rejecting Adam as inferior.

Chapter 191

Allah's Directive for Justice

Allah greatly emphasises the dispensation of justice. His directive to the Prophet Muhammad (peace be upon him), the head of the Muslim community, was to enforce justice, irrespective of any consideration. Accordingly, while speaking from the pulpit he told the congregation: "I would be the first to cut off the hands of my daughter, if she is ever found to be stealing." His relentless pursuit of justice and fairness turned the Muslim society of the day into an exemplary one, almost free from crimes: A comprehensive directive for justice features in the following verse:

> **Allah commands you to deliver trusts to those to whom these are due. Judge with justice when you judge among people. Allah gives excellent advice. Allah is All Hearing, All Seeing.**
>
> **(Al-Nisa 4: 58)**

Being all-just, Allah commands us to be fair and honest in our dealings. Justice is the corner-stone of a happy, peaceful society so Allah prescribes it for us. Warring or raiding was a way of life, rather a source of income in pre-Islamic Arabia. So there was an abundance of orphans in society. Their trustees, mostly sunk in moral degeneration, usurped orphans' belongings, of which they were guardians. Against this backdrop, Allah insisted that believers take special care of orphans. Contained in the Quran are several directives for their humane treatment.

The above advice is part of the same concern for doing justice to the helpless, weak orphans.

We should stand for fairness in all departments of human activity. The Prophet (peace be upon him) championed the cause of justice, particularly for women, widows, orphans and children.

Points to ponder

- As Allah is the best of judges, he commands fairness in our dealings. Generally speaking, injustice is the root cause of social unrest. Allah plugs this loophole with His insistence on transparency and justice in our dealings.
- Prophet Muhammad (peace be upon him) has said on record that justice done in a moment outweighs even years-long worship throughout nights. Justice helps keep the social order intact and stable.

Chapter 192

Variety in Our Languages: Allah's Sign

Speech is a great blessing conferred upon us by Allah. It distinguishes us from other creatures as our articulate speech is not only readily comprehensible for the ease of mutual dealings and relationships, it is retrievable, well-preserved for posterity, in both oral and written forms. We have a massive variety in languages and dialects employed by us in various regions. Some languages are special to their communities while some transcend national boundaries, for example, English, French, Arabic and Urdu. Allah makes it pointedly clear that any language does not signify any special status. They are, at best, markers of our identity. This should not therefore be a bone of contention among us.

> **It is one of Allah's signs that He created the heavens and the earth and variety in your languages and your colours. In this are signs for those who have knowledge.**
>
> **(Al-Rum 30: 22)**

The amazing variety in our complexion and languages is another sign of Allah's creative power. These labels should not cause any discord in our social fabric. It is shameful that language and colour, which simply distinguish some people from others, have become innocuous labels and cause discord on a wide and ugly scale. We have superimposed the notions of superiority and inferiority upon these. Much of the hostility in the world is owing to linguistic jingoism and apartheid. The all-wise, all-knowing Allah considers these superficial differences as merely a manifestation of variety or diversity in the world. For Him, our piety alone matters. He declares: "The most honourable one in the sight of Allah is the most pious among you." (The Quran 49:15). Among the Prophet Muhammad's favourite companions were Black Bilal (RA) and the Persian-speaking, Salman. Muslims represent a single community of believers across the world, without any distinction of colour, ethnicity or caste. Non-Arab Muslims heavily outnumber Arab Muslims, though Islam originated in Arabia.

We should foster mutual love and respect for all human beings, irrespective of their caste, colour, race or nationality.

Points to ponder

- It is our sincere devotion to our lord that matters, not the language in which we communicate with Him. It is usually metalanguage that conveys our innermost feelings.
- Regrettably language, like race, colour and religion, has been abused as a divisive force. Each language merits respect and justice. It should not be used for manipulating domination or fragmentation.

Chapter 193

We Owe Allah Our Total Obedience

Allah, our Creator and Lord deserves our full attention and obedience. Since we subsist wholly on His provisions, it is morally and legally binding on us to turn only to Him and adhere to His commands. Bear in mind that His commands are for our own good and success in both worlds. He is too lofty to gain anything from our worship. He continues to enjoy His most exalted place, irrespective of our obedience to His supreme reign in the universe. It is pressed home in this verse:

> **It is one of Allah's signs that the heavens and the earth stand by His command. When He will summon you from the earth, you will come forth. His is all that is in the heavens and on earth. All are obedient to Him. He originated creation and will create again, which is easier for Him. His is the highest attribute in the heavens and on earth. He is Almighty, the Wisest.**
>
> **(Al-Rum 30: 25-27)**

The above lines underscore Allah's might. Little wonder then that all of us will appear before Him on the Day of Judgement in order to render our account. Allah is the originator, master and lord of all that exists. Objects of Nature obey His command and follow the course ordained by Him. Since time immemorial, they have been functioning consistently. Disbelieving human beings are also bound by Allah's commands: they have no choice or control regarding their birth, death and fate.

The best course of action for us is to recognise our Creator and lord, the one true God, Allah. We would enjoy peace and inner happiness in both this and the next world by following His directives to us.

Points to ponder

- Those in the universe who do not enjoy free will toe Allah's line completely. We would earn His immense reward, if we willingly turn to Him in obedience. Viewed thus, we can excel even angels.
- Islam literally means to surrender. As we accept it, we are obliged to obey Allah unquestioningly. Islam exhorts us to reflect on Allah's signs around us. This sincere study would prompt us to align completely with His will.

Chapter 194

Stages of Our Lives: Allah's Wondrous Sign

We have to accept willy-nilly that each one of us has to undergo varied phases of life: from a helpless baby to a curious toddler, energetic teenager, stable young age, mature middle years, to frail, despondent in old age. Strikingly enough, we have no control over the slow yet steady passage of time and our transformation from one phase to another, no matter how hard we may try to resist or cover it up. Allah's absolute power and our helplessness are too obvious to be denied. The verse below sheds light on our evolution:

> **It is Allah Who created you from dust, then from a sperm drop, then from a blood clot. He brings you out as a baby. He then lets you grow to gain full strength. Then He lets you turn old. Some of you die early. He lets others reach their appointed term. All this so that you may think.**
>
> **(Al-Mumin 40: 67)**

It is Allah Who ordains our lifespan and its varied stages. Out of His boundless wisdom He has fixed our lifespan, over which we have no control. Millions of deaths every year, despite tremendous advances in medical technology and pharmaceutical industry, point to Allah's power. As the above Quranic verse was addressed first to the seventh-century illiterate Arabs, it presents only such a bare description of our creation/birth which they could grasp. It is a scientifically valid statement as well, though without finer details and jargon. What is more important is Allah's assertion about our helplessness in the following stages: as a baby, as an ageing frail person, as a victim of death in the prime of our life or in our ripe old age.

This makes us reflect on Allah's absolute power, our limitations and our ultimate return to Him. Our sincere thinking on these great questions of being is bound to prompt us to embrace true faith and adhere to the way of life shown so eloquently by Allah and His messenger, the Prophet Muhammad (peace be upon him).

Points to ponder

- Not only do we grow in age, we also undergo personality changes in every stage of life. Our thought patterns and even worldview are altered as well. This demonstrates Allah's total grip over our affairs.
- We yearn to return to childhood and youth as we face grim realities in our advanced years. Our longing in old age reaches its zenith. However, we cannot alter the situation even slightly, affirming our weakness and Allah's absolute, invincible power.

Chapter 195

No Help Possible Against Allah

Allah's absolute power is manifest before all of us. If He wants to do us a favour, no power on earth can withhold it. By the same token, if misfortune, disease, or death befalls us or our near and dear ones, we all are absolutely helpless. Medical help, no matter how good it might be, has its limitations. Had wealth been effective against all this, no rich or powerful person would have ever faced any crisis or death. At the end of the day, we realise that we cannot do anything, if Allah has decreed it. And He does not do so in order to torment us but as part of His grand plan, of which we have no knowledge. Our helplessness is conveyed pithily in this verse:

> **Had Allah willed so, He could have made all of them a single community, He has mercy on him whom He wills. There will be no helper or supporter for the wrongdoers. Do these Unbelievers take others as protectors besides Allah? Allah alone is the protector. He will bring the dead back to life. He has power over everything. Allah will decide all about which you differ. Such is Allah, my Lord. In Him I trust and to Him I turn.**
>
> **(Al-Shura 42: 8-10)**

This is Allah's scheme of things. He tests us all. Otherwise He is powerful enough to make all of us follow Islam alone. The disbelievers should realise the grim reality that if they do not follow Allah's guidance, no one will be able to help them in the hereafter. The presence of even the majority of disbelievers in the world should not be misconstrued as some reflection on His power. It was quite easy for Him to create all of us as believers, who would never be able to deviate an inch from His way. However, He has granted us free will and invested us with mental faculties and conscience to discern the truth about the one true God, of which the signs are found aplenty in our own selves and all around us. All power, however, rests solely with Allah. If we reject Him, we will be subject to His terrible punishment in the afterlife. No one, particularly false gods, will then be able to protect or help us against His chastisement.

We should emulate the Prophet Muhammad's affirmation: "In Allah I trust and to Him I turn." (The Quran 42:10)

Points to ponder

- Allah would exercise His power publicly and in full on the Day of Judgement. No one will dare to express their dissent to His decree. His word would be final and it would be absolutely fair and just.
- Allah's might and glory should humble us. It does not amount to fatalism. We should keep striving our level best to make our dreams come true. However, we should realise it all along that our Lord's decree is supreme. He does what He deems fit and we should reconcile to His will.

Chapter 196

Belief in Allah Is Innate in Our Nature

Despite all our posturing, and even professing atheism or betraying apathy to faith, we all experience a natural, strong, spiritual urge, looking for a support system, especially in a crisis, old age or during bereavement. No one can deny the sense of awe, dread and humility as they are reflected as signs around us which manifest Allah's presence, His munificence and power. While having many facilities and nutritious food, we find it incredible how millions upon millions of fellow human beings live, nay thrive, in seemingly adverse circumstances. Rags to riches stories are real, not fairy tales. All this persuades us instinctively of Allah's being and His oversight of everything:

> **So turn your face exclusively to true faith and follow the true nature on which Allah has created human beings. There is no change in Allah's creation. This is true faith. However, most of the people do not understand this. Turn to Allah and fear Him. Establish Prayer. Do not be among those who take partners with Allah.**
>
> **(Al-Rum 30: 30-31)**

This succinctly states the key Islamic belief—faith in the one true Allah—and to follow the natural straight way innate in our conscience. With full devotion we should pray to the one true God. In Islamic terminology it is called salah (prayer) obligatory for every adult Muslim male and female, preferably in congregation. Most of the new mosques in India and abroad have adequate facilities for women to pray. Almost an equal number of Muslim men and women perform Hajj (pilgrimage) in Makkah, Saudi Arabia. So do women fast and pay zakah (charity). Islam admits no gender injustice in matters of faith.

The most affectionate, most compassionate Allah has graciously invested all human beings with an innate, instinctive ability to recognise truth and follow the straight way. Owing to negligence or blind conformity to ancestral ways disbelievers suppress and blunt their quest for truth. It is all the more strange that in everyday worldly matters they display keen shrewdness and alertness. However, they deliberately turn a blind eye to matters of consequence such as faith in the one true God, abiding by divine guidance in life, concern for eternal life in the hereafter and Allah's reward and punishment after death.

Points to ponder

- Even the most wicked person recognises the superiority and excellence of virtue, though they may not profess the same.
- Throughout our life we come across amazing stories of poetic justice, reward for honesty and virtue, sincere repentance by evil persons, and the change of their heart etc.; these all impel us instinctively to believe in and proclaim Allah's glory.

Chapter 197

Allah Instructs Us to Offer Prayer

Prayer is the direct, personal and one-to-one contact with Allah. In the Islamic belief system, it occupies pride of place. We are encouraged to offer as many prayers as possible in addition to the five mandatory prayers in congregation. Allah points out the huge benefits of prayer: "O believers seek help with patience and prayer." (Al-Baqarah 2:153). In other words, we are spiritually reinvigorated as we pray. Prayer instils discipline in us, as some prerequisites such as a clean body and clothes and ablution (*wuzu*) are to be met and mandatory prayers are to be said at their appointed hours in congregation:

> **(O Prophet), recite the Book sent to you and establish Prayer. Prayer keeps one away from indecency and evil. Remembering Allah is the greatest thing. Allah knows all that you do.**
>
> **(Al-Ankabut 29: 45)**

Prayer being the direct communion between our lord and master, Allah and us infuses into us an acute realisation of Allah's power and the approaching Day of Judgement. This deep consciousness deters us from doing any evil. We know fully well that Allah is all-seeing and will hold us accountable for all that we do and say. Out of His infinite wisdom and overflowing love for us, Allah has prescribed obligatory prayer five times a day: at dawn, early afternoon, late afternoon, after sunset and early night. Believers pray at other hours as well, especially in the serene, spiritually nourishing small hours of night. As we pray, we recognise that we are in Allah's presence and that He watches us praying to Him. This imprints indelible Allah-awareness on our mind and heart. So those who pray sincerely cannot even think of committing any immorality or sin. They know that after only a few hours they have to stand again in front of the all-seeing, all-knowing Allah. Allah-awareness is our precious asset, as it keeps us steady on the straight way and fills our mind and heart with spiritual solace and tranquility.

May Allah enable us to pray to Him sincerely and regularly.

Points to ponder

- Allah has prescribed the five mandatory prayers to be offered daily in congregation. The proliferation of mosques in any Muslim locality is on account of the same. Moreover, congregation helps sustain and reinforce solidarity and unity among Muslims.
- Prayer is totally Allah-centric. We invoke only Him, recite His word and beseech Him earnestly for meeting all of our needs.

Chapter 198

How to Lead Life: Allah's Advice

Allah has provided in His book, the Quran and through His role model messenger, Prophet Muhammad (peace be upon him) comprehensive guidelines encompassing all facets of life about how to lead life. The first and foremost important truth to be borne in mind is that our life has a purpose and meaning and that we would be held accountable for all that we say and do. With this idea being uppermost in mind we are most likely to behave well, be kind towards everyone and be cautious in our actions. Needless to add, this would not only make our lives pleasant and cordial but also that of all those around us, in particular family and friends in particular. Our life should be an amalgam of faith and good actions, including earning our bread, as illustrated in this passage:

> **O believers, when the call (*adhan*) is made for Friday prayer, rush towards the remembrance of Allah. Give up all trading. That is best for you, if you knew. When the prayer is over, move about in the land, looking for Allah's favours. Remember Allah much so that you may get success.**
>
> **(Al-Jumuah 62: 9-10)**

These instructions are illustrative of a perfect blending between acts of devotional worship and all lawful worldly activities such as trade for earning our bread. Islam condemns monasticism. It repeatedly asks us to lead a full life, engaged in exploring and harnessing Nature, representing Allah's signs for our guidance. Prayer is the most effective means for drawing us closer to Allah. Prayer should be marked by our earnest, single minded devotion to Him. At the same time, He urges us to take up economic activity for sustaining ourselves and our family. Lawful worldly activities do not run contrary to believers' life of piety. Islam being the natural way caters to both our material and spiritual needs.

We should strike a balance between our religious and economic pursuits. Even the latter accrue the same reward from Allah which is due for acts of devotional worship. Islam does not admit any compartmentalisation between the holy and the profane. The entire life of believers is an act of worship that wins them Allah's pleasure.

Points to ponder

- Allah is so keen on our welfare and happiness in the social order that He instructs us how to treat our parents, spouses, children and the wider community well.
- Apart from better social relations Allah guides us in the political, economic, psychological and spiritual realms.

Chapter 199

Allah's Doors of Salvation Are Open for Everyone

Forgiveness and pardoning sinners, regardless of the quantum of wrongs committed by us, is Allah's outstanding attribute. In as many as 147 Quranic verses He declares Himself to be most merciful and oft forgiving. If we turn sincerely to Him in repentance and resolve not to repeat the wrongs for which we have sought His forgiveness, we are most likely to attain salvation. Our invocation for His mercy should, nonetheless, be before we are already in the throes of death, breathing our last. Allah's pronouncement of His salvation in the following verse is strikingly wide ranging:

> **The believers, the Jews, the Christians, and the Sabians–all those who believe in Allah, the Last Day and do good, they will have their reward with their Lord. There is no fear or grief for them.**
>
> **(Al-Baqarah 2: 62)**

The Islamic scheme of salvation is not specific to Muslims alone. It is abundantly clear that Allah promises reward to those Jews, Christians and Sabians (a community in Iraq in the Prophet Muhammad's day) as long as they believe in the one true God and resurrection. Allah's mercy and justice embrace everyone. After the advent of Allah's final messenger, the Prophet Muhammad (peace be upon him) in early seventh century, believers have to accept these three articles of faith: Belief in i) the one true God, Allah, ii) Prophet Muhammad (peace be upon him) and iii) life after death. With respect to those who lived before his messengership, their belief in Allah, the Day of Judgement and their good actions will suffice for their entitlement to Allah's reward in the afterlife.

Since Allah has clearly spelled out the belief system for us, we should exert ourselves to meet this standard. Our eternal happiness or damnation rests on this.

Points to ponder

- Allah alone is the redeemer. We need not look for someone to secure our deliverance. Our sincere repentance and remorse would suffice for our redemption.
- Allah has no doubt, provided room for intercession by His messengers, particularly Prophet Muhammad (peace be upon him). However, all intercession would be subject to Allah's clearance. Only by His leave would they be able to recommend clemency for someone. All power on the Day of Judgement would rest solely with Him.

Chapter 200

Allah's Hospitality for the Pious

The pious, who stood by faith and were ever engaged in doing good would be warmly welcomed by Allah in His paradise. In a moving passage Allah gives the glad tidings to His virtuous servants: They would be offered there the best which is beyond our imagination. This is the ultimate felicity which we can think of:

> **(It will be said): "O the soul at peace! Return to your Lord, well pleased (with you) and well pleasing (to Him). Be among My pious servants. Enter My garden (of Paradise)!"**
>
> **(Al-Fajr 89: 27-30)**

Allah's above promise to us is the highest privilege imaginable. Let us grab this opportunity with both hands and attain felicity on the Day of Judgement.

Allah's boundless love, affection and mercy are evident from the above generous promise. He does not overburden us with a taxing list of demands. True faith and good actions entitle us to His paradise and its eternal joys.

Notwithstanding His majesty and glory, Allah is seen here showering His praise and love on His obedient servants. As the most merciful, all-pardoning Lord, He is ever ready to bestow His reward on us, if we follow the straight way. Winning Allah's pleasure is not a herculean task, beyond our reach. It calls only for the sincerity and purity of our intention, and our discharging obligations due to Allah and to fellow human beings.

Allah's most attractive promise should prompt us to make the most of this golden opportunity. We cannot have a better bargain than this for our eternal success.

Points to ponder

- The pious would be lavishly rewarded for their self-control and exemplary conduct and their success in trials and tribulations in this world.
- As they were permeated with Allah-awareness in their sayings and actions, believers led life in accordance with Allah's will which resulted in such ample reward.

Chapter 201

Allah Is Immortal

The only immortal being is Allah: All others, great or small, are mortal, which is a common sight. Being the Lord and Creator Who is unique is every respect, Allah is eternal, without any beginning or end. There cannot be godhead without the essential feature of immortality. He has to settle everything. Moreover, death would betray His imperfection whereas He is the Creator and Master of death itself.

> **God alone will inherit the earth and all that is on it. Everyone will return to Him.**
>
> **(Maryam 19: 40)**

At the end of time everything will return to Allah, the real Master and Owner. We are only trustees of all that we have, and only during our lifetime. Being trustees we should be very careful, as we will be answerable for all our actions.

As the Lord, Master and Creator, Allah alone is immortal. He has always been there and will remain so. All else, including Allah's messengers are mortal as they faced death. Of His numerous unique attributes, Allah's eternality is very striking. He has brought everything into being, including this universe, as part of His grand design. He has created us, sent us to this world for an appointed term. However, on the last day He will end the present order, resurrect us and adjudge us, on the basis of our faith and actions and will accordingly award us eternal paradise or consign us to eternal hellfire.

We should keep in mind this divine scheme of things. It helps us adhere to the straight way. In Islam the purpose of our life and our fate in the next world are stated very clearly, free from any metaphysical, philosophical or mythological jargon or superstructure. We should remember all along the bare fact of Allah's Lordship and our return and answerability to Him.

Points to ponder

- Death represents our transition from this world to the next one. It is not synonymous with end.
- Allah will adjudge as all of us would return to Him on the Day of Judgement.

Chapter 202

Beneficiaries of Allah's Reward

Allah's reward and punishment system is both logical and elaborate. As the almighty lord, He is free to do whatever pleases Him. For our peace of mind, however, He has clarified who will earn His reward or incur His wrath. Our Creator knows well that we are vulnerable to committing lapses, and even sins. For tackling this issue, He has devised the exit route of His forgiveness and mercy, provided that the guilty turn to Him in repentance. He reiterates His role as the Creator and in the universe in this verse:

> **Those who avoid major sins and shameful actions, and make only minor lapses, Allah will be full of forgiveness to them. He knows you best as He produced you from the earth, and while you were inside your mothers' wombs. Do not consider yourselves as pious. He knows best who fears Him.**
>
> (Al-Najm 53: 32)

Out of His boundless mercy and compassion, Allah condones our minor lapses. We should, nonetheless, be constantly on guard and shun any violation of His commands. Since He has created us in the first place, He knows our motives and lapses well. The all-knowing Allah is aware of our innermost motives He knows us from our pre-birth, natal stage. Moreover, it is He Who has created us and hence He is fully cognizant of our psyche and instincts.

It is so gratifying that His retribution is neither instant nor too exacting even for a minor lapse which we may commit out of our humanness. His mercy is all-pervading and He has promised forgiveness to us, provided that we turn in sincere repentance to Him.

We should be on guard against boasting about our righteousness. Allah hates those who make a show of their piety. Being all-knowing, all-seeing He will recompense us fairly and fully.

Points to ponder

- Allah recognises that we as human beings are liable to err. He graciously condones our minor lapses committed in weak moments. However, He warns us sternly against moral disorder which corrupts the whole social order.
- Allah emphasises the nexus between our faith and conduct. Our belief in Him should be reflected in our good conduct. Our misconduct betrays weakness in our faith. We should strengthen our faith by way of developing Allah-awareness in our heart and mind.

Chapter 203

Allah Consigning People to Hell

Some persons appear perplexed over refrain-like references to Allah's punishment and hellfire in the face of Allah's boundless mercy. This should not sound as a contradiction in terms. Apart from being most merciful and most compassionate, Allah is also the all-just ruler and master. He has explained to us His scheme of things and bestowed upon us His numerous bounties on which we constantly draw. However, if someone still defies His commands and His warnings against following a self-destructive path, justice demands that they should be punished:

> **All that is revealed to you (O Prophet) from your Lord is the truth. However, most of the people do not believe. It is Allah Who has raised the heavens without any support which you may see. He established Himself on the throne. He has made the sun and the moon follow (a law). Each one runs its course for an appointed term. Allah governs everything. He has explained the signs so that you may have faith in meeting your Lord. It is Allah Who has spread out the earth, placing in it mountains and rivers. He has made every fruit in pairs. He causes the night to cover the day. In all these there are signs for those who think. There are nearby pieces of land, gardens of vines, corn fields, and date palms, some growing in clusters and some standing alone on earth. All of these are watered by the same water. Allah has made**

some fruits better in taste than others. In all these there are signs who use reason. You may be surprised over (their rejection of faith). More surprising is their saying: "What! Will we be created again after we are reduced to dust (after death)?" They are the ones who disbelieve in their Lord. There will be yokes round their necks. They are the people of the Hellfire. They will live in it.

(Al-Raad 13: 1-5)

We should always seek Allah's protection against all evil. It is so reassuring to note that Allah wards off evil from us. The detailed description of Allah's creative wonders which we note all around us is followed by observations on the silly, foolish disbelievers who reject Allah in the face of such evident signs. Is it not a miracle that the same soil and water help produce sweet, bitter and sour fruits in trees standing next to one another? Allah asks us to apply reason in studying and tapping Nature or His signs for our benefit and enlightenment.

Points to ponder

- Allah's punishment should not be misperceived as antithetical to His mercy. The most merciful lord is keen on enforcing order and happiness in society. Those who wilfully destroy the social fabric, oppress fellow human beings and commit heinous crimes against humanity deserve horrible punishment.
- Since Allah has eloquently warned against the dire consequences of evil, His punishment is fair and logical.

Chapter 204

Allah As Our Protector

We instinctively feel the need for protection, no matter how old we might have grown. Allah is our best protector and guardian in that He is all-powerful and all-knowing. All of us turn to some helper in a crisis, as we are weak and vulnerable. Allah affectionately reassures us, saying that we should invoke Him and that He listens to our supplications. Allah has arranged for guardian angels who look after us. However, if Allah has decreed some misfortune for us as part of our test, they are helpless:

> **(O Prophet), say: "I seek safety and protection with the Lord of all people, The King of all people, Allah of all people. I seek safety and protection from the evil of those who whisper secretly, who prompt evil into the hearts of people. I seek safety and protection from the evil ones among the Jinn and people."**
>
> **(Al-Nas 114: 1-6)**

As part of our trial, Allah has created evil as well, particularly Satan who is always bent on misguiding us. We should invoke Allah—the lord and king of everyone for His refuge against any evil. Out of His immense kindness and graciousness Allah has warned us eloquently against evil. Since we are vulnerable to doing wrong, His warning is a great blessing for us. Likewise, He has been caring enough to have taught us the above prayer. Its recitation is very reassuring and consoling. Above all, He has generously promised us His protection against all evil, if we turn sincerely to Him.

Evil is, no doubt, rampant and appears attractive too. As part of our test, it seduces us in many ways, at the same time, Allah has instructed us how to defend ourselves. The Quran cites the brilliant example of the Egyptian emperor pharaoh of Prophet Musa's day (thirteenth and fourteenth century BC). The pharaoh was worshipped as god-king in Egypt. In such a blatant polytheistic setting, living inside the pharaoh's palace, his wife greeted Prophet Musa's call to monotheism.

With faith in Allah and determination we can resist and overcome evil.

Points to ponder

- Allah has directed us to take every precaution against any eventuality and invoke Him for help and protection.
- Prophet Muhammad (peace be upon him), Allah's beloved servant, would often recite the Quranic Surahs Al-Masad (113) and Al-Naas (114) which constitute a plea to Allah for protection against all that is evil and harmful to us.

Chapter 205

Allah's Bounties Are for Everyone

Allah is most munificent in having granted His various bounties to all—believers and unbelievers alike. What is required for leading life are the basic necessities of air, water, food, etc., and physical and mental faculties in varying degrees. We fortunately get all these bounties for free and in plenty. Ironically enough, far from thankfully acknowledging these, we disobey our benefactor and abuse these bounties for defying Him and for causing corruption.

> **Allah does favours to everyone, these as well as those. The favours of your Lord are not denied to anyone. See, Allah has given more to some than others. In the Next Life some will have a higher position and excellence over others.**
>
> **(Isra 17: 20-21)**

Allah has generously provided much to each of us, though in order to test us He has granted more to some. As we serve Him gratefully, He will exalt our rank in the next life. Allah is the lord and master of the entire universe. He is not some local god of Arabs or Muslims alone. As is fairly evident from the above declaration, He does not discriminate among us on any grounds in heaping His bounties on the whole of humanity. He grants sustenance, natural resources and provisions to everyone, regardless of their religious or sectarian denomination, nationality, ethnicity or colour.

However, in the life after death, following His judgement, He will lavish choicest rewards on believers and punish disbelievers rigorously. His scheme of things is transparently clear, fair and logical.

It is for us to set our house in order and try to secure His pleasure.

Points to ponder

- No one can even enumerate and evaluate Allah's bounties which have been available since time immemorial to everyone. In return, He does not ask Him to pay anything. He urges us only to follow His guidance which is best-suited for us.
- Prophet Muhammad (peace be upon him) has instructed us to thank and praise Allah for His bounties. Hundreds of supplications for various occasions, in recognition of Allah's blessings, are on record for us to emulate.

Chapter 206

Allah Has Subjected Everything to Us

It is one of Allah's great favours that He has appointed human beings as His vice-gerent on earth. Invested with spectacular physical and mental faculties, down the millennia, we have been able to harness objects of Nature to our use and benefit. We have managed to unearth much and accomplish discoveries and inventions. Take travel for example. Initially we tamed animals, put them at our disposal for undertaking long and arduous journeys. Since the Industrial revolution, we have vastly improved means of transport. Using natural resources and by dint of our mental prowess and technological skills, we have been able to achieve swift and comfortable means of transport which has resulted in the overall progress and prosperity.

> **Do you not consider this—Allah has subjected for you all that is in the heavens and on earth? He has blessed you with many of His bounties, both visible and invisible ones. There are some people, however, who dispute regarding Allah, though they do not have any knowledge or guidance or book to guide them.**
>
> **(Luqman 31: 20)**

We cannot even count Allah's bounties on which we freely draw, particularly our mental and physical abilities. Out of His kindness He has made the forces of Nature subservient to us. As a result, we stand out above all other creatures. It is a great pity that some people refuse to acknowledge Allah's self-evident presence, knowledge, and power.

The all-merciful, provider lord has placed the entire universe at our disposal for exploration and harnessing everything for our benefit. For this He has equipped us with matchless physical and mental faculties. While drawing upon the same we have been able to discover and invent so much. In our times, the pace of ingenuity and progress, especially by tapping artificial intelligence (AI), has been pleasantly mind-boggling.

We should thank our lord, Allah from the depths of our heart for His munificence and benefaction.

Points to ponder

- With greater knowledge, we owe a heightened sense of responsibility, particularly related to animal rights and environment.
- We should not forget the important truth: we are only trustees of natural resources and would have to render account for any abuse, extravagance and imbalance.

Chapter 207

Cattle: Allah's Big Favour to Us

Allah has mercifully enabled us to domesticate cattle. For centuries it has been a thriving industry, boosting our economy and adding vastly to our dinner table with meat, milk, dairy and poultry products in particular. It is Allah alone Who instilled in us the knowledge and skills for subjugating cattle. With technology we have gained further mastery in this domain.

> **Do they not consider Allah's creation? He creates for them cattle which they own. Allah has subjected cattle to them. (As a result) they ride some of them while they eat some. They have other benefits and drinks from cattle. Will they then not thank (Him)?**
>
> **(Ya Sin 36: 71-73)**

On a little reflection we realise the bounty of cattle which Allah has provided to us. We derive many benefits from them, especially milk and meat. This should make us all the more appreciative of Allah's creative power and kindness to us.

For self-introduction, Allah presents simple examples from everyday life. Since time immemorial we have been drawing heavily upon cattle for a host of benefits. It is a pity that we take these bounties from Allah as granted and do not pay any heed to these in terms of appreciating these as Allah's creative wonders.

Full of gratitude, we should acknowledge our debt to the Lord. We could not survive without His numerous huge favours to us. Glory be to our most loving, guardian lord!

Points to ponder

- Through our mental prowess, which is a gift from Allah, we have managed to rein in cattle that otherwise outweigh us physically. The substantial role played by camels and horses in pre-modern times shows this.
- Apart from meat and dairy products we derive many benefits from cattle. We should turn in gratitude to Allah for this huge blessing which is still of much relevance and value in today's industrialised world. Moreover, we should take good care of cattle that provide so many benefits to us.

Chapter 208

Allah's Omnipresence

Since Allah is the only all-powerful, all-knowing lord, the belief in His omnipresence should not raise eyebrows. Rather, it is a natural corollary of His lordship. For us this attribute of His should serve as a deterrent. This makes us realise that He watches us, no matter where we might be. Take fasting for instance. We may pretend to be fasting in the company of others. However, in the privacy of home we may eat and drink freely. That Allah is omnipresent, keeping a vigilant eye on our actions in both private and public, is bound to have a deterrent effect. The following verse makes a pointed reference to the direction of our prayer:

> **The east and the west belong to Allah. To whichever direction you turn, you will face Allah. Surely Allah is All Embracing, All Knowing.**
>
> **(Al-Baqarah 2: 115)**

Apart from asserting Allah's absolute power, it strikes at the fallacious notion of some sacred direction worship. One may pray to Allah in any direction, as He is omnipresent. Some communities in the past sanctified certain directions, taking these as God's abode. As Allah is above and beyond time-place fixities, He clarifies that His command prevails everywhere and He is not confined to any particular direction. Allah declares that virtue lies in true faith and helping those in need, not in turning our faces to east or west. (The Quran 2:177) When Muslims pray, they face

Kabah in Makkah and from all parts of the world, they approach Kabah from all directions.

Allah does not give importance to rituals. He takes into consideration our sincere faith in Him as the one true God and our efforts towards the well-being of everyone around us—our family and friends, community, country and humanity at large.

Points to ponder

- The Quran remarks that it hardly matters which direction we face while worshipping. Rather than a mere, hollow form, Allah takes into account the spiritual content of our devotion to Him. Since He is omnipresent we may approach Him anywhere.
- Allah transcends spatio-temporal limits. Confining Him upwards in the Heavens or to His throne alone smacks of anthropomorphism which Islam denounces.

Chapter 209

Proceedings on the Day of Judgement

In the Quranic passage below, we are introduced to the actual proceedings on the Day of Judgement. At the end of time, at Allah's command, Israfeel, an angel will blow the trumpet causing everyone to die and destroying the present order. As it gets blown soon for the second time, Allah will revive all the dead, from day one to the last day. All of us will gather in the grand assembly. The next steps of Allah's reckoning are detailed in the passage:

> **Allah will question the people to whom the Messengers were sent. He will also question the Messengers. Then He will declare everything, based on knowledge. For He is never away from them. On that Day (of Judgement) there will be perfect weighing. Those whose scales are heavy will achieve success. And those whose scales are light, they will be losers. For they used to deny Allah's signs.**
>
> **(Al-Araf 7: 6-9)**

This clarifies Allah's scheme of things. He will ask His prophets about the response of their respective communities to the call to truth. He will then recount our record of deeds and recompense us with perfect justice. Since the seventh century, Allah's guidance has been available in its error-free, well-documented form in every language and in every nook and corner of the world. So Allah will ask all of us, though we did not have any of His messengers in our time, about our response to His well-preserved guidance. Since He is all-knowing and has put in place an elaborate, accurate system recording our conduct, He will judge us on that basis. His evaluation of our record of deeds will be transparently fair.

So our fate, our ultimate end is in our own hands. As we profess and practise true faith and good actions we will achieve felicity. Otherwise, eternal perdition awaits us.

Points to ponder

- Allah's scheme of the hereafter is highly systematic and logical. All power would be exercised solely by Allah. Messengers would be present to testify that they had faithfully conveyed Allah's message to their respective communities.
- Transparency and fairness would be the hallmarks of Allah's judgement. A faithful record of our faith and actions and messengers' testimony would be the main evidence for how we are recompensed.

Chapter 210

Allah's Promise to the Pious

Out of His limitless magnanimity, Allah has promised lavish reward for those who profess and practise faith and good. He is so generous to them that He has designated them as inheritors of paradise. It is His guidance alone which helps us steadily follow His way. Strikingly enough, He is highly appreciative and rewards us well even for nominally good actions. Since He is all-just and ever-true to His word. He has arranged for excellent hospitality for the pious:

> **As to those who believe and do good, Allah will admit them to the Gardens beneath which rivers flow. They will live there forever. Allah's promise is true. Whose word is truer than Allah's?**
>
> **(Al-Nisa 4: 122)**

Paradise awaits us, thanks to Allah's mercy and compassion, provided we abide by His commands in our lifetime. His promise is bound to come true. It is such an inspiration and solace to note His promise of paradise.

Almighty Allah is extremely kind and nice to His servants. After having created us out of His measureless mercy, He has informed us what pleases and enrages Him. For communicating His guidance, He has sent down His book and His final messenger, Prophet Muhammad (peace be upon him).

The ways of piety and evil stand distinct from each other. Moreover, Allah's signs in Nature and our own conscience deep down in our being constantly show us the way to Him. If we act on reason, we will reach the conclusion that Islam is the only natural way to reach Allah.

Divine guidance is for everyone, of all time and place. It is up to us to enlist ourselves among the fortunate ones who will get His reward. Since Allah never deviates from His word, His promise is bound to come true for each one of us.

Points to ponder

- Allah is so generous and large hearted that He has ensured our eternal felicity in the hereafter for a few good actions which we perform in this world. We cannot adequately thank such a highly appreciative patron.
- At one level, believers are entitled to such lavish rewards because they believed in Allah the unseen. Moreover, through history, forces of evil that glamourise materialism and actively promote Godlessness have flourished. In our time, celebrity syndrome, atheism or, at least, indifference towards religions have been rampant. Against such odds, the pious adhere to the straight path, resisting all temptations and distractions resolutely.

Chapter 211

The Way to Allah

The way to Allah calls for utmost devotion and sincerity of purpose. Moreover, it represents an amalgam of sound faith conforming to the Quran and the Prophet Muhammad's way (Sunnah) and excellent conduct. Unwavering commitment to and conviction in the oneness of Allah (tawheed) crowns their conduct. They stand out for fulfilling their obligation to Allah and fellow human beings. Apart from being obedient and kind to their parents who are very particular about Islamic upbringing of their children, considerate to neighbours, the weaker sections of society and orphans—their life is marked by revulsion to sin and evil and by simplicity, self-abnegation and contentment.

> **Say: "My Prayer, my acts of worship and my living and my dying are for Allah alone, the Lord of the universe. He does not have any partner. Thus I am commanded. And I am the first of those who submit themselves to Allah."**
>
> **(Al-Anam 6: 162-163)**

Devotion and sincerity should be the hallmark of our relationship with Allah. Actually, our whole life should be bound by our obedience and commitment to Him.

The above Quranic passage projects the ideal response of a sincere, believing servant of Allah. Full of humility and servitude, we should pledge our oath of allegiance to Him, and assure Him that we will do all we can for obeying, rather devoting ourselves—heart and soul—to win His pleasure. We should uphold His uniqueness and absolute power.

Allah's commands are forthright, without any ambiguity. We have to execute these with utmost sincerity and diligence. As His creatures, it is befitting for us to surrender to Him in all humility. Gracefully and mercifully, He has promised immense rewards to us.

Points to ponder

- The way to Allah is studded with championing truth and justice. Believers make no compromise regarding these.
- They consistently pursue Allah's ways, rejecting all other paths and do not care about any criticism against them by evil-minded persons.

Chapter 212

Norms of Invoking Allah

Generously enough, Allah has encouraged us to approach Him as and when we need His help, guidance and support. He has assured us that He always listens to our supplications and responds to us in the way He deems best. Obviously, He does not instantly grant in each instance what we seek for reasons beyond our comprehension. Even if our supplications are not answered, He would compensate us in this life or the next. In the passage below, He guides us how we should invoke Him:

> **Call upon your Lord with humility and in private. He does not love those who cross the limits. Do not spread mischief on the earth after it has been set in order. Call upon Allah with fear and hope. Allah's mercy is for those who do good.**
>
> **(Al-Araf 7: 55-56)**

We are instructed here how to pray to Allah. Both congregational prayer in mosques and invocation to Him privately, preferably in the small hours of the night are equally commendable. The above directive points to our duties. As Allah's creatures who are totally dependent on Him for everything, we should pray to Him humbly. Any violation of His commands should not even cross our mind. He is very heedful about maintaining a peaceful, cordial social order. It is in our interest that evil does not have any place in our social fabric. Otherwise, it will make our own life hellish, without harming Allah in any way.

Allah is not a revengeful entity, looking for an excuse to inflict His scourge upon us. He promises mercy, and reward for us if we lead a pious life marked by prayers and obedience to His commands. Allah is our loving well-wisher.

Points to ponder

- The opening Surah in the Quran, Al-Fatihah, which is recited in every cycle (rakah) of prayer, illustrates best how to address Allah and what to seek. Our invocation should reflect our subservience to and glorification of Him. More importantly, it should be characterised by our sincerity, fervour and devotion to Him.
- Supplications to Allah are the most effective means for connecting us to our most affectionate and most caring lord. We may recite the supplications recommended by the Prophet Muhammad (peace be upon him) and plead for anything sought by us from the depths of our heart.

Chapter 213

Never Forget Allah

Islam aims at infusing Allah-awareness into Muslims. It does not expect them to renounce life and be engaged in acts of devotional worship all the time. On the contrary, the Quran repeatedly exhorts us to explore and harness the forces of nature, to develop a critical faculty of inquiry and to work for the benefit of humanity. However, our belief in Allah, our Lord to whom we are accountable for all we say and do, should always permeate our heart and mind. The following verse asks us to develop our Allah-awareness:

> **O believers, fear Allah. Let everyone consider what he sends forward for the Hereafter. Fear Allah. Allah is aware of your actions. Do not be like those who forgot Allah. Allah made them forget their souls. They were evil people.**
>
> **(Al-Hashr 59: 18-19)**

This is valuable advice for us: our life and all actions should be Allah-centred. Those given to materialism and worldliness are liable to neglect Him. We are warned against this attitude—it would spell doom for us.

Allah-awareness is the key to our success. If this permeates our heart and mind, we are not liable to go astray. As Allah is all-knowing, all-seeing, He watches all of our actions. The earlier communities who were ravaged by divine penalty were guilty of having disregarded Him. They, like many of us, were lured by the Godless way of life which lets us satiate our unbridled, base desires.

We must abstain from such recklessness and lead life in accordance with Allah's directives. In this alone lies our happiness in both this and the next world.

Points to ponder

- Materialism is liable to engrossing us. That is why Allah constantly reminds us to set our eyes on the purpose of our life and our ultimate return to Allah for Judgement.
- A sense of Allah-awareness imbues us with self-confidence and tranquillity. We feel assured of Allah's protection and care. This goes a long way in our coping with crises.

Chapter 214

Let Us Thank Allah

It is common sense to thank our benefactor and patron. So in the case of Allah Who has bestowed everything on us, we cannot ever adequately thank Him. Yet we should try our level best to express our praise and gratitude for Him. We are too weak and helpless to accomplish anything on our own. Allah alone enables us to do anything. His bounties are so unique and numerous that He deserves accolades from the depths of our being:

> **Every good thing you have is from Allah. When any hurt touches you, you call Him. When He removes the hurt from you, some of you take partners with Him. They do not thank Him for what He has given them. So enjoy briefly. Soon you will know the truth.**
>
> **(Al-Nahl 16: 53-55)**

It portrays the mindset of ungrateful people. We may abuse our free will in this world. But we will have to pay very dearly for our misconduct. Let us devote ourselves to Allah and thank Him for our better prospects in the next life. It portrays the conduct of ungrateful persons. They turn a blind eye to the enormous favours done to them by Allah. Illness, some loss or the death of near and dear ones are part of the test and trial ordained by Allah for us. As sincere, discerning servants of Allah, put up with some ordeal while reposing faith in Him. He may grant us relief in this world or compensate for it in the next life.

So we should act with resilience and perseverance. As human beings, without any real power, we are liable to suffer some loss. Our response should be its gracious acceptance, with prayers for ease and compensation. This alone will and can grant us solace. We cannot fight against our fate. We should repose unflinching faith in the most compassionate, most merciful Allah.

Points to ponder

- Allah places a premium on the virtue of expressing gratitude. This trait instils into us humility, positivity and concern for fellow human beings. Thanking Allah profusely blesses us with psychological and spiritual bliss.
- Allah is so keen on developing this virtue that in another Quranic verse He asks us to thank Him as well as our parents. A relationship built on thanksgiving is enviably durable and mutually rewarding.

Chapter 215

Servants of Allah

Everything in the universe is in servitude to almighty Allah. The colossal celestial bodies do not and cannot deviate even an inch from Allah's laws to which they are bound. We can excel with these and even the holy angels, if we choose to serve and worship Allah. This would bring felicity to us in both the worlds, particularly in the next life as we would be eternally blessed with all the joys imaginable. Some traits of Allah's servants are listed in the following passage:

> **It is Allah Who has made day and night, which follow each other. This is a sign for him who wants to take a lesson or to thank Him. The servants of the Most Compassionate One walk on earth in humility. When the ignorant persons address them, they say: "Peace." They spend the night prostrating and standing before their Lord in prayer. They pray. "O our Lord, keep away from us the punishment of Hell. Its punishment is total destruction." Hell is indeed an evil end and an evil resting place.**
>
> **(Al-Furqan 25: 63-66)**

This presents before us the role model of those whom Allah loves. They stand out for their humility, their single-minded devotion to Allah and their fervent invocation to Him for protection against hellfire. Apart from engaging in prayer, invoking Allah's help and glorifying Him, they reflect also on Allah's signs for strengthening their faith and devotion to Allah. The alternation of day and night is adduced above as one of the numerous marvels brought into being by Allah. It is nothing short of a miracle how smoothly and effortlessly Allah merges night into day and day into night. The two stand poles apart in their features and each of the two is of immense benefits to us.

As dedicated servants of Allah, also seek Allah's protection against horrible Hell. Only Allah, our guardian and protector, can save us against it.

Points to ponder

- Servants of Allah stand out for their utmost devotion to Allah, unwavering adherence to His way and conscientious fulfilment of obligations to Allah and fellow human beings, specifically their family.
- They are remarkable also for their shunning any sin out of their deep-seated Allah-awareness and their fear of answerability on the Day of Judgement.

Chapter 216

Allah's Favourites

It is the highest privilege imaginable for us to be reckoned among Allah's favourites. Allah the most compassionate has kindly set out the criteria, fulfilling which we can earn proximity with Him. This exalted rank would fetch us unthinkable rewards, particularly in the next life. Amazingly enough, Allah does not specifically mention only His devout worshippers as worthy of winning His pleasure. Ordinary Muslims leading life in accordance with His guidance while being engaged in their professional career would also be considered. Some traits of His favourites are described in the following passage:

> **They spend yet they neither waste nor act as misers. They follow the middle path. They do not call on any god besides Allah. Nor do they kill any whom Allah has forbidden, except with justice. They do not have sex outside marriage. He who does so will face its punishment. His punishment will be double on the Day of Judgement. He will live there in humiliation. However, if he repents, believes and does good, Allah will replace his sins with good actions. Allah is Most Forgiving, Most Merciful. He who repents, believes and does good, he turns to Allah in a true way.**
>
> **(Al-Furqan 25: 67-71)**

This is how Allah will deal with us on the Day of Judgement. What is best is that the doors of repentance are wide open for us. Allah is most merciful, all-forgiving and will greet His sincere servants. Believers stand out for their moderation. In money matters they are neither misers nor squanderers. They realise that they are only a trustee of the money granted to them by Allah. On the Day of Judgement, they will have to render a thorough account of their actions. Allah will reward or punish us with reference to our record of deeds. Polytheism, killing and sex outside marriage are some of the major sins which will incur Allah's stringent punishment.

It is so gratifying that Allah promises forgiveness, even for grave sins, if we repent sincerely and never indulge in these again. We must praise and glorify such a compassionate and affectionate lord.

Points to ponder

- Among Allah's favourites are those who are successful in striking a balance between their sound faith and good conduct. They are not given to any extremism: renunciation of life or finding no time at all to connect with their Lord, Master for their spiritual reinvigoration.
- Allah loves those who lavishly give to charity. Prophet Muhammad (peace be upon him) would advise his companion to spend in Allah's way all that was excess of their needs, including those of their family.

Chapter 217

Allah's Messengers for Everyone

For apprising humankind of His guidance, which is pivotal to their success in this and the next life, Allah sent down a series of His messengers since time immemorial upto 633 CE, the Prophet Muhammad (peace be upon him) being His final messenger who carried out this mission in and around Arabia from 610 CE to 633 CE. His demise marked the end of messengrership. Allah's final guidance was preserved in its pristine purity for all time and place. The Bible mentions hundreds of prophets down the millennia. We note the appearance of sages in other non-Biblical communities in every part of the world. They may originally have been Allah's messengers who are now mistaken for His incarnations or semi-gods. The series of messengers and their function are described in this verse:

> **Allah sent a Messenger to every community who talked to them in their own language. This was in order to explain (Allah's commands) to them clearly.**
>
> **(Ibrahim 14: 4)**

Out of His affection and concern for humankind Allah sent down many prophets in all time and place. They explained divine guidance in their own language to their respective communities. Allah's system of guidance is simple and direct. It is up to us to derive benefits from it. The series of Allah's messengers ended with the Prophet Muhammad (peace be upon him). As Allah's final, latest guidance, the Quran and the Prophet's detailed role model are accessible to everyone, and with recent advancements in technology it is easier to study and decipher Allah's signs in Nature. The divine guidance preserved in its pristine purity suffices for humanity until the last day.

Now the natural way to truth, Islam stands distinct from all other "isms". No one can now plead before Allah that His message had not reached them so they should not be taken to task.

Points to ponder

- Messengers are not to be misconstrued as supra beings, God's incarnation or enjoying godhead. Allah chose pious members of their own community to be His messengers and revealed His guidance.
- Since Allah's final, eternally valid guidance, the Quran and its brilliant exposition by the Prophet Muhammad (peace be upon him) known as Sunnah (his practice and *Hadith* (his sayings) are available to everyone in different languages, the institution of messengership has come to an end.

Chapter 218

Allah Appreciates Our Faith and Good Conduct

Notwithstanding His absolute sovereignty and power, Allah is so loving and clement towards us that He lauds our sound faith and good actions and rewards us amply. He has promised His choicest reward for pious believers in paradise. Moreover, He blesses them with inner peace and tranquillity in this life, though they may be mired in adverse circumstances. He facilitates their noble actions in this life and enables them to work for their deliverance in the hereafter:

> **Those who recite the Book of Allah, establish Prayer, and spend (in Allah's cause) both privately and publicly out of what Allah has given them, they look forward to a trade that will not face any loss. Allah will reward them for their actions and may give them even more out of His grace. He is Most Forgiving, Most Appreciative.**
>
> **(Fatir 35: 29-30)**

Throughout the Quran, Allah encourages us to give in charity. He has promised immense reward for those who help fellow human beings. Far from being indifferent to human beings, Allah closely watches all that we believe and do. For the sake of transparency, objectivity and fairness, He has devised a foolproof recording system which will serve as irrefutable evidence on the Day of Judgement.

To our good fortune, our Lord is most appreciative of our sound beliefs and excellent conduct. He has promised the highest felicity imaginable to those who are devoted to Allah, His book, the Quran, acts of worship and charity. They will be rewarded even more than what is due to them.

Let us celebrate the glory of such a generous and gracious lord, Allah, Who has devised best possible measures for promoting good and happiness in this world. By disobeying Him, we have made our life miserable and agonising.

Points to ponder

- Of the many good actions, Allah is mightily pleased with our charity. Apart from relieving to some extent, the plight of the underprivileged, it reinforces the social fabric and curbs the dire consequences of a sense of deprivation.
- Charity provides us the "feel-good" factors. More importantly, it contributes to acquiring Allah's pleasure which would be our only bulwark on the Day of Judgement when everyone would be struck with panic and dread. We would then look forward to His compassion and forgiveness.

Chapter 219

The Unbeliever's Plight on the Day of Judgement

In its exposition of the hereafter which is quite extensive in the Quran and Hadith, unbelievers have been clearly forewarned against their intolerable ordeal on the Day of Judgement. With hellfire staring them in the face, they would be aghast over the loss of their expectations which they had reposed in their false gods and deceptive so-called religious figures. All power would be wielded on the Day of Judgement by Allah alone and their false gods would be the first to disown them. So Satan, the great deceiver, would declare that the evil people had committed wrongs themselves and knowingly, as he had no real authority over them. This would aggravate the unbelievers' agonising remorse and sense of devastating loss:

> **The Unbelievers imagine that they will not be brought back to life. (O Prophet), tell them: "Certainly, by my Lord, you will be surely brought back to life. Then you will be informed about your actions. It is quite easy for Allah." Believe in Allah, His Messenger and the light (the Quran) which He has sent. Allah is aware of your actions.**
>
> **(Al-Taghabun 64: 7-8)**

It explains Allah's retribution system which is easy to understand. It does not have any convoluted notion of the cycle of rebirth, with little chance of salvation. The belief in the hereafter is highly effective in making us Allah-conscious.

It is worth realising that the most forbearing, most compassionate Allah does not seize and punish culprits instantly. He grants all of us a long respite, with ample time and opportunities to mend our ways. He lets the wicked even kill His chosen messengers. So the apparent glamour or flourishing of evil should not alarm or frustrate us. It should not give rise to any doubt about Allah's power and justice. This freedom, though for a very limited period of time, is part of our test.

Soon after their inescapable death, these culprits will taste horrid punishment. They would love to die but death will not be granted to them. They would undergo the eternal plight of life-in-death.

May Allah protect us against His scourge and help us consistently follow the straight way.

Points to ponder

- As unbelievers would stand doomed for their eternal perdition, apart from their painful punishment, the lack of even a ray of hope of absolving themselves would hurt them most.
- In contrast, believers, even when faced with the worst crisis and suffering in this life, always have hope of a bright future and all joys awaiting them. They look forward to reunion with their near and dear ones.

Chapter 220

Allah's Exhortation for Charity

Next to having faith and doing good, Allah exhorts us most to give in charity. Non-Muslim readers of the Quran are struck by its refrain-like directives for helping the poor and the needy, orphans and widows, and taking good care of parents, children, kith and kin, neighbours and even those with whom we have chance meetings. Allah likens charity to giving a good loan to Him! More amazing is His munificent promise to return it manifold in the hereafter. All that we have is from Him alone. Yet for helping the poor and the needy, He seeks a loan from us. This underscores His overflowing love and affection.

> **O believers, spend in Allah's way the good things you have earned and also what Allah has produced for you from the earth. Do not choose for spending any bad things which you yourselves will not accept, or will accept only after overlooking (their defects). Bear in mind that Allah is Self Sufficient, Most Praiseworthy.**
>
> **(Al-Baqarah 2: 267)**

These are valuable pieces of advice regarding charity. Allah does not need anything. For strengthening the social fabric, He asks us to give good quality things in charity, which may please beneficiaries. Throughout Allah's book, the Quran, we are urged to give to charity generously, in private or public, and without expecting anything in return. Islam has institutionalised charity as it has prescribed zakah (2.5% on wealth annually) for all believers, men and women alike. It has also introduced charity as expiation for our lapses, at child birth, prior to Eid and on all celebrations.

Allah is so caring and sensitive about the rights of the underprivileged that He insists that what we give in charity should be of good quality. The Prophet Muhammad (peace be upon him) is on record exhorting Muslims to meet one another with a smiling face, as this too, represents an act of charity. Our needy relatives, neighbours and friends should get our charity on priority. Islam makes no distinction between believers and disbelievers as recipients of charity. This underscores the humane, universal outlook of Islam.

Points to ponder

- Allah makes it absolutely clear that we should give to charity selflessly, only for the sake of Allah. It should not be a ploy for gaining something in return.
- Allah binds us to maintain the self-respect of the beneficiaries of our charity. We should neither disclose their names. Nor should we cause any hurt to their feelings or insult them in any way. We are only custodians, passing on Allah's bounties to them as directed by the real owner.

Chapter 221

Allah's Advice to Us on Spending Money

We believe that as owners of our money we are free to spend it as we wish. Allah, however, removes this common misconception, asserting that we are only its trustee. Allah has bestowed it upon us as part of His test in order to ascertain how we behave regarding money. His advice is it that should be spent prudently; we should meet our own and our family's needs with it, without indulging in extravagance or miserliness. Above all, we should cheerfully share it with the poor and the needy.

> **The example of those who spend their wealth in the way of Allah is that of a grain of corn which grows seven ears, and in each ear there are one hundred grains. Allah grants many times increase to whom He wills. Allah is Limitless, All Knowing.**
>
> **(Al-Baqarah 2: 261)**

This is another forceful Quranic directive for generous charity. Allah has promised manifold reward for our help to our underprivileged brethren and sisters. The analogy for manifold reward for charity underscores Allah's generosity and mercy. As part of His plan for testing us, He has, no doubt, not eliminated poverty, inequality and even evil altogether. These are grim realities of life. He has, nonetheless, devised a mechanism for us which, if implemented honestly and vigorously, lessens and alleviates the misery of the poor. Charity, including the mandatory duty of paying zakah, goes a long way in protecting society against discontent, hostility and class wars. The first Islamic state headed by the Prophet Muhammad (peace be upon him) in seventh-century Arabia, was a robust welfare state, catering adequately to the needs of orphans, widows, the physically challenged and weaker sections of society.

As trustees, not owners, of the resources granted kindly to us by Allah, we should strictly follow our master, Allah's directives about spending lavishly on charity.

Points to ponder

- As indicated in the above-quoted Quranic verse, Allah blesses our charity and will lavishly repay us in the next life.
- We should bear always in mind that Allah would ask us altogether on the Day of Judgement. The Prophet Muhammad (peace be upon him) instructed: "Remember! The first question you would be asked on the Day of Reckoning would be: "how did you spend your youth, money and energy?" This realisation greatly helps us to follow the middle, straight way.

Chapter 222

Allah's Norms for Charity

While giving money in Allah's cause, in view of the emphasis placed by Allah on this noble act, certain norms should be followed. Otherwise, it would render our charity as null and void. The first and foremost point is our sincerity. It should only be for the sake of Allah, without even an iota of desire for name and fame. The Prophet Muhammad (peace be upon him) pressed home the same point figuratively: "You should give charity with one hand in a way that your other hand does not know about it." We should not have any ulterior motive behind our charity:

> **Those who spend their wealth in the way of Allah and do not follow up their charity with a reminder of their favours and do not cause any hurt, they will have their reward with their Lord. There is no fear and grief for them. Kind words and overlooking faults are better than charity followed by causing hurt. Allah is All Sufficient, Most Forbearing.**
>
> **(Al-Baqarah 2: 262-264)**

Allah instructs us in this important norm of charity: not to hurt the self-respect of beneficiaries. Nor should we expect anything in return. Allah alone will reward us for our sincere charity. Allah is very particular about maintaining decency and order in our social life. Not only does He ask us to help the underprivileged, He also advises how to help them without hurting their dignity: not to remind or offend beneficiaries of our charity and not to receive anything in return from them. Allah has promised everlasting reward for our sincere charity in the afterlife.

Significantly enough, Islam clarifies that Allah is independent and, self-sufficient and all-resourceful. He does not demand for Himself any material goods from us. All charity is for those in need. As it will be amply rewarded in the next life, we should donate as much as we can in Allah's cause.

Points to ponder

- We may donate publicly if our announcement is likely to motivate others to give charity.
- We should ensure the self-respect of the beneficiary. Our charity should first reach those who are close to us because we know their plight first-hand. Charity is to be distributed among all, irrespective of their religion. Charity consists also in guiding all, helping people in every way, not always monetarily.

Chapter 223

Wisdom: Allah's Precious Gift to Us

While Allah has bestowed mental faculties on all, He grants wisdom to select ones. As a result, they stand out for their piety and excellent conduct. They are a source of strength, inspiration and support for their family and community. With reflection on the meaning of life, Allah's bounties and signs and study we may gain wisdom even at a young age. Wisdom carries broad connotations. It should not be narrowly construed as one's knack for minting money. It is termed as Allah's huge favour in the following verse:

> **Allah grants wisdom to whom He wills. He who is granted wisdom is granted much good. Only the people of understanding take a lesson.**
>
> **(Al-Baqarah 2: 269)**

It must be clarified at once that wisdom is not a synonym for the highest academic degree or professional skills. Wisdom consists in gaining true knowledge of ourselves, of our Creator, and of the purpose of our life and duties in this world, which will yield success to us in the next world. Let us strive to attain this true variety of wisdom.

The most gracious, most generous Allah has overwhelmed us with the bestowal of numerous bounties upon us. One of His outstanding gifts to us is our intellect. This enables us to think rationally, perceive things in a proper context, reach sound conclusions and thus make this world a better place not only for ourselves but also for humanity at large. Our mental faculty should direct us first to the great questions of being: Who is our Creator? What is His guidance for us? What kind of life should we lead? How to tackle the thorny issue of death? etc.

Allah guides genuine seekers of truth to Himself, enabling them to discover the meaning of life and realise Allah's plan and their role in this world.

We should invoke Allah for granting us wisdom which helps us adhere to the way prescribed by Him.

Points to ponder

- The study of the Quran, complemented and supplemented with reading the Quran interpretation (*tafsir*) and wisdom literature, including literary masterpieces in various languages, contributes to accumulating wisdom.
- A careful observation of others' behaviour, both pleasing and delinquent, is another effective means for developing discernment and maturity.

Chapter 224

No Support for Us on the Day of Judgement

Allah has provided sufficient details about the Day of Judgement. He has made it absolutely clear time and again that our credentials in this world, no matter how impressive these might be, would be of no avail in the hereafter. We know it too well that at death we leave behind all that we possess. In Allah's fair and transparent reckoning only our faith in Him and our good actions would carry weight. Even messengers, saints and family members, would be totally helpless as we would face Allah's interrogation. His judgment based purely on merit would be final.

> **The Day of Judgement is the appointed time for all. On that Day one's friend will be of no use to them. Nor will they get any help, except those on whom Allah may have mercy. He is Almighty, Most Merciful.**
>
> **(Al-Dukhan 44: 40-42)**

It is a categorical declaration about the Day of Judgement. No worldly tie, status or consideration will be of any worth at that time. One's family and friends will be totally helpless and lost in their own misery. We should strive for only Allah's mercy for our deliverance.

In this transient world we lead our lives, with much help and support from everyone around us, particularly our parents and children. Our social contacts go a long way in securing many good opportunities for our success. This networking is, however, ephemeral. As we die, each one of us will have to bear the consequences of our faith or its lack, and actions, be these good or evil. Even Allah's messengers will not be in a position to plead on our behalf without Allah's permission. Allah alone will judge and reward or punish us, without consideration for our social status in this world.

We should imbibe well the truth about our accountability on the Day of Judgement. This is essential for our success in the afterlife. Otherwise we will be damned forever.

Points to ponder

- Since the life in the hereafter would be eternal and any reprieve would be dependent wholly on Allah's mercy, we should devote ourselves to Him.
- All of us have a support system in this life that rescues us. However, the moment we die, no one can benefit us in any way. Only our faith and conduct would determine our fate. We should pay more attention to it.

Chapter 225

Social Norms Prescribed by Allah

Out of His vast mercy and affection for humanity, Allah has laid down in His book an elaborate code of conduct for forging, maintaining and strengthening social relations. The Prophet Muhammad (peace be upon him) acted on the same and hence we should emulate him. These norms contribute to a balanced, cordial social order which makes life happy and peaceful. These directives instruct us how to behave with our parents, children, relatives, neighbours, friends and the broader community. The following verse forbids bad manners which poison our social life:

> **O believers, let not some men among you laugh at others. It may be that they are better. Let not some women among you laugh at others. It may be that they are better. Do not defame one another. Do not taunt one another by (offensive) nick names. After having faith it is bad to commit any sin. Those who do not repent are wrongdoers.**
>
> **(Al-Hujurat 49: 11)**

Allah asks us to construct a cordial, empathetic social order, free from such evils as offending, defaming or taunting fellow human beings. He brands these offences to be discordant with faith. The all-caring, the most graceful Allah has laid down an extensive code of socio-moral conduct for believers. He expects believers to lead a purposive, pious life—free from social evils which cause discord and shatter the social and moral fabric.

Backbiting, malicious gossiping and offensive chatting are fairly common in our everyday life, committed by men and women alike. Allah, on the contrary, asks us to lead a pious life, characterised by love, affection and concern for all those around us. The above directives seek to strengthen the socio-moral order. It is unthinkable that believers, who have pledged their allegiance to Allah and the Prophet (peace be upon him) may indulge in any sin, particularly misbehavior with other human beings who deserve respect as Allah's creatures.

Points to ponder

- Allah accords equal importance to both: the obligations due to Him and to fellow human beings. If we commit any lapse regarding these, on the Day of Judgement He may forgive our non-performance of duty. However, unless a victim of our wrongdoing pardons us, He would not condone our wrong.
- Allah's exhortations about social relations accentuate the ideals of human fraternity and unity. No one should be looked down upon and all should be helped and supported.

Chapter 226

Allah Forbids Backbiting

Backbiting is a highly common yet horrendous social evil. It gives rise to souring relations and hostility and hatred which, at times, have ghastly consequences. We all are bound by social links and have to interact with others at numerous levels. All of us are not angels or saints and have our human failings and weaknesses. We should, however, adapt to these. Speaking ill of someone badly hurts the person concerned and he repays it in the same coin, which opens the floodgates for further vices, even violence. For our welfare Allah forbids it explicitly in the following verse:

> **O believers, avoid suspicion as much as possible. For suspicion in some cases is a sin. Do not spy on or backbite against one another. Would any of you like to eat the flesh of his dead brother? No, you would surely hate it. Fear Allah. He accepts repentance and is Most Merciful.**
>
> **(Al-Hujurat 49: 12)**

This is another emphatic directive from Allah to shun despising and backbiting people. He employs a highly evocative imagery in likening backbiting to a loathsome act like eating the flesh of one's dead brother. Allah has imparted extensive advice about forging and developing friendly social relations. These valuable pieces of advice are in our own interest. Since mutual distrust, backbiting and slandering poison the social fabric and give rise to a host of menacing problems (feud, fighting, and even violence and bloodshed), Allah nips it in the bud. As our Creator and thoroughly familiar with our response system and instincts, He employs psychological strategies for deterring us against these social evils, especially backbiting. If we momentarily lose self-control and commit a lapse, we should repent our mistake at the earliest and turn to Allah in sincere repentance. Being most merciful and most compassionate, He may forgive us.

Leading a pious, peaceful life is in our own best interest. Then we can focus on constructive, positive work.

Points to ponder

- Allah employs a very telling and evocative simile for instilling into us revulsion against the reprehensible vice of backbiting—He likens it to eating the flesh of one's deceased brother.
- While speaking ill of someone is forbidden, when someone's credentials are checked, particularly for entering into a business transaction or matrimonial alliance, Allah instructs us to give a truthful opinion, even though it may entail adverse comments. This is to ensure greater good and protect one against loss.

Chapter 227

Allah's Justice System

Like any other dispensation of Allah, His justice system is perfect. Some persons feel perplexed, rather disturbed over the rampant injustice and wanton wrongdoings in this world and question Allah's inaction or even His existence. Were Allah to seize us instantly for every wrong committed by us, it would defeat the very purpose of His creation of this world for our test and trial. It is part of His justice system that He grants equal opportunities to everyone, including the wicked. However, at the end of time, He would strictly exact justice:

> **Allah will set up perfect scales on the Day of Judgement. No one will be wronged at all. If one has done something equal to the weight of a mustard grain, He will take it into account. He is enough to take account.**
>
> **(Al-Anbiya 21: 47)**

Fairness is an outstanding attribute of Allah. It will be manifest at its sharpest on the Day of Judgement when He will recompense us with perfect justice. Allah's perfection is reflected amply in His justice. In providing sustenance and other bounties, including physical and mental faculties, Allah makes no distinction between believers and those who openly oppose and mock Him. His forbearance lets the latter even prosper.

However, He will apply exacting standards of justice in dealing with us on the Day of Judgement. In the face of this incontrovertible evidence about disbelief and evil actions, the culprits would not be able to contest, or refute the evidence. For their deliberate lifelong intransigence and their disregard for the divine guidance available to them, they would be severely punished for ever. On the contrary, Allah being the most appreciative would grant the choicest reward to those who do good.

We should salute such a magnificent and generous lord, Allah.

Points to ponder

- In Islam, this and the next life are inextricably linked. The universal law of cause and effect is at work. If we embrace faith and do good, we would enjoy emotional and spiritual bliss in this life and eternal rewards in the next.
- Allah's justice system stands out for its fairness and transparency. He would reward and punish us on the basis of our own record of deeds. Moreover, no one would be able to influence His judgement in any degree.

Chapter 228

Allah Constantly Tests Us

Our life is a constant test. Numerous, varied situations and conditions evaluate our mettle. One of Allah's fairly common tests is our financial condition. He places us in both prosperity and adversity. Both of these conditions are equally tough. If we do not possess Allah-awareness, we are more likely to go astray. Affluence breeds arrogance and apathy towards the deserving people. Poverty impels one to degrade oneself and commit unlawful acts for survival. Allah speaks of "good and bad times" as a test for us in this verse:

> **Allah divided them into various communities on earth. Some of them were pious while others were not. He tested them with both good and bad times so that they may turn to Him.**
>
> **(Al-Araf 7: 168)**

It gives us some idea of Allah's plan for testing us. Both prosperity and adversity for us are part of our trial. These should not be misconstrued as His favour or displeasure. He will adjudge us according to our conduct, irrespective of our financial condition. The natural division of human beings into tribes and nations is inconsequential. Allah is not concerned with our appearance or markers of caste, colour, language or ethnicity. What concerns Him is the choice we make—opting for belief and piety or go astray. To ascertain our mettle He subjects us to adversity and prosperity. Our miserable circumstances should not turn us into skeptics, distrusting Allah's mercy and justice. By the same token, prosperity should not make us complacent and arrogant, assuming that we have got everything by dint of our own merit and hard work.

We should devote ourselves to our Lord, regardless of our good or bad times and set our eyes on winning His pleasure in all circumstances.

Points to ponder

- Allah's test mechanism is so tough that His beloved final messenger Prophet Muhammad (peace be upon him) had to undergo all sorts of suffering: he was an orphan, his mother died when he was only 6 years old; he faced horrible persecution at the hands of his own tribe, Quraysh, for 13 years, including three years of long rigorous social and economic boycott; his exile to Madina, 450 kms away from his hometown, and battles thrust upon him by unbelievers.
- Allah has promised immense rewards for us if we rise to the occasion and keep following His straight way.

Chapter 229

Loss for Unbelievers in the Hereafter

As Allah is all-just and the fairest master, He has clearly explained what pleases and displeases Him. He would not act arbitrarily or whimsically in rewarding or punishing us on the Day of Judgement. Since He is our Creator, He knows best our psyche and thought patterns. Our actions are governed by their value: benefit or loss. We naturally opt for the former and discard the latter. Accordingly, throughout the Quran, Allah has made it absolutely clear to us that if we do not follow His way, we would end up as losers in the eternal hereafter:

> **Allah is Most Glorious, the True King. There is no god besides Him. He is the Lord of the honourable throne. He who calls another god besides Allah, without any authority, his account will be taken by his Lord. The Unbelievers never get success.**
>
> **(Al-Muminun 23: 116-117)**

Allah is the truth. The brief respite granted by Him to disbelievers should not blind them to the impending reality: their death and answerability to Allah. Allah's absolute power and judgement in the hereafter are undeniable realities. Numerous signs both in ourselves and around us testify to His lordship. Given this, disbelievers have been following a self-destructive path. No creature can obviously escape their Creator Who alone reigns supreme in the universe.

There is nothing logical or plausible to suggest the plurality or absence of God. Death and the Day of Judgement are imminent. Disbelievers may enjoy some benefits in this world as granted by the most forbearing and most gracious Allah. However, they would be interrogated and punished in the Hereafter.

May Allah grant us the strength to revere Him as the only true king of the universe. May He shower His mercy upon us.

Points to ponder

- Besides horrible physical agony in Hell, unbelievers would feel further tormented over the missed opportunity. Remorse would haunt them badly. They would see believers thriving in the hereafter whom they would dismiss scornfully.
- Worse, they would face eternal punishment, with no hope of redemption. Despair would aggravate their plight. It is high time we reorient ourselves to Allah's way.

Chapter 230

Attaining Allah's Pleasure

Our success in both the worlds depends on us earning Allah's pleasure. We can gain it. This does not call for any onerous, arduous, regimented spiritual excises or renouncing life. While leading our routine life, no matter how we earn bread lawfully, we can draw proximity with Him. It is perhaps needless to add that it is the highest felicity imaginable for us. Our success in the hereafter would be eternally joyful life, with every bounty at our disposal. The adherence to Allah's ways is stressed in this verse:

> **One who turns fully to Allạh and lives piously holds the firmest handle. With Allah rests the decision of all affairs.**
>
> **(Luqman 31: 22)**

Allah assures us of His reward to us if we live in obedience to Him. As all power rests with Him alone, He will reward us amply for our faith in Him and good actions. The key to our success lies in our recognition of Allah's excellent attributes, specifically as our lord, master and provider. As we owe everything to Him, we should serve and worship only Him. Moreover, since He is the master of the Day of Judgement, realise that His pleasure and mercy alone can help us achieve deliverance. This calls for our total devotion to Him and leading life in accordance with His directives, available to us in the Quran and the Prophet

Muhammad's teachings. This guarantees our eternal success and happiness in the afterlife.

Points to ponder

- The way to securing Allah's pleasure is simple and practical: to profess and practise faith and good deeds. This itself would lead to shunning evil.
- The details of the straight way prescribed by Allah are easily accessible in the Quran and the Prophet Muhammad's sayings, Hadith, which are available in translation in English and other world languages. We cannot thus plead our ignorance of truth and its inaccessibility on the Day of Judgement.

Chapter 231

Allah's Recompense for Unbelievers

Allah has made the rules of the game patently clear. He alone is the master, creator, sustainer and lord of the universe Who has created the world with a definite purpose: to test us if we obey Him, the unseen. He has prescribed the straight way, recorded in even its minute details in the Quran and the Prophet Muhammad's exemplary life and sayings. He has invested us with free will and necessary means for leading life. If we deliberately and maliciously choose to reject Him, we stand doomed for eternal perdition in the next life. It does not betray any injustice or bias towards believers, as is clarified in this verse:

> **(O Prophet), do not be sad about him who disbelieves. All of them have to return to Allah. He will then inform them what they used to do. Allah knows even the secrets of the hearts. He has allowed them to enjoy life for a while. He will then drive them to a harsh punishment.**
>
> **(Luqman 31: 23-24)**

The all-powerful, all-wise Allah has this scheme of things for those who refuse to accept Him. He lets them enjoy this life. However, they would face the consequences of their disbelief in the next life. The Prophet Muhammad (peace be upon him) sent down by Allah as mercy unto humanity, felt distressed to note the rejection of Allah by some of his own close relatives and his tribe, Quraysh. He knew well that their disbelief would land them in eternal hellfire. Allah comforts him by saying that guidance rests solely with Him. As He notes some good in us, He enables us to profess and practise true faith and good actions. Disbelievers would be confronted by dire consequences of their evil conduct. Allah would punish them on the basis of their record of deeds.

The all-knowing Allah has been magnanimous enough to let them enjoy their brief life. He would recompense everyone fairly.

Points to ponder

- The most forbearing Allah keeps sustaining even staunch atheists and unbelievers and does not annihilate them here and now for their defiance of Him. However, justice demands exemplary punishment for them which would be their fate in the next world.
- In view of His transparently clear plan regarding our reward and punishment in the next life, the unbelievers' perdition should not come as a surprise. Rather, it reinforces Allah as the all-just, most magnanimous and most forbearing lord.

Chapter 232

Variety in Allah's Creation

Allah's creation stands out for its many features: its grandeur and splendour, beauty and glory, beneficence and multipurpose dimensions, wide range and colourfulness. Take human beings as an example. Presently there are billions while many billions passed away at an earlier date. Yet each human being is unique in his complexion, hair, colour of the eye, physique, shape, size, features, voice, pace, mental and physical faculties, taste, outlook, thought pattern, likes and dislikes, clothes, food habits, social relations, hobbies, addictions, accomplishments, dreams, financial condition, DNA and biometrics, to mention only a few. Only almighty Allah could bring about such mind-blowing variety, of which some instances are identified in this verse:

> **Do you not consider this—how Allah sends water from the sky. Then with it He brings out fruits of various colours. In the mountains there are shades of white and red, and of various shades of colours, and also intensely black. Likewise, men, animals and cattle are also of various colours. Among Allah's servants only those gifted with knowledge fear Him. Allah is Almighty, Most Forgiving.**
>
> **(Fatir 35: 27-28)**

Pay attention to another creative wonder of Allah: the amazing variety of colours in His creation. His creative power is boundless. Allah does not employ any philosophical argument or mythological story for introducing and describing Himself. Far from it, He adduces self-evident, clearly visible examples which are as familiar to us today as they were in the seventh century when they were presented first. Variety on account of multiplicity of the colour of mountains, flowers, trees, soil, human complexion, animals, birds, insects, sea creatures and other objects of Nature point to the presence and dexterous working of a super designer, fashioner and creator marked by originality, ingenuity and abundance.

Attention is drawn here to the various colours of fruits, produced from the same rainwater and grown from the same soil, and mountains in the same region. Our perception of these marvels should make us all the more Allah-aware and obedient to Him. This would ensure our success in the eternal afterlife.

Points to ponder

- Astronomy and cosmogony represent other superb spectacles of Allah's majesty and creativity. The sheer number and size of galaxies is staggering; between 100 billion and 2 trillion. Most of these are approximately 3,000 to 3,00,000 light years away.
- The variety in the animal, plant and marine worlds are observable to some extent by all. Topography is another amazing facet, with mountains, hills, glaciers, volcanoes, rivers, forests, plains, deserts, plateau, valleys, landscape and sky scape.

Chapter 233

Allah Is Self-Subsisting

Apart from His omnipresence, omnipotence and omniscience, another highly astounding attribute of Allah is His being eternal, without a beginning or end! He is entirely self-subsisting, not dependent on anything or anyone in any sense. This is something unique to Him and befits the supreme lord. Had He been made of something, it would have called for a maker who would have been, of course, superior to Him. Moreover, if He was created of some substance, it could decay, which is something improbable for someone as perfect as the lord. Allah's eternalness is stated in the following verse:

> **Whoever is on earth will die. Only the face of your Lord will remain forever. Allah is full of glory and honour.**
>
> **(Al-Rahman 55: 26-27)**

Mortality or death is an undeniable fact. Allah alone is eternal and self-subsisting. To Him we should turn humbly for our deliverance. Decline and death are unmissable pointers to our helplessness and dependence on Allah for our emotional and spiritual health and tranquility. The reality of death should not make us feel dejected, or despondent. Nor should we mistakenly construe it as the end of our being. Allah has clearly explained that while death is ordained for each one of us, it is only a passing stage of the larger phenomenon—the everlasting afterlife. Allah has granted us life in this world in order to examine if we believe in Him, the unseen, with the aid from His numerous signs around us, and His guidance available in the form of His book, the Quran and His final messenger, the Prophet Muhammad's teachings.

If we respond to the call to truth which is innate in our conscience, Allah would lavishly reward us in the next life. However, if we are lost in the illusory glitter and materialism of this world and neglect or reject truth, we would have to pay very dearly for this: eternal loss and perdition, without any hope of redemption.

Points to ponder

- On little reflection, we realise that Allah's eternalness is not something mysterious, unfathomable. Since He is unique and peerless in every respect, His self-subsistence should not raise brows.
- It is logically essential that the master lord Who has created everything must be everlasting. Only such an entity could take care of such a vast universe, with numerous creatures.

Chapter 234

Allah Would Bestow Felicity on Us

Allah's generosity and grace knows no bounds. Though we are His creatures and owe everything to Him, He has promised felicity in the hereafter to those of us who are devoted to Him. In so doing, He is absolutely fair and objective. All of us who come up to His criteria, regardless of our colour, ethnicity, era or any other label would enjoy the felicity conferred by Him. His criteria basically include: our conformity to His way and our fulfilling obligations to family, community and country:

> **Allah has made the abode of the Hereafter exclusive for those who do not seek glory on earth and do not cause any mischief. The pious will have the best end.**
>
> **(Al-Qasas 28: 83)**

Allah aims to inculcate humility and piety in us. These traits are essential for constructing a happy social order. It is in our own interest to develop these qualities which bring about success in both the worlds. The way to the eternal joys of the next life is neither difficult nor complicated by a maze of rituals, offerings and mythology. On the contrary, it is simple and doable. Allah asks us only to lead a life free from polytheism and evil. He expects us to believe in Him and do good to everyone with whom we come into contact in life—our parents, children, friends, neighbours and members of our community, country and all humanity and all life forms. Humility and piety save us against pride and wrongdoing which lie at the heart of every discord.

Accordingly, Allah has promised the highest reward for those of us who are obedient to Him and pious. Our good conduct would enrich our society and all of us would enjoy a happy life.

Points to ponder

- Allah is so appreciative of the pious that He designates them as "the inheritors of paradise" (Al-Muminun 23:11).
- Allah exalts those who are humble, help fellow human beings and promote and reinforce all that is good. They actively discourage immoral, evil acts and help construct a pious social order which is a blessing for everyone. They create such an ambience that good and virtues thrive and people do not feel inclined towards community evil.

Chapter 235

Allah's Requital

Allah's justice is fair and generous. He watches all we say and do. As part of His grand design He does not force anyone into adopting the straight way. Nor does He compel anyone into going astray. However, He facilitates the path we choose and lets us fulfil our heart's desire. In the Quran, while He urges the Prophet Muhammad (peace be upon him) to carry out vigorously His mission, He cautions him as well that he should not impose faith upon anyone. It should be our own decision to acknowledge Allah's glory and serve Him our level best. Allah spells out the basis of His requital:

> **He who brings a good action will be rewarded with something better. However, those who do evil will be punished only to the extent of their actions.**
>
> **(Al-Qasas 28: 84)**

As Allah is immensely merciful and appreciative, He will reward those who profess and practise sound faith and good actions. We will get much more than what we actually earn on the basis of our faith and good action. However, Allah punishes the guilty only in proportion to their wrongdoing. He is not vindictive or tyrannical.

This asserts Allah's absolute power and control. Since He is all-knowing, He will recompense us perfectly. Notwithstanding His limitless power, His judgement is marked by justice and fairness. Mercy is Allah's outstanding attribute, as is evident from the above promise. The Prophet

Muhammad (peace be upon him) elucidated Allah's abundant mercy thus before his companions: He told them that a mother's love for her child is, no doubt, immense. However, Allah's affection towards His creatures is 100 times more than the proverbial motherly love.

Allah insists on good action. He does not approve ascetism, retiring from life and engaging all the time in worshipping Him. Needless to add, good actions will help construct a better world for us to live in.

Points to ponder

- Allah's reward is not only for devotion to Him. If we help fellow human beings financially or in other ways, we are entitled, thanks to His graciousness, to lavish reward. He has promised His generous hospitality to those who give in charity, privately or publicly.
- His punishment is not out of any vindictiveness on His part. Nor is He biased towards anyone. The rules of the game are unmistakably clear. Those who stray into error, notwithstanding His explicit warnings, would be consigned to eternal punishment.

Chapter 236

Allah's Guidance

We are fortunate enough to have Allah's guidance in its pure unadulterated form: His book, the Quran and His final messenger, Prophet Muhammad's directives are available to all in different languages across the world. Like air, water, food and other basic necessities of life, this elaborate guidance is of immense value. This alone can crown us with success in both the worlds. It is of particular relevance to the hereafter. For our adherence to it alone guarantees our deliverance and eternal happiness in the next life:

> **Allah, there is no god besides Him. He is the Ever Living, Self Subsisting. (O Prophet), Allah has sent down the Book to you in truth. It confirms the earlier Books. Allah also sent down the Torah and the Gospel before this, for the guidance of people before this. He has sent down the criterion (i.e. the Quran to distinguish between truth and error). There is terrible punishment for those who reject the signs of Allah. Allah is Almighty, the Lord of retribution.**
>
> **(Ali Imran 3: 2-4)**

We get a clear picture here of how Allah will deal with us. He has put in place an extensive system for guidance: divine signs in and around ourselves, prophets, and holy books, of which the Quran is the final, latest version valid until the last day. Prior to its corruption, the Bible held this position. If we refuse to follow His guidance, we are doomed for disaster in the next life.

Throughout history, Allah, out of His infinite love and mercy for humanity, sent down His books and messengers to all parts of the world for showing us the straight way. Since 610 CE until today and the last day, the Quran revealed to the Prophet Muhammad (peace be upon him) is the source of guidance for us. It has replaced all the earlier dated and corrupted books. Allah has made an error-free arrangement for the accurate preservation of His final book, the Quran. Apart from its authentic, published form of a book, it is recorded also in the memory of millions of Muslims, men and women alike, known as hafiz (those who have memorised the entire Quran).

If some unfortunate persons reject Allah's precious gift of guidance, they would face its consequences in the next life which is eternal.

Points to ponder

- Throughout history through His enlightening books and messengers, the most compassionate Allah has provided for our guidance so that fair treatment is meted out to us on the Day of Judgment.
- The final, well-preserved guidance from Allah is before all of us in the form of the Quran and the Prophet Muhammad's role model who led his illustrious life in the full light of history. The American scholar, Michael H. Hart acclaims him as the most influential person in history in his book, *The 100: A Ranking Of The Most Influential Persons in History (1978).*

Chapter 237

Allah's Power and Glory

Allah's power and glory is undeniable. We do not have to be a scientist or anatomist to find out His greatness. His signs, manifesting His splendour are scattered all around us. Let us look at our body. It is a super machine on one hand, performing and producing so much and on the other, it is a spiritual entity, abounding in tender feelings and emotions. Allah alone could accomplish such a feat. We see so many super specialists unable to fathom even its working, let alone its creation:

> **Allah's is the kingdom of the heavens and the earth. Allah has power over everything. In the creation of the heavens and the earth and in the alternation of night and day there are signs for people of understanding. They keep remembering Allah—standing, sitting and lying on their backs. They reflect on the creation of the heavens and the earth (saying): "O our Lord, You have not created all this without a purpose. Glory be to You. Save us from the Hellfire. O our Lord, he whom You throw into the Hellfire stands humiliated. There is indeed no helper for wrongdoers."**
>
> **(Ali Imran 3: 189-192)**

As we constantly witness Allah's power and glory, we should celebrate His greatness. The creation reflects a deep purpose, to which we should be alive and discharge our duty as submissive creatures of Allah.

Allah asks us to be mindful of Him all the time. As His loyal servants we should keep Him in our heart and mind, regardless of the posture of our body and the nature of any mundane job in which we are engaged. Likewise, our study of Nature and its resources and our inventions and discoveries should be permeated with our appreciation of His creative power, and His mercy for us, in having provided for us such bounties.

Allah seeks our acknowledgement of His favours to us in order to instill into us humility and a sense of answerability to Him. This contributes to making us better human beings who are conscientious and responsive to fellow human beings.

Points to ponder

- Allah-awareness at all times is the real objective. A particular posture is not essential. While we may be engaged in doing something mundane, we should bear the thought of Allah in our heart and mind.
- Those of us who decode the rationale behind Allah's creation are really fortunate. He has not brought everything into being for sport. There is a purpose behind His creation: we recognise Him, obey Him and thus ensure our eternal felicity.

Chapter 238

Allah Is Not Unjust to Anyone

Being most compassionate, most kind, Allah is all love and affection for everyone. His creation and sustenance for everyone evidences His overflowing concern and care. It is He who instils filial love, marital bliss and friendly affection. His mercy accounts for the perfect functioning of the universe. Equally amazing is His delivery system of provisions for all living beings. It is incredible how animals, birds, underwater creatures and insects have their fill:

> **Neither your desires nor the desires of the people of the Book matter. One who does evil will be punished for it. He will not find for himself any protector or helper, other than Allah. One who does good, male or female, and is a believer will enter Paradise. They will not be wronged at all.**
>
> **(Al-Nisa 4: 123-124)**

It is illustrative of Allah's fair treatment of all human beings. Gender parity is present in Allah's judgment. He will admit the pious, be they men or women, to paradise. Some people erroneously believe that their conformity to their ancestors, saints or earlier books, which have been suppressed by the revelation of the Quran and the advent of the Prophet Muhammad (peace be upon him), would suffice for their deliverance. Allah declares plainly that only our belief in Him as the one true God and good actions carry any weight. Being the best judge and lord of all creatures, He makes no discrimination between men and women, or people of various colours, languages, races and regions. He would recompense everyone fairly.

Let us prove ourselves deserving of His reward which He has promised us out of His overflowing mercy and love for us.

Points to ponder

- Apart from being most merciful, Allah is also the master and ruler of the universe. He enforces order and discipline and tests us in a variety of ways which might appear taxing to us.

- His justice is so perfect that all of us would be fairly recompensed on the Day of Judgement. In rewarding and punishing us He would not wrong anyone in the least. We should praise and glorify such a unique Lord.

Chapter 239

Allah Commands Us to Be Just

Such is Allah's concern for enforcing justice and fairness that even in the heat of Muslims' persecution and oppression at the hands of Makkan unbelievers, the Quran asked the beleaguered Muslims: "O believers, stand up firmly for Allah as witness to justice. Let not the hatred of any people move you away from justice. Do justice. It is closer to piety. Fear Allah. Allah is aware of all that you do." (Al-Maidah 5:8) Accordingly, the Prophet Muhammad (peace be upon him) dealt with Jews in Madina with justice. He declared them as equal partners as members of a single community in the first written constitution of the world, as he headed the nascent Islamic state of Madina. Allah's insistence on professing and practising justice is evident in this verse:

> **O Believers, stand firmly for justice. Testify for the sake of Allah, even if it be against yourselves, your parents or your close relatives, be they rich or poor. Allah is more concerned with their well-being. Do not follow your desires so as to act unjustly. If you twist or turn away (regarding testimony), remember that Allah is aware of all that you do.**
>
> **(Al-Nisa 4: 135)**

As justice ensures peace and happiness in society, Allah lays particular emphasis on it. His command to us to dispense justice to everyone, irrespective of our ties of kinship, underscores His deep concern for justice. In His dealings, He displays perfect justice, without an iota of any partisanship. He is just and asks us to be just and fair in all our dealings. Since we are liable, out of our humanness, to take sides with our near and dear ones, Allah warns us strictly against any unfair practice. As the munificent lord and provider, He would take care of everyone. We should not try to favour our family, friend or anyone to give them an unfair advantage. This is not specific to only legal matters or court proceedings. All of our interactions and speech should be characterised by justice, equity and non-partisanship.

Allah values fairness on our part and would reward us immensely on the Day of Judgement.

Points to ponder

- While emphasising the pivotal importance of justice for us the Prophet Muhammad (peace be upon him) remarked: "A just, fair ruler excels a devout worshipper who spends nights in devotional prayer".
- Justice in Islam is a very wide-ranging, all-inclusive directive. Apart from the legal domain, it should be practised in our interpersonal relations, business and dealings and performance as a professional and a member of our society, community and country.

Chapter 240

Error in Allah's Eyes

As part of His all-inclusive guidance, Allah has identified precisely what constitutes error in His eyes, apart from spelling out the straight way. We are obliged to shun all that He brands as evil. The unbelievers' main error is their wilful disregard for Allah's signs which are littered around us. Their deliberate failure to employ their reason or even common sense to realise the presence and oneness of Allah works to their detriment. They are so lost in the trivia of this world, materialism, pleasures of the flesh and minting money that they have no time or inclination for grasping truth and the purpose of their life:

> **O believers, believe in Allah, His Messenger, the Book that He has revealed to His Messenger, and the Books He sent down before. He who disbelieves in Allah, His angels, His Books, His Messengers and the Last Day, he goes far into error.**
>
> **(Al-Nisa 4: 136)**

Allah spells out the articles of Islamic faith clearly. These are simple, easy to understand and appeal to reason. These present a complete picture of Allah's scheme of things: His guidance and final recompense. In Islam there is nothing convoluted regarding matters of faith. The beliefs are logical and interconnected and provide us with a clear perspective on everything. The Creator and His creation which is all before us; the agency of the palpable, accessible book, the Quran and the human messenger, the Prophet

Muhammad (peace be upon him, 570 CE–633 CE) who lived in the full light of history and whose brilliant life and elucidation of all things Islamic, has been and would be the role model for billions of Muslims in every aspect of our life; the chain of messengers and books reflecting the continuity of Allah's identical message for all time and place, the invisible angels who instantly execute Allah's commands and, above all, the hereafter to which all of us are destined after our death. Allah will decide our fate on the basis of our faith and actions.

Points to ponder

- Since unbelievers reject Allah in the first place, they are unable to appreciate other articles of faith: messengership, the next life and Allah's book. They turn a blind eye to these self-evident truths.
- Worse, they form convoluted, irrational notions of divinity. Credulously enough, they ascribe partners and associates, which puts their god in very poor light. If someone is dependent on others, how can he be perceived as the lord. By definition, God must be perfect and unique.

Chapter 241

Allah Is All-Knowing

Omniscience is a basic prerequisite of godhead. Only the all-knowing God could be the endless marvellous Creator, massive sustainer of all beings, ever-responsive to numerous needs of His billions of creatures and the perfect judge on the Day of Judgement. He knows the past, present and future. His foreknowledge embraces our misconduct, sins, calamities and sufferings in this world. He lets all this happen as a part of His grand scheme, though He does not endorse these. He has devised these as part of His test. Allah's knowledge of even minute details is pressed home in this verse:

> **With Allah are the keys of the Unseen. No one other than He knows the Unseen. He knows all that is on the land and in the sea. Every leaf that falls is in His knowledge. Every grain in the darkness of the earth or anything fresh or dry is recorded in the clear book (of destiny).**
>
> **(Al-Anam 6: 59)**

This is a comprehensive, nay awe-inspiring description of Allah's might and total control over all that exists. Always be mindful of the all-seeing, all-powerful Allah. The Islamic concept of Allah rests mainly on His mercy, knowledge and power. Out of His boundless mercy He sustains billions of life forms and He has been doing so since time immemorial, without diminishing His resources. His knowledge is all-encompassing. The verse refers to even seemingly trivial points about a leaf and a grain. Coupled with His absolute power, He watches everything.

This should make us all the more cautious about Him passing judgement on our faith and actions. Since nothing is beyond His ken of perception, His reckoning would be accurate and absolute. We better prepare ourselves for our inevitable encounter with Him at our death and our fate, which is totally in His hands.

Points to ponder

- Allah projects an awesome description of His godhead. Take His knowledge as an example. Today with the latest skills for intelligence gathering, including night vision, thermographic camera, infrared illumination, etc. and their storage and retrieval systems, we can form some idea of His sweep over vision.
- Allah's perfect knowledge would be at its sharpest as He would judge us on the day of recompense. Nothing big or small would be out of His purview and hence perfect fairness would mark His judgement.

Chapter 242

Allah's Responsiveness to Us

Notwithstanding His majesty and His mastery over billions of galaxies, He is always responsive to us. He watches all of our actions, listens to us and takes good are of us. He welcomes us warmly, as we turn to Him. The Prophet Muhammad (peace be upon him) is on record, having informed people: "When a repentant person approaches Allah, He is immensely pleased." What magnanimity! How reassuring! His omnipotence accounts for His oversight of each one of us. His comforting words shine through this verse:

> **(O Prophet), when My servants ask you about Me, tell them: "I am close to them. I respond to the call of the caller when he calls Me. They should respond to My call, and believe in Me. Perhaps they may be guided."**
>
> **(Al-Baqarah 2: 186)**

We are very fortunate to have such a caring, affectionate lord. He listens to our supplications. He has shown us guidance, following which we may earn His pleasure. Notwithstanding His might and glory which is unimaginable for us, our most merciful, most affectionate lord has an open, direct line of communication with us. Without any clergy or intermediary, ritual or offering, we can reach Him 24x7. Out of His graciousness He listens to our pleas, grants these if He deems these fit for us, and would compensate for these in this or the next world, if in His infinite wisdom He does not accept these. This concept of direct access to the Lord all the time is special to Islam. At another place in the Quran, He declares that He is closer to us than our own jugular vein (The Quran 50:16). He listens to our whisperings and notes the thoughts crossing our mind.

The Islamic concept of Allah is marked by this unique proximity between our lord and us. We should make most of it by winning His pleasure and acting on His directives, which will bring us eternal success in the hereafter.

Points to ponder

- Islam does not admit any intermediary (some incarnation, clergy or saint, etc.) between Allah and us. Each one of us can approach Him directly and He pays us due attention. His care and concern for us are both bewildering and deeply touching.
- The Islamic concept of Allah is remarkably personal. We feel mightily reassured and comforted that He is beside us, particularly when we are in distress. We may not always get immediate relief, for reasons known only to Him, He would definitely compensate us for turning to Him in this world or the next.

Chapter 243

Allah Consigns People to Hell

The Quran carries some dreadful passages, detailing the agonising punishment which would be inflicted on the evil, unbelieving people: raging and ravaging hellfire, highly disgusting food that would choke; such water that would not quench thirst and many other horrible forms of scourge. It is, however, gratifying that each of these descriptions is immediately followed or preceded by an account of the joys of paradise. Hell and paradise are mentioned an amazingly equal number of times in the Quran. This balance is to the fore in the following verses:

> **Allah put inner peace into the hearts of Believers so that they may grow stronger in faith. To Allah belong all the forces of the heavens and the earth. He is All Knowing, the Wisest. He will admit the believing men and women to the gardens (of Paradise) beneath which rivers flow. They will live there. He will remove their sins. With Allah this is great success. He will punish the hypocrite men and women and the polytheistic men and women. For they have evil thoughts about Allah. Misfortune will overtake them. Allah's wrath and curse are upon them. He has prepared Hell for them. What an evil end!**
>
> **(Al-Fath 48: 4-6)**

It illustrates Allah's love and kindness towards believers: firmness of faith, inner peace and happiness and paradise as their eternal abode, with unimaginable joys. The most caring Allah blesses us with peace of mind, tranquility and spiritual serenity, as we sincerely believe in Him and pursue the straight way shown by Him.

On the contrary, if out of ignorance, bigotry and stubbornness, some reject the most merciful Allah's message, His wrath would afflict them, subjecting them to a gruesome plight on the Day of Judgement, followed by eternal damnation. In so doing, He would fulfill the dictates of justices and fair play. For He had graphically conveyed to disbelievers His warning and their disaster in the next life.

Points to ponder

- Since Allah has eloquently forewarned who will enter Hell, He cannot be accused of being tyrannical or callous: He does not derive any pleasure from punishing us.
- Allah is so compassionate that He would reward the pious many more times than what they deserve. In contrast, He would punish the guilty exactly equal to the evil committed. Moreover, out of His boundless mercy He is ever-ready to forgive us, if we turn sincerely to Him and do not indulge in sins again.

Chapter 244

The Way to Paradise

Allah has graciously arranged for paradise, the abode of eternal joys and limitless bounties in the next life. More remarkably, He has specified the way. If we follow it, we can be eligible for dwelling in it for ever. The way consists, in the main, in

- Professing and practising sound beliefs, as spelled out in the Quran and explicated in Hadith (Prophet Muhammad's sayings).
- Good actions by way of fulfilling our obligations and doing good to fellow human beings. Allah places a premium on us if we are kind and engaged in serving our family, community and humanity at large. Patience is stressed as a prerequisite in the following verse for entering paradise:

> **Do you think you will enter Paradise, without Allah testing who among you fought hard and remained patient (in His cause)?**
>
> **(Ali Imran 3: 142)**

The way to paradise is strewn with tests and trials. With our strong faith and good conduct, we may earn a place in paradise. We should develop self-restraint and self-purification in Allah's way. The specific reference to fighting has its historical circumstantial setting. In the early days of Islam, there were only a handful of Muslims who were brutally persecuted. They were killed, dragged on scorching sand and subjected to socio-economic boycott for years. Even when they migrated to a town, Madina, 450 kms away from Makkah, their hometown, the disbelieving Makkans came all the way to Madina to annihilate them. Against this backdrop and for self-defence, Allah allowed Muslims to defend themselves. In the first battle at Badr, a few miles away from Madina, 313 resourceless Muslims were pitted against a well-equipped 1,000-strong army of Makkan disbelievers. Aided by Allah's mercy, Muslims fought valiantly and won this and subsequent battles thrust upon them by disbelievers. However, the above directive stands also in its general, universal sense, urging Muslims to profess and practise self-restraint and perseverance. This would win them Allah's pleasure and entry into paradise.

Points to ponder

- Our ultimate excellent end is in our own hands. As our benefactor and sincere guardian, Allah has instructed us in the acts which would facilitate our entry into paradise.
- Self-restraint is the key to good conduct. We cannot achieve anything without sacrificing what is very dear to us: time, money, energy, comfort, etc. There is Allah's immense reward for self-abnegation.

Chapter 245

Faith and Its Reward by Allah

Allah urges us to embrace faith. This is in our own interest. Faith instils inner peace and strength into us. It impels us to do good and resist all temptation. Life is a constant trial. At every stage we need help and support. Faith enables us to overcome all hurdles and inspires us to undertake even seemingly hard tasks. It proves to be a pillar of resilience and perseverance in every crisis. It constantly comforts us as we realise that we are under the care and protection of the omnipotent, omnipresent and omniscient Lord. Faith accrues to us lavish, everlasting rewards, as promised in this verse:

> **There is forgiveness and big reward for those who fear their Lord, though without seeing Him.**
>
> (Al-Mulk 67: 12)

Faith consists in our belief in Allah, without seeing Him. He has granted us ample intellect to perceive His omnipresence, omnipotence and omniscience in and around ourselves. We will be immensely rewarded for our consciousness of Him, deep in our heart and mind. Allah employs in the Quran simple, easy to understand examples and signs which lead us to recognising Him as the one true God and glorifying and worshipping Him as a token of our gratitude to Him. This quest for truth, of which the doors are open to each one of us, also persuades us of His mercy and love for us, His wisdom in guiding us how to live and how to attain felicity in the next life which is everlasting. A study of Allah's messenger, the Prophet Muhammad's illustrious example and his life-giving teachings is also helpful in attaining true faith. Our belief in Allah inspires and activates us to perform our religious duties and observe the norms laid down by Him. As a result, we discover the meaning and purpose of our life and are consistently engaged in doing good which helps create a better society, a cordial community and a happy country and world.

Points to ponder

- If we are blessed with faith, it provides invaluable consolation when we lose our near and dear ones. In the absence of belief in the afterlife we are inconsolable as we face bereavement.
- Faith has its own reward: inner happiness and tranquillity. Moreover, Allah has promised His choicest reward, for faith in the next life. That would be our only high return premium, as we have to leave behind all that we have when we die.

Chapter 246

Allah Is All-Aware

Such is the sweeping range of Allah's knowledge that He is fully aware not only of all our actions but also of our underlying motives and innermost thoughts. We may conceal our plans, even actions from everyone, including our family and close friends. However, Allah notes even the thoughts crossing our mind. We should therefore be on our guard in all that we say and do. Allah's omniscience is underscored in this verse:

> **It is all the same what you say publicly or privately. Allah knows even the secrets of hearts. Will He not know? It is He Who has created (you). He understands the finest points and is All Aware.**
>
> **(Al-Mulk 67: 13-14)**

Dramatically this question is posed about Allah's knowledge of our actions and their underlying motives. Since He is our Creator, He knows every fibre of our being. His judgement will therefore be perfectly objective. Since Allah is all-knowing, all-powerful, He knows well whatever we do or say, no matter how secretly and privately. More amazingly, He has devised a foolproof recording system of our speech and action, and even our innermost motives, which would be presented on the Day of Judgement as evidence against us. As He is the best judge and most non-partisan, He will reward or punish us in proportion to our faith and actions. Being all-aware, He perceives even our innermost thoughts. However, He will judge us only on our actions, not stray thoughts which sometimes come to mind.

That Allah is all-aware should govern our conduct. This would protect us against falling into error. We will thus have a better report card on the Day of Judgement.

Points to ponder

- Allah's omniscience is a prerequisite for dispensing perfect justice on the Day of Judgement. Without His all-inclusive knowledge He could not reward or punish us. Had He done so, His judgement would have been flawed, something unthinkable of the almighty lord.
- Allah's foreknowledge of everything is not synonymous with His endorsement of all that happens. If we abuse the faculties and resources granted to us by Allah as a part of His trial, He is not responsible for the evil committed by us. His retribution would, nonetheless, be based on His omniscience.

Chapter 247

Allah's Expectations from Us

Allah is not a hard taskmaster, bent on pulverising us. Nor does He forbid us the joys of life, in a balanced way within the limits set by Him. Nor does He compel us into giving all our belongings to Him. He, nonetheless, expects each one of us to use reason, reflect on His signs and abide by His directives which streamline both our individual and collective life. His expectation from us is summed up in this pithy verse:

> **Worship Allah alone and thank (Him)**
>
> **(Al-Zumar 39: 66)**

Islam is a strictly monotheistic religion. It does not have any room, even in the slightest, for any partner, helper or equal of Allah. Even messengers, including Prophet Muhammad (peace be upon him) are Allah's obedient servants and answerable to Him. As His creatures, it is our first and foremost duty to worship and praise Allah. Islam makes no compromise on this cardinal belief that Allah is the one true God Who is the lord, master and provider of all that exists. Only He causes our life and death, loss and gain, and ordains our fate. Again, it is He alone Who would bring us back to life for judgment which He would dispense, to the exclusion of everyone. In Islam, angels, saints or clergy have no place. It is an Allah-centric religion. Intercession for us on the Day of Judgment depends on His will.

As obedient servants of Allah we should serve and thank Him for His numerous favours to us.

Points to ponder

- In Islam, worshipping and thanking Allah has very broad connotations. It does not imply retiring to a prayer mat, with a rosary bead in our hands and uttering some invocations and supplications in Arabic. As long as we carry out routine activities, including work, maintaining family and social relations, eating and drinking and even sleeping with the thought of Allah permeating our heart and mind, we are engaged in serving Him as His devout servants.
- Allah likes most this vocation on our part: praising and thanking Him, as He deserves it the most. Moreover, this induces into us humility, purposiveness and positive thinking, which is good for us and for those around us.

Chapter 248

Unbelievers' Lot on the Day of Judgement

In the long Quranic passage quoted below, the psychological and emotional trauma of unbelievers on the Day of Judgement when the truth would dawn on them, as the hellfire would stare them in the face has been described. Despite having wasted their lifetime, endowed with Allah's faculties and bounties, they would then try to disown clinging to falsehood. Their remorse would be too little and too late. They did not pay heed when they had ample time and opportunity:

> **The Disbelievers prevent others from it (Allah's Message) and they themselves keep away from it. They thus destroy themselves and they do not realize it. If you could see when they will be made to stand before the Hellfire. They will then wish: "Would that we were sent back to the world. This time we will not reject the signs of our Lord. Rather, we will be among the believers." (They will say so because) the truth which they had concealed before it will be revealed to them. If they were sent back, they will do again what was forbidden to them. They are indeed liars.**
>
> **(Al-Anam 6: 26-28)**

Allah recounts here a harrowing scene of the Day of Judgement, when some people will face His wrath for their disbelief. Their pleas will be to no avail. However, now there is still time for us to brace ourselves for our accountability to Him. We should make the most of this opportunity available to us.

This graphic description recounts the disbelievers' pitiable response on the Day of Judgement. Throughout their lives they willfully and maliciously rejected truth. Worse, they erected all sorts of barriers in the cause of truth. However, on the Day of Judgement on witnessing the spectacle face to face they would turn panicky. The truth of Islam and their falsehood will manifest before their eyes. To escape punishment, they would fervently entreat for granting them another chance. However, it would be pointless after the test and its result are over.

May Allah, the most merciful, save us against disgrace and punishment of the Day of Judgement.

Points to ponder

- Falsehood or unbelief is a thin veneer which vanishes in no time. In contrast, faith is rock-solid and overcomes all trials and tribulations, even life-threatening challenges. The unbelievers abandoning disbelief on the Day of Judgement is illustrative of the same truth.
- What would hurt unbelievers most in the hereafter, apart from their horrid punishment, the tormenting sense of loss, lack of any hope of reprieve and betrayal by their leaders who had encouraged them to commit disbelief and assured them of their protection, yet would leave them in the lurch at the drop of a hat.

Chapter 249

Allah Is Most Compassionate

The entire universe exists because of Allah's mercy and compassion. Otherwise, we would not have been blessed with such invaluable bounties, free of any charge: air, water, sunlight, food and drink, the earth as suitable habitat, caring and loving ambience cultivated by our parents, kith and kin and the broader community. We get numerous opportunities and openings, once again, thanks to His kindness and care for us. On our own we could not even survive as a baby or carve out a niche for ourselves without the affection instilled into the people concerned by Allah. The striking facets of Allah's mercy are stated in this verse:

> **(O Prophet), when they who believe in Allah's signs come to you, tell them: "Peace be upon you. Allah has prescribed for Himself mercy. If any among you does evil out of ignorance and then repents and improves his conduct, he (will find) Allah Most Forgiving, Most Merciful."**
>
> **(Al-Anam 6: 54)**

Throughout, the Quran speaks of Allah as most compassionate, most merciful. This comes out from the declaration that He overlooks our lapses, accepts our repentance and will treat us kindly on the Day of Judgement. Out of His infinite kindness, Allah makes full allowance for our humanness. He generously accepts our repentance, provided that it is genuine and we do not indulge again in that sin. The doors of His forgiveness are wide open, even for die-hard disbelievers in their lifetime. Many staunch enemies of Islam at an early date repented and were accepted as Muslims. An instance in point is of a towering Muslim ruler and one of the best companions of the Prophet (peace be upon him), Caliph Umar ibn Al-Khattab (RA). He had gone out with his unsheathed sword in order to kill the Prophet (peace be upon him). However, on the way he heard the Quran recitation and was so deeply moved by its profound message and the heroic behavior of his believing sister and her husband, that on reaching the Prophet's door he was transformed into a devout believer. He devoted the rest of his life to the cause of Islam and is held in high esteem by Muslims for his accomplishments.

Points to ponder

- Forgiveness and justice are the most prominent manifestations of Allah's mercy towards us. We are liable to err. However, He is ever-ready to embrace us in His mercy.
- Had Allah not put into place His elaborate justice system in the next life, our suffering and misery in the present life, caused by the wicked ones, would have gone unrequited. However, thanks to the Day of Judgement proceedings, no one, however mighty they may be in this life, would be able to escape His terrible punishment, and that too, eternally.

Chapter 250

What Happens after Death?

The idea of death haunts each one of us. Generally speaking, we instinctively fear death. Allah causes our death at the hour preordained by Him. He alone knows our lifespan. More importantly, Allah has allayed our misgivings and fears about death, as He clarifies that death is not to be dreaded. It is an inevitable stage and marks the transition from this world to the next. Until the Day of Judgement, of which the date is known only to Allah, all the dead, rather their souls, are placed in *barzakh* (the intervening stage between our death, and the Resurrection and the Recompense). On the basis of faith and conduct in this life, we would be rewarded or punished in *barzakh* and final requital, on the Day of Judgement. The post-death stages are described in this verse:

> **Allah is supreme over His servants and sets angels as guardians over them. When death comes to any of you, they take your soul. They never fail in their duty. All of them will be returned to Allah, their true Protector. His alone will be the judgement. He is the Swiftest in taking account.**
>
> **(Al-Anam 6: 61-62)**

At Allah's command, the angel of death seizes our soul. Allah will evaluate our performance, particularly our faith and good conduct. Since He is severe in retribution, we should lead a pious life. Death is common knowledge. Every day we note death overtaking us, the rich and the poor, the young and the old, and believers and disbelievers alike. Yet it is a great pity and surprise that we do not prepare ourselves for this imminent eventuality. For every other business, be it related to work, family, investment, shopping, food, entertainment and what not, we plan meticulously and devote our time, energy and money, which are very dear to us, to these. However, we turn a blind eye to death and what will follow it.

It is high time to bear constantly in mind the grim reality of death. This would deter us from all that is trivial and evil. Believers do not fear death. Rather, they look forward to it, representing the stage to return to our Creator and lord. We should prepare better ourselves for our meeting with our lord and we should entitle ourselves to His mercy and reward.

Points to ponder

- Instead of speculating about death and feeling depressed, we should focus on our ultimate, eternal end after death. Turn to Allah, lead life as prescribed by Him and look forward to His forgiveness and mercy.
- Be constantly aware of impending death. This is not to suggest to stop working and neglecting our obligations. Our engagement in our routine life should not however, make us negligent of death which is bound to overtake us sooner or later.

Chapter 251

Allah Cautions Us against This Ephemeral Life

As we grow up, we see the vast world, with its varied vocations and temptations. We choose a career and get engrossed in it and other material pursuits—family and friends, and in our time, social media and entertainment. We hardly have the time or inclination to think over such basic questions: Who are we? From where did we come? Where do we go back from here? What is this world? What is the purpose behind our life? Out of His care and concern Allah has answered all these questions of being in the Quran: companions' queries on these issues were resolved by the Prophet Muhammad (peace be upon him) as recorded in the *Hadith* corpus. Allah cautions us in this verse against our negligence:

> **Leave alone those who take their religion to be a mere sport and amusement. The life of this world has deceived them. But remind them (with the Quran) lest one be caught for what he does. He will not have any protector or intercessor besides Allah. Even if he offers any ransom, it will not be accepted (on the Day of Judgement). They will be questioned for what they used to do. They will get boiling water to drink and painful punishment for their unbelief.**
>
> **(Al-Anam 6: 70)**

We are liable to be engrossed in our mundane, worldly pursuits, especially in making money and leading a luxurious life, without any regard for Allah, faith, good conduct and our next life. Our wealth and high social rank will be of no worth on the Day of Judgement. We are warned here explicitly about the horrendous punishment in the next life.

Throughout the Quran, Allah asks us to be serious about the great questions of our being: our faith, our way of life and our fate in the next life. We are mortal and will leave behind everything at our death, particularly wealth for which we exert ourselves so much. The Prophet Muhammad (peace be upon him) served, in the main, as a warner for his community, alerting them to the impending death and terrible punishment in the hereafter for our lack of faith and sins. As a result, the early Muslims, his companions turned into noble, pious souls.

Let us pay heed to Allah's eloquent warnings and improve our prospects in the everlasting next life.

Points to ponder

- This world with its glitter is liable to mislead us. Many of us are trapped by materialism and consumerism, which blinds us to the truth and our fast-approaching death. We should keep soul-searching.
- Let us be absolutely clear about the truth that this world is transitory; we may stay in it for a while. Like those before us, we are destined for death. More importantly, we would be recompensed most generously and lavishly, provided we have faith and good actions to our credit.
- Allah often warns us against worldliness. For it would have dire consequences in the next life.

Chapter 252

Allah's Creation with a Purpose

The realisation that Allah has created us with a purpose induces in us a positive outlook. We value our time and energy more and contribute significantly to our self-development, family, community and humanity. This in turn, creates such ambience which benefits everyone. The crime rate declines sharply; women and weaker sections feel secure and happy. Its most important impact is on class differences, as social and economic discord is reduced. The following verse brings into sharper light Allah's scheme for us:

> **It is Allah Who has created the heavens and the earth with a purpose. The Day He says: "Be", it (the Day of Judgement) will be. His word is the truth. His will be the authority on the Day when the trumpet is blown. He knows the Unseen and the open. He is the Wisest, All Aware.**
>
> **(Al-Anam 6: 73)**

Let us not forget the purpose of life: to lead it in accordance with Allah's will. Allah will exercise His total power on the Day of Judgement. Being all-knowing, He will decide our rank, with reference to our faith and actions. The all-wise Allah has created everything with a purpose. Nothing in Nature is useless, without a goal. In the face of this truth, which we note all around us, we should fashion our life wedded to the objective of serving and pleasing our Lord and helping and supporting fellow human beings in every possible way.

Our death and the Day of Judgement are bound to happen. Only our true faith and good actions would bring about our deliverance and eternal bliss in the next world. The sooner we imbibe this truth, the better it is for us.

Points to ponder

- The Quran recounts the believers' exclamation, based on their reflection on Allah's creation: "O our Lord! You have not created all this without a purpose. Glory be to You! Save us from the hellfire." (Ali Imran 3:191)
- In the face of Allah's assertions about a definite purpose behind the creation of this amazingly vast universe, we should not harbour this silly notion that everything has come into being on its own and that it would end in time, without any accountability. We should recognise and celebrate Allah's grandeur and glory.

Chapter 253

Unbelievers' Agony on the Day of Judgement

We see unbelievers and even staunch atheists prospering, enjoying all bounties. This should not astonish or depress us. Allah declares that He would bestow His provisions, in a certain measure ordained by Him, to everyone, irrespective of their creed, colour, ethnicity or any other consideration. He is most forbearing, all-wise. The unbelievers' affluence deceives them further, obstructing them from any reflection on or realisation of Allah's plan and the real purpose of their life. The truth would dawn on them only on the Day of Judgement when they would be in the midst of the hellfire, as foretold in this verse:

> **(Allah will tell Disbelievers on the Day:) "Now you have come to Us alone as We had created you for the first time. You have left behind all that We had given you. We do not see any of your intercessors about whom you claimed that they were Our partners. All relations between you and them have now been cut off. All those whom you imagined to be the partners with Us have vanished."**
>
> **(Al-Anam 6: 94)**

This graphic scene of the Day of Judgement should jolt us into thinking about the horrible consequences of: our rejection of Allah, our utter helplessness and resourcelessness on the Day of Judgement, and our misplaced belief in Allah's partners, and intercessors whom we take to be our saviours. It is high time to follow Allah's true guidance and attain everlasting success.

On the Day of Judgement we would realise our individual accountability. Today we feel safe and secure in the company of our near and dear ones, and on account of our wealth, social status and connections. We rely also on the patronage from those whom we take as gods and intermediaries with God (idols, saints and God's imaginary incarnations, etc.). However, all these illusions would shatter as soon as we die and face Allah.

Out of His immense mercy and affection Allah has forewarned us against such delusion and shown us the straight way which guarantees our joyful end.

Points to ponder

- Allah's generosity and forbearance comes out in this instructive dialogue between Him and Prophet Ibraheem (peace be upon him). When the latter built a house for Allah, Kabah in Makkah, Saudi Arabia, he prayed to Him to ensure provisions for his believing progeny in the arid town of Makkah. Allah corrected him, saying that He will grant sustenance to all of his progeny, be they believers or not.

  The above passage presents a graphic picture of the sheer helplessness, trauma and remorse of unbelievers on the day they appear before their lord for judgement.

Chapter 254

Allah's Commands

Islam is an action packed religion. It does not consist of only some spiritual exercises or a litany of supplications or local superstitions, rituals and customs. On the contrary, it is a complete way of life, instructing us in all domains, from maintaining personal hygiene to urging us to harness the forces of Nature for improving the quality of life and deriving benefits for humanity. Accordingly, Allah has laid down a range of commands, guiding our personal, collective, social, economic, moral and spiritual life. Some of His life-giving commands feature in this passage:

> Tell them: "Come, let me tell you what your Lord has forbidden—Do not join anything as equal with Him. Do good to your parents. Do not kill your children out of the fear of poverty. For Allah provides you and will provide them also with sustenance. Do not even go near anything shameful, be it open or secret. Do not take life which Allah has made sacred, except through the due process of justice. Allah has commanded you all this so that you may understand. Do not go near the orphan's property, except to improve it, until he comes of age. Give measure and weight with justice. Allah does not burden anyone beyond his capacity. When you speak, speak with justice, even though it may concern a near relative. Fulfil the pledge to Allah. He has commanded you all this so that you may take a lesson.
>
> (Al-Anam 6: 151-152)

This explains to us what Allah approves and disapproves. The items forbidden by Him underscore His concern for order, mutual sympathy, fairness and probity. All of these commands are geared towards constructing a joyful social life for us.

It is significant that in this cluster of Allah's commands, only the first one is related to faith, of not associating any partner with the one true God. All other commands concern our everyday life in a very elaborate way—kindness to parents and children, shunning immorality in any form, regarding all life as sanctified, taking good care of orphans, honesty and fairness in all business transactions, standing for justice, non-partisanship and keeping our word. Needless to add, these virtues are essential for a happy social order.

How considerate and compassionate Allah is to us! Glory be to Him!

Points to ponder

- Allah's commands are applicable to all adult believers. However, the most compassionate Lord has made due allowance for menstruating, pregnant women, the sick and the old and blessed them with exemption from some toilsome devotional worship duties.
- Since these commands are from our Creator Who knows best our mindset, our needs and our welfare, their implementation is in our own interest.

Chapter 255

We Are Allah's Trustees on Earth

While identifying our status in this world, Allah has graciously and munificentally designated us as His khalifah (trustee or vicegerent). It is the highest privilege imaginable for us to hold such an exalted rank in the eyes of our Lord. However, this coveted position, not available to any of His numerous other creatures on earth, has its own set of obligations. If we do not discharge these duties, we forfeit our status. Allah's bestowal of trusteeship on us is proclaimed in this verse:

> **It is Allah Who has appointed you (O humankind) vicegerent on the earth. He has raised some of you above others in rank. This is so that He may test you in what He has given you. Your Lord is strict in punishment. Yet He is Most Forgiving, Most Merciful.**
>
> **(Al-Anam 6: 165)**

Allah has done a huge favour to humankind in having made human beings the best creatures on earth and His vice-gerent. This important position calls for us to strive to accomplish this role. Out of His infinite wisdom, Allah has granted us abilities in varying degrees, which is part of Him testing us. If we fail to perform our duty, though being endowed with so much, He will take us to task on the Day of Judgement. We should seek His forgiveness and mercy for overlooking our failings.

Allah's message to us is loud and clear: we are His trustee in this world. He has granted us much (physical and mental faculties, money, and other provisions in varying degrees). We would be held accountable on the Day of Judgement for their use or abuse. As to His bestowal of His bounties, as part of His plan, He has blessed some more than others. He seeks to examine our conduct in both prosperity and adversity. So we should not begrudge the inequality in our financial and social status.

What is more important is that we realise our role and obligations as Allah's trustee so that we do not face His displeasure on the Day of Judgement.

Points to ponder

- As a trustee, perform your role conscientiously. To begin with, bear this fact in mind that we are not free to act as we wish. Other creatures and the environment have their rights. We must respect their space. Allah asks us to maintain ecological balance.
- In our personal life we should be ever-conscious of our accountability to Allah as a trustee. For example, our income, no matter how hard-earned it might be, is not for any extravagance. Others, particularly the weak and the poor have their share in what Allah has generously given us.

Chapter 256

Allah Disapproves Compulsion in Religion

Allah has prescribed Islam as the religion for humanity. He, no doubt, urges all of us to embrace Islam. However, He leaves the matter of faith to our choice. While exerting our free will and in recognition of the truth emanating from Allah's signs within and around us, we should accept Islam in self-surrender to Him. Allah is powerful enough to have made everyone Muslim. However, out of inexhaustible wisdom He lets everyone flourish, including unbelievers and atheists. Allah's prohibition of coercion in religion is evident from this verse:

> **There is no compulsion in religion. Guidance stands clear from error. He who rejects the evil ones and believes in Allah takes hold of the firm handle that never breaks. Allah is All Hearing, All Knowing.**
>
> **(Al-Baqarah 2: 256)**

While Allah has approved Islam as the only religion for humankind, He does not compel anyone into believing in Islam. Rather, Islam upholds the principle of "live and let live", as we have freedom to accept or reject faith. Allah, nonetheless, warns us against terrible consequences in the next life for those of us who refuse to believe in Him.

Islam stands for peaceful co-existence. Jews and Christians and other non-Muslims have thrived for centuries in the Muslim majority countries. When the Prophet Muhammad (peace be upon him) migrated to Madina and was its head, he enacted the first written constitution of the state of Madina. He granted equal rights and religious freedom to Jews and branded them as members of the single community of Madinans which included both Jews and Muslims. When a delegation of Christians from nearby Najran called on him in Madina, he let them pray inside his mosque (For details see Craig Considine's (Professor of Sociology at Rice University, USA) *People of the Book: Prophet Muhammad's Encounters with Christians 2021).*

Points to ponder

- Since Prophet Muhammad (peace be upon him) was a very kind, merciful person, he often prayed to Allah that everyone should turn to Islam, which would save them against hellfire, Allah plainly told him that it is not for him to impose guidance on anyone. Allah alone may show people the straight way.
- The Quran recounts that Prophet Nuh's son, Prophet Lut's wife, Prophet Ibraheem's father and Prophet Muhammad's affectionate uncle, Abu Talib, who was his guardian, were not believers. Allah grants choice to everyone. It is ironical that even in the face of these pronouncements, Islam is misperceived by some as a religion which spread by sword.

Appendix

99 Excellent Names and Attributes of Allah			
Sr. No.	Arabic Name	Transliterated Name	Meaning
1	الله	Allah	Allah
2	الرَّحْمَنُ	Al-Rahmān	Most Merciful
3	الرَّحِيمُ	Al-Raheem	Most Compassionate
4	الْمَلِكُ	Al-Malik	True King
5	ٱلْقُدُّوسُ	Al-Quddūs	The Holiest
6	ٱلسَّلَامُ	Al- Salām	All-Peace
7	ٱلْمُؤْمِنُ	Al-Mu'min	All-Security
8	ٱلْمُهَيْمِنُ	Al-Muhaymin	All-Overseer
9	ٱلْعَزِيزُ	Al-Ázīz	Almighty
10	ٱلْجَبَّارُ	Al-Jabbār	All-Overpowering
11	ٱلْمُتَكَبِّرُ	Al-Mutakabbir	All-Great
12	ٱلْخَالِقُ	Al-Khāliq	Best Creator
13	ٱلْبَارِئُ	Al-Bāri'	Best Designer
14	ٱلْمُصَوِّرُ	Al-Musawwir	Best Fashioner
15	ٱلْغَفَّارُ	Al-Ghaffār	Most Forgiving

99 Excellent Names and Attributes of Allah (cont.)			
Sr. No.	**Arabic Name**	**Transliterated Name**	**Meaning**
16	ٱلْقَهَّارُ	Al-Qahhār	Most Irresistible
17	ٱلْوَهَّابُ	Al-Wahhāb	Most Munificent
18	ٱلرَّزَّاقُ	Al-Razzāq	Best Bestower
19	ٱلْفَتَّاحُ	Al-Fattāh	Best Judge
20	ٱلْعَلِيمُ	Al-'Aleem	All-Knowing
21	ٱلْقَابِضُ	Al-Qābiz	Best Restrictor
22	ٱلْبَاسِطُ	Al-Bāsiṭ	Best Expander
23	ٱلْخَافِضُ	Al-Khāfiz	Best Degrader
24	ٱلرَّافِعُ	Al-Rāfey	Most Elevated
25	ٱلْمُعِزُّ	Al-Mu'iz	Most Exalted
26	ٱلْمُذِلُّ	Al-Mudhill	Best Humiliator
27	ٱلسَّمِيعُ	Al-Samee	All Hearing
28	ٱلْبَصِيرُ	Al-Bāseer	All Seeing
29	ٱلْحَكَمُ	Al-Ḥakam	Best Decreer
30	ٱلْعَالِمُ	Al- 'Ālim	Best Knower
31	ٱللَّطِيفُ	Al-Laṭeef	Most Subtle
32	ٱلْخَبِيرُ	Al-Khabeer	All-Aware
33	ٱلْحَلِيمُ	Al-Ḥaleem	Most Forbearing
34	ٱلْعَظِيمُ	Al- 'Aẓeem	Most Splendid

99 Excellent Names and Attributes of Allah (cont.)			
Sr. No.	Arabic Name	Transliterated Name	Meaning
35	ٱلْغَفُورُ	Al-Ghafūr	Most Pardoning
36	ٱلشَّكُورُ	Al-Shakūr	Most Appreciative
37	ٱلْاعَلِىٰ	Al-Aʿlā	The Highest
38	ٱلْكَبِيرُ	Al-Kabeer	The Greatest
39	ٱلْحَفِيظُ	Al-Ḥafeeẓ	All-Watchful
40	ٱلْمُقِيتُ	Al-Muqeet	All-Sustainer
41	ٱلْحَسِيبُ	Al-Ḥaseeb	All-Reckoner
42	ٱلْجَلِيلُ	Al-Jaleel	Most Magnificent
43	ٱلْكَرِيمُ	Al-Kareem	Most Bountiful
44	ٱلرَّقِيبُ	Al-Raqeeb	All-Observer
45	ٱلْمُجِيبُ	Al-Mujeeb	Ever Responsive
46	ٱلْوَاسِعُ	Al-Wāsey	All-Embracing
47	ٱلْحَكِيمُ	Al-Ḥakeem	All-Wise
48	ٱلْوَدُودُ	Al-Wadūd	Most Loving
49	ٱلْمَجِيدُ	Al-Majeed	Most Glorious
50	ٱلْبَاعِثُ	Al-Bāʿith	Best Sender
51	ٱلشَّهِيدُ	Al-Shaheed	Best Witness
52	ٱلْحَقُّ	Al-Ḥaqq	All-Truth
53	ٱلْوَكِيلُ	Al-Wakeel	Best Guardian

99 Excellent Names and Attributes of Allah (cont.)			
Sr. No.	Arabic Name	Transliterated Name	Meaning
54	ٱلْقَوِيُّ	Al-Qawee	All-Powerful
55	ٱلْمَتِينُ	Al-Mateen	All-Strong
56	ٱلْوَلِيُّ	Al-Walee	Best Protector
57	ٱلْحَمِيدُ	Al-Ḥameed	Most Praiseworthy
58	ٱلْمُحْصِي	Al-Muḥṣee	Best Record Keeper
59	ٱلْمُبْدِئُ	Al-Mubdee	Best Commencer
60	ٱلْمُعِيدُ	Al-M'īd	Best Restorer
61	ٱلْمُحْيِى	Al-Muḥyī	Best Giver of Life
62	ٱلْمُمِيتُ	Al-Mumeet	Best Taker of Life
63	ٱلْحَىُّ	Al-Hayy	Ever-Living
64	ٱلْقَيُّومُ	Al-Qayyūm	The Self Subsisting
65	القريب	Al-Qarīb	The Nearest One
66	ٱلْمَاجِدُ	Al-Mājid	Most Gracious
67	ٱلْوَاحِدُ	Al-Wāhid	The Indivisible One
68	ٱلْأَحَد	Al-Ahad	The One
69	ٱلصَّمَدُ	Al-Samad	The Unique
70	ٱلْقَادِرُ	Al-Qādir	The Omnipotent
71	ٱلْمُقْتَدِرُ	Al-Muqtadir	The Mightiest

99 Excellent Names and Attributes of Allah (cont.)			
Sr. No.	Arabic Name	Transliterated Name	Meaning
72	ٱلْمُقَدِّمُ	Al-Muqaddim	Best Warner
73	ٱلْمُؤَخِّرُ	Al-Mu'akhkhir	Best Deferrer
74	ٱلأَوَّلُ	Al-Awwal	The First One
75	ٱلْآخِرُ	Al-Ākhir	The Last One
76	ٱلْظَّاهِرُ	Al-Ẓāhir	The Manifest
77	ٱلْبَاطِنُ	Al-Bātin	The Hidden
78	ٱلْمُتَعَال	Al-Muta'āl	The Highest
79	ٱلْبَرُّ	Al-Barr	Most Benign
80	ٱلْتَّوَّابُ	Al-Tawwab	Most Relenting
81	ٱلْمُنْتَقِمُ	Al-Muntaqim	Best Retributor
82	ٱلْعَفُوُّ	Al-'Afuww	Most Lenient
83	ٱلْرَّؤُفُ	Al-Ra'ūf	The Most Tender
84	مَالِكُ ٱلْمُلْكُ	Mālik Al-Mulk	The Lord of All Dominion
85	ذُو ٱلْجَلَالِ وَٱلْإِكْرَامُ	Dhū Al-Jalāl Wa Al-Ikrām	Full of Majesty and Splendour
86	ٱلْمُقْسِطُ	Al-Muqsiṭ	All-Just
87	ٱلْجَامِعُ	Al-Jāmey	Best Gatherer
88	ٱلْغَنِيُّ	Al-Ghanī	All-Sufficient
89	ٱلْمُغْنِيُّ	Al-Mughnī	The Enriching One

99 Excellent Names and Attributes of Allah (cont.)			
Sr. No.	**Arabic Name**	**Transliterated Name**	**Meaning**
90	ٱلْمُعَطِي	Al-Mu'ttī	Best Giver
91	ٱلْمَانِعُ	Al-Māney	Best Forbidder
92	ٱلنَّافِعُ	Al-Nāfey	Most Beneficent
93	ٱلنُّورُ	Al-Nūr	All-Light
94	ٱلْهَادِي	Al-Hādī	Best Guide
95	ٱلْبَدِيعُ	Al-Badiy'	Best Originator
96	ٱلْبَاقِي	Al-Bāqī	Ever To Remain
97	ٱلْوَارِثُ	Al-Wārith	All-Owner
98	ٱلرَّشِيدُ	Al-Rasheed	Best Mentor
99	ٱلصَّبُورُ	Al-Ṣabūr	Most Persevering One

Further Reading (chapter-wise)

1. The Quran, Al-Anfal 8: 34
   The Quran, Al-Ankabut 29:45
2. The Quran, Fatir 35:45
   The Quran, Al-Nisa 4:147
   The Quran, Hud 11:117
3. The Quran, Ibraheem 14:34
   The Quran, Al-Nahl 16:72
4. The Quran, Al-Zumar 39:53-54
   The Quran, Al-Baqarah 2:222
5. The Quran, Hud 11:6
   The Quran, Al-Talaq 65:3
6. The Quran, Qaf 50:4
   The Quran, Al-Baqarah 2:186
7. The Quran, Al-Raad 13:28
   The Quran, Luqman 31:26
8. The Quran, Saad 38:28
   The Quran, TaHa 20:81
9. The Quran, Al-Qiyamah 75:3
   The Quran, Al-Hadeed 57:1-2
10. The Quran, Al-Baqarah 2:222
    The Quran, Al-Tawbah 9:108
11. The Quran, Hajj 22:23
    The Quran, Al-Taghabun 64:9
12. The Quran, Al-Muminun 23:6
    The Quran, Al-Nur 24:30-31
13. The Quran, Al-Zumar 39:66
    The Quran, Al-Nahl 16:22
14. The Quran, Hud 11:117
    The Quran, Al-Qalam 68:35
15. The Quran, Al-Baqarah 2:156
    The Quran, Fatir 35:4
16. The Quran, Al-Baqarah 2:216
    The Quran, Al-Mulk 67:13
17. The Quran, Saad 38:28
    The Quran, Al-Araf 7:156
18. The Quran, Al-Baqarah 2:255
    The Quran, Al-Mumin, 40:3
19. The Quran, Al-Qiyamah 75:3-4
    The Quran, Al-Baqarah 2:164
20. The Quran, Ali Imran 3:90
    The Quran, Yunus 10:6
21. The Quran, Ali Imran 3:54
    The Quran, Al-Anfal 7:30
22. The Quran, Al- Isra 17:55
    The Quran, Al-Mujadalah 58:7
23. The Quran, Saba 34:50
    The Quran, Hud 11:61
24. The Quran, Al-Qiyamah 75:3-4
    The Quran, Al-Hadeed 57:1-2
25. The Quran, Al-Nahl 16:22
    The Quran, Al-Ikhlas 112:1-4
26. The Quran, Fatir 35:15
    The Quran, Al-Maidah 5:54
27. The Quran, Al-Jumah 62:8
    The Quran, Qaf 50:43
28. The Quran, Al-Ahzab 33:17
    The Quran, Al-Ankabut 29:2
29. The Quran, Al-Talaq 65:3
    The Quran, Ali Imran 3:159
30. The Quran, Al-Nahl 16:12-16
    The Quran, Al-Nahl 16:79-81
31. The Quran, Al-Zumar 39:52
    The Quran, Al-Isra 17:20
32. The Quran, Al-Isra 17:97
    The Quran, Al-Dahr 76:3
33. The Quran, Ali Imran 3:86
    The Quran, Al-Anam 6:160
34. The Quran, Al-Talaq 65:8
    The Quran, Al-Anam 6:62
35. The Quran, Al-Anbiyya 21:47
    The Quran, Al-Jathiyah 45:26
36. The Quran, Al-Talaq 65:11
    The Quran, Ya Sin 36:17
37. The Quran, Al-Mumin 40:15
    The Quran, Al-Kahaf 18:56

38. The Quran, Luqman 31:30
The Quran, Qaf 50:42

39. The Quran, Al-Anam 6:113
The Quran, Al-Nisa 4:131

40. The Quran, Al-Kahf 18:49
The Quran, Al-Hujurat 49:18

41. The Quran, Al-Shuara 26:154
The Quran, Ibraheem 14:42-48

42. The Quran, Al-Baqarah 2:152
The Quran, Al-Ahzab 33:3

43. The Quran, Fatir 35:5
The Quran, Al-Rum 30:60

44. The Quran, Al-Isra 17:53
The Quran, Al-Isra 17:31

45. The Quran, Al-Shura 42:9
The Quran, Al-Raad 13:26

46. The Quran, Al-Anam 6:162
The Quran, Al-Araf 7:54

47. The Quran, Al-Imran 3:2
The Quran, Hud 11:6

48. The Quran, Al-Zumar 39:62
The Quran, Al-Hashr 59:24

49. The Quran, Al-Hadeed 57:4
The Quran, Ali Imran 3:5

50. The Quran, Yunus 10:37
The Quran, Al-Sajdah 32:2

51. The Quran, Ali Imran 3:102
The Quran, Al-Nisa 4:56

52. The Quran, Al-Araf 7:87
The Quran, Al-Baqarah 2:281

53. The Quran, Al-Anbiyya 21:47
The Quran, Al-Maidah 5:47-53

54. The Quran, Al-Nisa 4:171
The Quran, Al-Hajj 22:62

55. The Quran, Saba 34:28
The Quran, Al-Anbiyya 21:107

56. The Quran, Al-Nur 24:36
The Quran, Al-Baqarah 2:255

57. The Quran, Al-Araf 7:153
The Quran, Al-Furqan 25:70-77

58. The Quran, Hud 11:61
The Quran, Al-Mumin 40:60

59. The Quran, Al-Hujurat 49:18
The Quran, Al-Maidah 5:109

60. The Quran, Al-Ikhlas 112:1-4
The Quran, Ali Imran 3:64

61. The Quran, Ibraheem 14:42-48
The Quran, Al-Tawabah 9:68

62. The Quran, Al-Baqarah 2:152
The Quran, Al-Zumar 39:53

63. The Quran, Al-Araf 7:87
The Quran, Al-Anbiyya 21:47

64. The Quran, Al-Hijr 15:26
The Quran, Al-Alaq 96:1-5

65. The Quran, Fussilat 41:37
The Quran, Yunus 10:6

66. The Quran, Al-Araf 7:54
The Quran, Luqman 31:11

67. The Quran, Al-Nur 24:41
The Quran, Ali Imran 3:26

68. The Quran, Al-Maida 5:120
The Quran, Al-Hadeed 57:2

69. The Quran, Al-Baqarah 2:207
The Quran, Al-Talaq 65:3

70. The Quran, Al-Furqan 25:43
The Quran, Al-Raad 13:2

71. The Quran, Al-Talaq 65:3
The Quran, Ali Imran 3:159

72. The Quran, Al-Zumar 39:53
The Quran, Al-Nisa 4:48

73. The Quran, Al-Araf 7:35-36
The Quran, Al-Ahzab 33:28-34

74. The Quran, Al-Anbiyya 21:16-17
The Quran, Fatir 35:41

75. The Quran, Al-Anfal 8:60-61
The Quran, Al-Nur, 24:40

76. The Quran, Al-Anam 6:141
The Quran, Yunus 10:31

77. The Quran, Al-Hadeed 57:3
The Quran, Al-Baqarah 2:255

78. The Quran, Ya Sin 36:36
The Quran, Al-Dhariyat 51:49

79. The Quran, Al-Hajj 22:58
The Quran, Al-Ankabut 29:17

80. The Quran, Al-Shura 42:26
The Quran, Al-Shura 42:40

81. The Quran, Al-Araf 7:8-9
The Quran, Yunus 10:54

82. The Quran, Al-Najm 53:32
The Quran, Al-Talaq 65:12

83. The Quran, Ali Imran 3:27
The Quran, Al-Qasas 28:84

84. The Quran, Al-Araf 7:53
The Quran, Qaf 50:12

85. The Quran, Al-Nahl 16:25
The Quran, Al-Nahl 16:27

86. The Quran, Al-Jumah 62:4
The Quran, Yunus 10:58

87. The Quran, Al-Nahl 16:38-40
The Quran, Al-Isra 17:49-52

88. The Quran, Al-Nahl 16:38-40
The Quran, Al-Isra 17:49-52

89. The Quran, Al-Zumar 39:53
The Quran, Al-Anam 6:54

90. The Quran, Al-Anfal 8:52
The Quran, Ha Mim Sajdah 41:50

91. The Quran, Hud 11:7
The Quran, Al-Shura 42:16

92. The Quran, Al-Jathiya 45:24-26
The Quran, Ali Imran 3:145

93. The Quran, Fatir 35:27-28
The Quran, Al-Zumar 39:5

94. The Quran, Al-Maidah 5:48
The Quran, Ha Mim
Sajdah 41:2-4

95. The Quran, Al-Ankabut 29:56
The Quran, Al-Hijr 15:19-20

96. The Quran, Al-Araf 7:57
The Quran, Al-Muminun 23:18

97. The Quran, Al-Nahl 16:66
The Quran, Al-Mumin 40:79-80

98. The Quran, Al-Saffat 37:164-166
The Quran, Al-Mumin 40:7-9

99. The Quran, Al-Isra 17:111
The Quran, Al-Baqarah 2:116

100. The Quran, Al-Talaq 65:11
The Quran, Al-Mumin 40:78

101. The Quran, Al-Hadeed 57:3
The Quran, Al-Anbiyya 21:34

102. The Quran, Al-Qasas 28:59
The Quran, Al-Zumar 39:25

103. The Quran, Luqman 31:34
The Quran, Ali Imran 3:29

104. The Quran, Al-Qiyamah 75:3-4
The Quran, Al-Naba 78:37

105. The Quran, Fatir 35:31
The Quran, Al-Shuara 26:197

106. The Quran, Al-Hadeed 57:11
The Quran, Al-Layl 92:15

107. The Quran, Al-Zumar 39:53
The Quran, Al-Najam 53:32

108. The Quran, Al-Nisa 4:124
The Quran, Al-Maidah 5:119

109. The Quran, Al-Muminun 23:1-11
The Quran, Al-Imran 3:17

110. The Quran, Al-Jathiyah 45:49
The Quran, Ali Imran
3:10 and 14

111. The Quran, Al-Shura 42:12
The Quran, Al-Dhariyat 51:57-58

112. The Quran, Al-Taghabun 64:15
The Quran, Al-Isra 17:31

113. The Quran, Al-Munafiqun 63:9
The Quran, Al-Kahaf 18:103-105

114. The Quran, Al-Mulk 67:15
The Quran, Al-Nahl 16:13

115. The Quran, Al-Ahqaf 46:35
The Quran, Al-Nur 24:21

116. The Quran, Al-Ahqaf 46:35
The Quran, Al-Nur 24:21

117. The Quran, Al-Mutaffifeen 83:4-6
The Quran, Al-Maryam 19:86

118. The Quran, Al-Shura 42:47
The Quran, Al-Araf 7:182-183

119. The Quran, Al-Hajj 22:5
The Quran, Al-Hijr 15:26

120. The Quran, Al-Nisa 4:8-9
The Quran, Al- Nisa 4:11-12

121. The Quran, Al-Shura 42:22
The Quran, Al- Jathiya 45:30

122. The Quran, Al-Nisa 4:48
The Quran, Al- Maidah 5:72-73

123. The Quran, Al-Araf 7:180
The Quran, Al- Buruj 85:14

124. The Quran, Al-Araf 7:110
The Quran, Al- Hashr 59:22-24

125. The Quran, Ibraheem 14:34
The Quran, Al-Kahaf 18:18

126. The Quran, Al-Baqarah 2:110
The Quran, Al-Baqarah 2:263

127. The Quran, Al-Nahl 16:58-59
The Quran, Al-Takweer 81:8-9

128. The Quran, Al-Nisa 4:135
The Quran, Al-Nisa 4:58

129. The Quran, Al-Nahl 16:94
The Quran, Al-Tahreem 66:2

130. The Quran, Al-Hujurat 49:10-13
The Quran, Al-Humazah 104:1-6

131. The Quran, Al-Hijr 15:85
The Quran, Al-Anbiyya 21:16-17

132. The Quran, Al-Rum 30:21
The Quran, Al-Araf 7:189

133. The Quran, Ibraheem 14:34
The Quran, Al-Nahl 16:18

134. The Quran, Al-Shura 42:31
The Quran, Al-Buruj 85:12

135. The Quran, Al-Hajj 22:28
The Quran, Al-Muminun 23:21

136. The Quran, Al-Anam 6:151-153
The Quran, Al-Isra 17:23-24

137. The Quran, Al-Muminun 23:18
The Quran, Al-Araf 7:57

138. The Quran, Al-Isra 17:70
The Quran, Fatir 35:12

139. The Quran, Ta Ha 20:105-107
The Quran, Al-Anbiyya 21:31

140. The Quran, Al-Baqarah 2:172
The Quran, Al-Maida 5:88

141. The Quran, Al-Baqarah 2:157
The Quran, Al-Nisa 4:96

142. The Quran, Al-Anam 6:95
The Quran, Al-Rum 30:24

143. The Quran, Al-Muminun 23:1-11
The Quran, Ali Imran 3:17

144. The Quran, Al-Tawbah 9:111
The Quran, Al-Muminun 23:10-11

145. The Quran, Al-Rum 30:21
The Quran, Al-Araf 7:189

146. The Quran, Al-Muminun 23:6
The Quran, Al-Nur 24:2

147. The Quran, Al-Dukhan 44:54
The Quran, Al-Tur 52:20

148. The Quran, Al-Hijr 15:19-20
The Quran, Al-Ṣhura 26:7

149. The Quran, Al-Araf 7:194-198
The Quran, Al-Nahl 16:20-21

150. The Quran, Al-Baqarah 2:164
The Quran, Ibraheem 14:32

151. The Quran, Al-Hashr 59:20
The Quran, Al-Maidah 5:72

152. The Quran, Al-Furqan 25:71
The Quran, Al-Nisa 4:129

153. The Quran, Fatir 35:11
The Quran, Al-Nisa 4:29

154. The Quran, Al-Maidah 5:54
The Quran, Yunus 10:62-64

155. The Quran, Al-Nahl 16:70
The Quran, Al-Zumar 39:42

156. The Quran, Al-Hashr 59:22-24
The Quran, Al-Ikhlas 112:1-4

157. The Quran, Al-Anfal 8:30
The Quran, Ali Imran 3:54

158. The Quran, Qaf 50:19
The Quran, Al-Anbiyya 21:35

159. The Quran, Al-Mumin 40:55
The Quran, Al-Mumin 40:77

160. The Quran, Al-Buruj 85:11
The Quran, Yusuf 12:90

161. The Quran, Al-Nahl 16:8
The Quran, Al-Muminun 23:18-22

162. The Quran, Al-Nisa 4:4
The Quran, Al-Nahl 16:72

163. The Quran, Al-Nahl 16:12-16
The Quran, Al-Nahl 16:79-81

164. The Quran, Hud 11:18-22
The Quran, Hud 11:101-104

165. The Quran, Ali Imran 3:185
The Quran, Al-Anbiyya 21:47

166. The Quran, Al-Taghabun 64:9
The Quran, Al-Saff 61:12

167. The Quran, Al-Hadeed 57:3
The Quran, Ta Ha 20:46

168. The Quran, Al-Nahl 16:106
The Quran, Al-Maidah 5:60

169. The Quran, Al-Baqarah 2:156
The Quran, Al-Anam 6:108-118

170. The Quran, Al-Araf 7:180
The Quran, Al-Hadeed 57:3

171. The Quran, Yunus 10:44
The Quran, Yunus 10:55-56

172. The Quran, Al-Qasas 28:73
The Quran, Al-Muminun 23:18-22

173. The Quran, Al-Hajj 22:65
The Quran, Al-Rum 30:48-49

174. The Quran, Al-Raad 13:11
The Quran, Al-Nur 24:34

175. The Quran, Al-Anam 6:127
The Quran, Al-Araf 7:53

176. The Quran, Al-Hajj 22:18
The Quran, Al-Dhariyat 51:56

177. The Quran, Al-Zumar 39:21
The Quran, Al-Rahman 55:10-13

178. The Quran, Al-Nisa 4:1
The Quran, Al-Rum 30:20-22

179. The Quran, Al-Anam 6:141
The Quran, Al-Nahl 16:11

180. The Quran, Al-Nahl 16:22
The Quran, Luqman 31:30

181. The Quran, Ta Ha 20:14
The Quran, Al-Baqarah 2:163

182. The Quran, Al-Baqarah 2:201
The Quran, Al-Baqarah 2:286

183. The Quran, Al-Anfal 8:56
The Quran, Al-Hijr 15:2

184. The Quran, Al-Muminun 23:1-11
The Quran, Ali Imran 3:17

185. The Quran, Al-Araf 7:179
The Quran, Al-Tawbah 9:68

186. The Quran, Al-Anbiyya 21:30
The Quran, Al-Waqiah 56:68-70

187. The Quran, Al-Zumar 39:66
The Quran, Al-Nahl 16:22

188. The Quran, Al-Isra 17:44
The Quran, Al-Hajj 22:18

189. The Quran, Al-Nisa 4:37
The Quran, Al-Tawbah 9:34-35

190. The Quran, Al-Baqarah 2:8-20
The Quran, Al-Baqarah 2:204-206

191. The Quran, Al-Nisa 4:65
The Quran, Al-Nisa 4:105

192. The Quran, Al-Hujurat 49:13
The Quran, Al-Nahl 16:13

193. The Quran, Al-Nisa 4:59
The Quran, Al-Nur 24:54

194. The Quran, Al-Rum 30:54
The Quran, Al-Kahf 18:45

195. The Quran, Ali Imran 3:165
The Quran, Al-Hadeed 57:2

196. The Quran, Al-Araf 7:172
The Quran, Al-Dhariyat 51:56

197. The Quran, Al-Baqarah 2:152-153
The Quran, Al-Muminun 23:1-2

198. The Quran, Al-Baqarah 2:45
The Quran, Al-Baqarah 2:177

199. The Quran, Al-Maidah 5:70
The Quran, Al-Zumar 39:61

200. The Quran, Yusuf 12:90
The Quran, Al-Baqarah 2:197

201. The Quran, Ali Imran 3:27
The Quran, Al-Zumar 39:10

202. The Quran, Al-Muminun 23:63-77
The Quran, Al-Shuara 26:200-209

203. The Quran, Hud 11:57
The Quran, Al-Qalam 68:51-52

204. The Quran, Al-Zumar 39:21
The Quran, Al-Rahman 55:10-13

205. The Quran, Al-Araf 7:54
The Quran, Al-Tur 52:18

206. The Quran, Al-Nahl 16:66
The Quran, Al-Mumin 40:79-80

207. The Quran, Al-Baqarah 2:177
The Quran, Al-Mujadalah 58:7

208. The Quran, Yunus 10:54
The Quran, Ibraheem 14:21

209. The Quran, Fatir 35:5
The Quran, Al-Mumin 40:77

210. The Quran, Al-Baqarah 2:286
The Quran, Ibraheem 14:40-41

211. The Quran, Hud 11:61
The Quran, Al-Baqarah 2:186

212. The Quran, Al-Tawbah 9:76
The Quran, Al-Qasas 28:77

213. The Quran, Ibraheem 14:7
The Quran, Al-Baqarah 2:152

214. The Quran, Al-Muminun 23:1-11
The Quran, Al-Ahzab 33:35

215. The Quran, Ali Imran 3:17
The Quran, Al-Dhariyat 51:16-19

216. The Quran, Yunus 10:47
The Quran, Al-Nahl 16:36

217. The Quran, Al-Nisa 4:147
The Quran, Fatir 35:34-35

218. The Quran, Al-Nahl 16:25
The Quran, Al-Nahl 16:27

219. The Quran, Al-Baqarah 2:110
The Quran, Al-Baqarah 2:117

220. The Quran, Al-Baqarah 2:110
The Quran, Al-Baqarah 2:117

221. The Quran, Ali Imran 3:92
The Quran, Ali Imran 3:134

222. The Quran, Al-Anam 6:89
The Quran, Al-Baqarah 2:129

223. The Quran, Al-Raad 13:18
The Quran, Yunus 10:54

224. The Quran, Al-Tahreem 66:5
The Quran, Al-Maarij 72-35

225. The Quran, Al-Humaza 104:1-6
The Quran, Al-Anam 6:98

226. The Quran, Al-Nisa 4:58
The Quran, Al-Nisa 4:65

227. The Quran, Al-Baqarah 2:155-157
The Quran, Al-Mulk 67:2

228. The Quran, Al-Kahf 18:102-106
The Quran, Al-Nur 24:39

229. The Quran, Al-Saff 61:12
The Quran, Al-Taghabun 64:9

230. The Quran, Al-Nahal 16:25
The Quran, Al-Nahal 16:27

231. The Quran, Al-Hujurat 49:13
The Quran, Ha Mim Al-Sajdah 41:11

232. The Quran, Al-Hadeed 57:3
The Quran, Al-Qasas 28:88

233. The Quran, Al-Nisa 4:13
The Quran, Al-Maidah 5:119

234. The Quran, Al-Nisa 5:32
The Quran, Al-Teen 95:4-6

235. The Quran, Al-Isra 17:97
The Quran, Al-Ahqaf 46:10

236. The Quran, Al-Mulk 67:16-17
The Quran, Al-Ahzab 33:17

237. The Quran, Saad 38:28
The Quran, Al-Nisa 4:58

238. The Quran, Al-Nisa 4:105
The Quran, Al-Nisa 4:135

239. The Quran, Al-Nisa 4:51-55
The Quran, Yunus 10:27-30

240. The Quran, Ali Imran 3:109
The Quran, Al-Baqarah 2:284

241. The Quran, Ta Ha 20:14
The Quran, Al-Araf 7:3

242. The Quran, Al-Araf 7:51
The Quran, Saad 38:55-58

243. The Quran, Ali Imran 3:15
The Quran, Al-Nisa 4:124

244. The Quran, Al-Nur 24:38
The Quran, Al-Ankabut 29:7

245. The Quran, Al-Anam 6:3
The Quran, Al-Raad 13:8-10

246. The Quran, Al-Maun 107:2-7
The Quran, Al-Baqarah 2:243

247. The Quran, Al-Haqqah 69:25-29
The Quran, Al-Naziat 79-35-39

248. The Quran, Al-Anam 8:95-104
The Quran, Al-Tawbah 9:104

249. The Quran, Al-Qasas 28:83
The Quran, Al-Ankabul 29:64

250. The Quran, Al-Jathiya 45:36
The Quran, Al-Hadeed 57:20

251. The Quran, Al-Dhariyat 51:56-57
The Quran, Al-Dahr 76:2

252. The Quran, Al-Araf 7:8-9
The Quran, Al-Raad 13-18

253. The Quran, Al-Nahl 16:90
The Quran, Al-Isra 17:23-24

254. The Quran, Al-Baqarah 2:30
The Quran, Al-Anam 6:165

255. The Quran, Al-Kafirun 109:6
The Quran, Yunus 10:99

Bibliography

A study of these books may help form a better idea of Allah and the Islamic worldview:

- Draz, M.A, *The Quran: The Basics*. Oxford, Routledge, 2009.
- Gibbon, Edward, *The Decline and Fall of the Roman Empire*. London, Wordsworth Edition, 1998.
- Gwynne, R. Ward, *Logic, Rhetoric and Legal Reasoning in the Quran*: God's Arguments. New York, Routledge, 2004.
- Hammad, Zaki, *The Gracious Quran*. LA, USA, Lucent International, 2007.
- Hart Michael, *The 100: A Ranking of the Most Influential Persons in History*. New York, Citadel Press, 1992.
- Irving, T. B. et. al, *The Quran: Basic Teachings*. Leicester, UK, Islamic Foundation, 1992.
- Izutsu, Toshihiko, *Ethico-Religious Concepts in Islam,* Montreal, McGill University Press, 1966.
- Khalidi, Tarif, *The Quran: A New Translation*. London, Penguin, 2008.
- Khattag, Mustafa, *The Clear Quran*. Lombard, Illinois, USA. Book of Signs Foundation, 2015.
- Kidwai, Abdur Raheem, *31 Blessed Names and Characteristics of Prophet Muhammad*, Leicester, UK, Kube Publication, 2016.
- Kidwai, Abdur Raheem, *365 Sayings of Prophet Muhammad,* Jaico Publishing House, Mumbai, 2008.
- Kidwai, Abdur Raheem, *365 Sayings of the Quran*, Jaico Publishing House, Mumbai, 2014.
- Kidwai, Abdur Raheem, *The Quran Speaks to You: 60 Great Lessons from Islam*, Jaico Publishing House, Mumbai, 2022.
- Kidwai, Abdur Raheem, *Blessed Names and Attributes of Allah,* Leicester, UK, Kube Publication, 2016.
- Kidwai, Abdur Raheem, *Daily Wisdom Saying of the Companions of the Prophet*, Leicester, Kube 2023, pp. 415.
- Kidwai, Abdur Raheem, *Daily Wisdom: Selections from Prayers and Supplications*. Leicester, Islamic Foundation, UK. 2013.

- Kidwai, Abdur Raheem, *Daily Wisdom: Selections from the Hadith.* Leicester, Islamic Foundation, UK. 2010
- Kidwai, Abdur Raheem, *Daily Wisdom: Selections from the Quran.* Leicester, Islamic Foundation, UK. 2011.
- Kidwai, Abdur Raheem, *Essential Teachings of the Quran.* Leicester, Islamic Foundation, UK. 2005. Also published by Jaico Publishing House, Mumbai, 2006.
- Kidwai, Abdur Raheem, *Muslim Woman: What Everyone Needs to Know,* Edited by Abdur Raheem Kidwai and Juhi Gupta, (New Delhi, Viva Books, 2019).
- Kidwai, Abdur Raheem, *What is in the Quran? Message of the Quran in Simple English,* New Delhi, Viva Books, 2013.
- Kidwai, Abdur Raheem, *Women in Islam: What the Quran and Sunnah Say*, Kube Publishing, Leicester, UK, 2020.
- Lawrence, Bruce B. *The Koran in English.* New Jersy, Princeton University Press, 2017.
- Murad, Khurram, *Way to the Quran.* Leicester, UK, Islamic Foundation, 1985.
- Nadwi, Syed Abul Hasan, *Guidance from the Holy Quran.* Leicester, Islamic Foundation, 2005.
- Sarton, George, *Introduction to the History of Science.* Florida, Kreiger Publishing, 1975.
- Siddiqi, Mona, *How to Read the Quran.* London, Granta Books, 2007.
- Toynbee, A. J., *A Study of History.* New York, OUP, 1988.

About the Author

Professor Abdur Raheem Kidwai (b. 1956), Honorary Director, KAN Centre for Quranic Studies, Aligarh Muslim University, Aligarh, has written on Islam/the Quran, including his English translation of the Quran in simple English.

Professor Kidwai, earned his Ph.D. in English from the University of Leicester, UK, served as Professor of English, and Director, UGCHRDC, AMU, Aligarh and was Visiting Professor, School of English, University of Leicester, UK.

Other books by him include:

The Quran: Essential Teachings

365 Gems from the Quran

365 Sayings of the Prophet Muhammad

The Quran Speaks to You: 60 Great Lessons from Islam